T0193152

Other Titles in the Smart Pop Series

The Battle for
AZERTH

Adventure, Alliance and Addiction
Insights into the **World of Warcraft**

EDITED BY
Bill Fawcett

An imprint of BenBella Books, Inc.
Dallas, Texas

"Elegant Game Design: Fishing for Those Missing Hours" Copyright © 2006 by Scott Cuthbertson

"Underworld of *Warcraft*" Copyright © 2006 by James John Bell

"*World of Warcraft*: Timesink of the Gods" Copyright © 2006 by Justina Robson

"LFG…And a Little More" Copyright © 2006 by Nancy Berman

"Reframed Relationships: MMORPGs and Societies" Copyright © 2006 by Mel White

"The Economy of *World of Warcraft*" Copyright © 2006 by Jerry Jackson

"Ancestors and Competitors" Copyright © 2006 by IMGS, Inc.

"Maps and Mapping" Copyright © 2006 by James M. Ward

"Should We Sell *World of Warcraft* by Prescription Only?" Copyright © 2006 by Maressa Hecht Orzack and Deborah S. Orzack

"Altaholics Not So Anonymous" Copyright © 2006 by Doranna Durgin and Nancy Durgin

"I Play Like a Girl: Yes, That Level 60 Night Elf Warrior Is Mine" Copyright © 2006 by Nancy Berman

"Advice to the *WoW*lorn" Copyright © 2006 by Jody Lynn Nye

"*World of Warcraft* Classes" Copyright © 2006 by IMGS, Inc.

Additional Materials Copyright © BenBella Books

Lyrics of "*World of Warcraft* Is a Feeling" Copyright © 2006 by http://www.purepwnage.com/music.html

Lyrics of "Stonehenge" Copyright © 2006 by Spinal Tap

Interior illustrations Copyright © 2002 by David Cherry, Ensign Entertainment Ltd.

Any mention of the game *World of Warcraft*™ in any manner in this book is the trademark of Blizzard Entertainment.

Smart Pop is an imprint of BenBella Books, Inc.
10440 N. Central Expressway, Suite 800
Dallas, TX 75231
www.benbellabooks.com
Send feedback to feedback@benbellabooks.com

BenBella and *Smart Pop* are federally registered trademarks.

Printed in the United States of America

Library of Congress Cataloging-in-Publication Data

The battle for Azeroth : adventure, alliance and addiction: insights into the World of Warcraft / edited by Bill Fawcett.
      p. cm.
   ISBN 1-932100-84-9
   1. Computer games. 2. World of Warcraft. I. Fawcett, Bill.
   GV1469.27.B375 2006
   793.93'2—dc22

                                                        2006012224

Proofreading by Stacia Seaman and Jennifer Thomason
Cover design by Mondolithic Studios Inc.
Text design and composition by John Reinhardt Book Design

Special discounts for bulk sales are available. Please contact bulkorders@benbellabooks.com.

CONTENTS

Part One: The Game

Part Two: *World of Warcraft* Classes
CHRIS McCUBBIN

Part One
The Game

ELEGANT GAME DESIGN:
Fishing for Those
Missing Hours

SCOTT CUTHBERTSON

World of Warcraft, *like all overnight successes, took years of hard effort to create. In fact, it took a surprisingly large number of years in an industry where time is big money and a two-year development cycle is considered unacceptably long. Amazing as it may seem today,* World of Warcraft *was, for a while, in danger of being considered Vaporware, that is, a promised product that never actually gets done. Parts of the game were shown and it was announced or rumored as planned for release the next year at the E3 show, the major trade event of the game industry, for a few years running. We now know, as is shown in later articles, that the determination of Blizzard to get the game right was a large part of this lengthy process. But at the time there were more than a few jokes by competitors at the yet-to-be-released game's expense. Some dismissed the game out of hand because the art was "too cartoony." Others said there really wasn't room for another fantasy game since* Asheron's Call 2™ *would suck up what was left of that market. As the quality of the game became more apparent over the years they are laughing less and instead studying why* World of Warcraft *is the most successful, by a factor of ten, Massive Multiplayer Online Role-Playing Game (that mouthful being normally referred to as "MMORPG" or just "RPG") ever created. When* WoW *came out* EverQuest® *was the ideal most companies wanted to approach. With a subscriber base of nearly half a million players, it was gen-*

1

erally regarded as being about as large as an online game could get. That was the prevailing wisdom, and profit projections were all based upon that assumption. We were so, so wrong. So what happened and why did it happen? What is it about World of Warcraft *that makes all the difference? In the pages that follow we asked a range of talented and knowledgeable game designers, authors and sociologists to give insights into* World of Warcraft, *how and why it was designed, why the game is designed the way it is and just what about* World of Warcraft *makes you, and about five million other players, so excited about a game…a sleep-depriving, mind-warping, life-changing game.*

L ET ME ADMIT ONE THING before I get in too deep here: I like to fish. Not the real me, mind you—I'm not actually into the whole kill-the-worm-then-kill-the-fish thing—but my *World of Warcraft* alter-egos have to while away the hours while I practice a kind of Zen Fishingness. Perhaps they would rather be out exploring treasures and caves or mines for bad guys, but I'm the one in control here.

There are very few shores in Azeroth that haven't been fished by my characters in *World of Warcraft.* Up and down the beaches of many lands, or on the many docks that most adventurers use to catch their transport to far-off places, you will find Claemor, my latest favorite character, whiling away the hours as he serenely casts and catches. Oh, sure, he's just a Level 15 Night Elf Druid, not really much to write home about in terms of might or power, but more often than not, he's the character I play when I log-on these days. Of course, what you don't know is that while Claemor is Fishing, I'm working on the phone, or perhaps thinking about the next thing I'm going to write on my latest project, or generally doing something else constructive. And it's the fact that I *can* fish whenever it suits me that makes *World of Warcraft* such a draw. I know I'm not the only person who has come to, after what I thought was only an hour of playing, stunned as I check the clock and wondering how a *WoW* session makes hours melt away like a Night Elf Rogue slipping into the shadows of Ashenvale. So much for productivity in the real world. But where do those hours go?

While the majority of gamers who sit down to enjoy a new game are hoping their new purchase will provide hours of enjoyment, they aren't spending too much time wondering about the intricacies of the game's design, saying to themselves: "I really hope this is an elegantly designed entertainment experience that will hold my interest for hours on end." Let's assume that they are, at the very least, hoping that it will be a fun diversion, and maybe they are hoping it will be an experience that will hold their attention for hours, maybe days, hopefully weeks, but more often than not, there is something not quite there; something's missing. Usually that something is a factor of elegant game design. And usually, it costs you fifty bucks to determine whether or not a game has it. Disproportionate to the cost, however, most gamers know in about fifty seconds if the game is going to be played or quickly sold back to the retail gaming store from which it so recently came.

In the case of a Blizzard-developed game, the gamer knows the "it" is going to be there. What they may not know is that it's not there by mere chance. How is it that, in an era where many games are made but few hit the mark, Blizzard has consistently hit it squarely on the nose?

It's All About the Q

Blizzard has a devastating one-two punch. They are at the pinnacle of the world's game-development community in a corporate alliance that few of their peers can equal, and they have an uncompromising history of releasing quality products despite the restrictions imposed in the harsh and highly competitive world of modern game development.

To understand the basics of today's game development, and how Blizzard and *World of Warcraft* stand apart, you need a little background. Here's a quick course in Game Development 101 for the uninitiated. . . .

Before you get to see the title screen on a game, you see what are called "splash screens," usually the Publisher's logo first, followed by the Developer's logo. Publishers and Developers are the main players in the modern game industry. Their relationship is a pretty simple formula, at least on paper: Developers make the game; they design it, program it, make the art and write the words. Publishers pay to have the game made, packaged, marketed and shipped to your local retail store. Depending on your point of view, Developers are poor souls desperately seeking funding to craft their creative vision, while Publishers are large corporations with money to fund said poor Developers. (I'll leave it up to you to figure out which fish usually gets eaten in this relationship, but here's a hint: it isn't the one with the big bank account.)

The complex mating ritual between corporate giant and starving artist traditionally begins, appropriately enough, in the springtime at the annual Electronic Entertainment Expo in Los Angeles—a place of painfully loud music, overly excited and underclothed models and sharply dressed Marketing types who hire well-endowed, underclothed models to stand in their display booths, some of which are so large they could house up to sixty families if constructed outdoors (meaning the booths, of course, not the models). While the show is traditionally a place to demonstrate new technology and release new games, away from the convention floor, it's also where Developers pitch their skills to Publishers (which frequently involves a combination of extravagant promises mixed with groveling). After months of follow-up meetings, Publishers end up sealing deals with the developer who displays the best plumage (or in this case, sexy, high-poly CG models in lush, rendered, dynamic 3D environments so real you wonder why you aren't simply watching television).

For Blizzard, life is very different. They are one of the few Developers out there who do not need to grovel, because they are actually owned by a major publisher. The aforementioned publishing arrangement comes ready-made for whatever game they choose to develop. The current trend in the game industry is for major Publishers to purchase the best Developers ("snapped up" is a standard term), thereby taking the Developers off the market for the competition; once a publisher finds a good developer, they do not want to let them go. Few of these "kept" companies, however, are allowed to use their own management to run their operation, let alone survive with their original company name intact. Developers are usually absorbed by these Publishers and given a suitably corporate tag, often one that defines their geographical relationship with their new parent, such as SuperCorp West. Blizzard, despite being bought in 1998 by Havas (now known as Vivendi/Universal), maintained its management and its name, and even managed to acquire smaller Developers of its own along the way (one of which was christened "Blizzard North," but that's a longer story). A sign of Blizzard's power even in a subsidiary relationship is that theirs is the only logo on the splash screen of *World of Warcraft*. You will note that Blizzard's logo is the only logo that appears when *World of Warcraft* opens, not even making room for the publisher/parent company in the tiny fine print at the bottom of the screen. They have achieved what few Developers have: they have superseded their publisher and flipped the traditional tail-dog relationship.

Defining this unique relationship is important in understanding the environment in which Blizzard is allowed to create. In traditional Developer-Publisher relations, excluding Blizzard for a moment, it is common for the Publisher to impose some standard restrictions on their new development "partner." Using the standard T-C-Q triangle from business school (which asserts that Time, Cost and Quality are all interrelated and one cannot be maximized without detracting from the other two), Publishers will almost always pick Time or Cost at the expense of Quality, especially because a company's quarterly forecasts tend to drive the creative process. When a Publisher and Developer begin discussing their grand designs for the game-to-come, the initial conversation is always about the Q and usually starts with the Publisher saying, "We're going to publish fewer games this year, so we can spend our money wisely to create a triple-A game experience of the highest possible quality." Notice that the original intent is always focused on the Q. Sadly, poor old Q more often than not finds itself left out in the winter cold later in the development process.

Assuming that the negotiation phase went smoothly and a contract was signed by the end of July, the Publisher begins to change its focus as the holidays approach:

> PUBLISHER: If we're going to make our quarterly projections, we'll need you to scale back on the design and remove some levels. Probably some characters, too.
> DEVELOPER: But those levels are critical to the gameplay experience!
> PUBLISHER: Our Marketing people say that it won't really hurt the game that much, and leaving the levels in could affect the bottom line and our ability to make your monthly milestone payment.
> DEVELOPER: We completely agree that your vision of a streamlined gameplay experience is a far better idea and will greatly benefit the gaming public. Okay, we'll make the changes right away.

Farewell to Q—Hello bargain bin.

But going way back to Blizzard's entrée into the game world, their philosophy has always been about the Q. From its early days, Blizzard adopted its now-famous mantra: "We will not ship a game until it's done," and over the years (which have been phenomenally successful), they have been able to stay true to their goal and protect the Q. Needless to say, this has made their publisher very happy financially and allowed Blizzard to flip-flop the traditional Developer-Publisher relationship. Let's try the same conversation above, only this time we'll see how it probably goes between Blizzard and their publisher/parent company):

> PUBLISHER: If we're going to make our Q4 projections, we'll need you to scale back the design and remove some levels. Probably some characters, too.
> BLIZZARD: No.

And that, I would imagine, is pretty much where it ends. Time and again, Blizzard is allowed that rare freedom to work on a project until it is done to their internal quality standards and the results are consistently positive, both in terms of gamer satisfaction and the bottom line.

So how did Blizzard achieve their unique position in the industry? Their history is written by the games they've created. Blizzard started by developing a few small, but well-reviewed, games with now-defunct publisher Interplay before self-publishing their first major offering: *Warcraft: Orcs and Humans*™, a straight-to-the-point name for a straight-to-the-point fantasy combat game. Unashamed of the overt influence of *Dungeon & Dragons*® and the works of J. R. R. Tolkien (Orcs are bad, Humans are good), the player was immediately immersed in a familiar world of swordplay, castles, knights and goblins. Before there was a genre called "Real-time Strategy," *Warcraft* was a breath of fresh air that gave the player an easily accessible and instantly satisfying experience, without needing to crack open the instruction manual (although everyone should because Blizzard's attention to quality and detail also extends to their printed material).

Warcraft was not the only game of its kind (*Populous*™ and *Dune II*™ had come before it, and *Command & Conquer*™ would soon follow), but it was polished and elegant in its simplicity. Click on a character, he responded with a pleasant greeting, ready for action. Click again, he moved where you sent him. Click on an enemy, the characters grunted and clashed as expected and continued to do so until one was dead or you decided to break it off. When you finished a level, you were rewarded with a tiny but nicely pre-rendered cinematic and a concise tally of your statistics. Even the sound effects, from the grunts and the sword-rings to the frustrated "Why do you keep touching me?!" when you over-clicked a character, were crisp and not at all out of place in a fantasy world. The public responded, of course, and Blizzard was on its way.

Blizzard's attention to detail was not only reflected in the game, but in the management of their company as well. Back in 1994, I had the privilege of meeting several Blizzard staffers at the precursor to E3—the Consumer Electronics Show in Las Vegas. In those days, the video-game portion of this massive convention was confined to a portable tent-like building in the parking lot of the convention center, and in a tiny little booth—and by booth I literally mean a booth, a table with three little walls—were proud members of the Blizzard team, standing beside their work along with a moderate but not overwhelming stream of visitors. I sought them out, actually, and they were pleased to say hello. They gave me a guided tour of *Warcraft* (even though I already owned the game), and they were kind enough to give me a mouse pad and a T-shirt for stopping by.

In hindsight, two things stood out about Blizzard even back then. The first was the team's genuine passion. One team member proudly pointed out that not only was he the game's designer, but also the Orcs' voices (which he performed on the spot). These guys were eager to show off their work, and for good reason. It was clear that even though their game was already on the shelves, they themselves continued to play it (which, believe it or not, is a rare thing in this industry). Secondly, even though their booth was tiny, that small space was pristine, polished in every way, right down to good quality mouse pads and T-shirts. Passion and attention to detail—that is the foundation of the company.

As the inevitable hype built for *Warcraft II: Tides of Darkness*™, Blizzard had its first opportunity to trumpet their "We'll ship it when it's done" attitude. This was met by disbelief from Publishers and gamers alike. If Blizzard pulled this off, would the game industry say farewell to deadlines and quarterly numbers and happy stockholders, and be forced to adopt this bohemian notion of the shattered T-C-Q triangle? Release dates would go out the window. Panic at the Electronics Boutique! (Yes, this was pre—EB Games.)

Then another strange thing happened. *Warcraft II*™ was delayed, and delayed, and delayed again. Games are delayed all the time, but in this case the public waited. Then it was delayed again. And still the public waited while the retailers screamed in agony at lost revenue projections. The game finally hit the shelves in May of 1995, and lo and behold, Blizzard had released another gem. It may not have been quite as perfect as the first in the series, having many bells and whistles that added considerably to its complexity, but it still sold in record numbers. Was this a harbinger of revolution in the Publisher-Developer relation?

No. Blizzard held out for the Q and were rewarded, but continue, to this day, to be the exception rather than the rule. And so now, *World of Warcraft*.

Crafting an Addiction

What is it about *World of Warcraft* that makes it so compelling to players around the world? There are many factors, including a track record that shows how well Blizzard understands its audience, as you might expect, but one key component helps it to stand out from the rest: outstanding game design. Good MMORPG (Massive Multiplayer Online Role-Playing Game) design is not rocket science, but it does require an unflinching commitment to attention to detail, and a firm commitment to the fans, to listen to their desires and adapt accordingly.

Good game design should be invisible to the player: while they are playing, they may not be consciously aware of the game's quest design, the way tasks are strung together, the risk-reward ratio and other structural factors that provide the game's foundation. Much of what a player experiences in a typical session of a well-designed game, whether they realize it or not, has been carefully orchestrated to hold their interest and guide them by the hand until they are comfortable with the controls—and committed to the game.

The character advancement ramp starts out simple, allowing the new player to gain levels very quickly as they get acquainted with their avatar's abilities and get comfortable with their new alter ego. Regardless of character class and affiliation (Horde or Alliance), every starter character gets a series of linear missions designed to teach the basics of movement and combat with little chance of getting killed. Beginning players usually don't need to venture far from home, and the enemies they face all but fall at their feet, which leads to lots of dramatic special effects animations and a good deal of starter loot (okay, not a lot of glamor to be found in rotted, rusted armor, but it's better than what you started with and based on what you see on other players, it's all up from here!).

This invisible hand-holding is critical to hooking the player into the game. No matter the player's skill level, the reward of instant gratification and increased power are very seductive.

These initial "linear" missions create the second layer of immersion and build the network of stories that pulls the player deeper into the game. From the moment they enter Azeroth, avatars receive quests that deepen in their complexity and ultimately keep players coming back for more. Linear missions are, by definition, quests strung together one after the other to form a larger "Quest Arc"—the player has to complete task "A" before moving to task "B" and so forth, until the arc is completed and the reward received. Linear missions keep characters in a controlled line of progression that increases in difficulty as quests are completed and the avatar gains levels. Quests are consistently at, or just above, the player's skill level, offering challenges to succeed without making the game boring throughout the player's time in Azeroth—that's definitely the hallmark of good game design.

At the lower levels, linear quests tend to be stand-alone and self-contained, but as the game progresses, these quests become layered and interconnected. At higher levels, the number of simultaneous quests increases until it seems like you have more jobs to do than time to do them and the stories about the quests become ever more engaging. This layering of quests serves two purposes: first, it answers the question that most players ask themselves regularly in MMORPGs: "What do I do next?" In *World of Warcraft*, this question is always just a click away. Rarely is a player questless, because each arc is specifically designed to guide the player to higher and higher levels. The second—and perhaps most important factor in quest design—is the almost perfect risk-reward ratio, the "carrot" that tempts a player to complete just one more mission before turning in for the evening. When this ratio is maximized, one little quest leads to one more little quest until the quest arc is completed and the sun is coming up and it's time to go to work after (another) sleepless night.

Beyond the linear quests and scripted story events, *World of Warcraft* has one additional element that gives the game its life, and it's a biggie: Fishing, my favorite in-game recreation. Fishing may seem insignificant next to the allure of those purple, orange and gold rare items or acquiring that full suit of well-matched armor, but it is, I would argue, the most important element of the game. Okay, it's not Fishing specifically that holds the power, but the ability to fish if you want to. Fishing not only makes this virtual world real, it encourages a player to take a game-sanctioned break from questing and just relax. Blizzard says it's okay to ignore their carefully crafted story arcs to perfect casting from the docks and beaches of Azeroth. This may seem like an unremarkable element of game design, but tasks like Fishing, Skinning, Tailoring and all the other "things to do" have been carefully designed to truly bring the world to life, by not only creating a pleasant diversion, but by creating a realistic virtual economy in which each player can participate as deeply as he or she likes, or not at all as it suits him or her. These elements also fill in the story gaps in a realistic way and subtly encourage players to spend their valuable time within the game, relaxing and contributing in their own way to the growth of a living, breathing world. And as the world grows and matures, we all have fun, which is the fundamental point of a game, isn't it?

All of this may seem like common sense and unremarkable when it's broken down into its basic components, but if it were that easy, why do so many games fail to adopt this basic level of good game design? Ask many "hard-core" gamers how they feel about the game's design, and they will likely tell you that *World of Warcraft* lacks sufficient depth or the complexity of many of the top-tier games on the market today. I suspect this attitude comes from a general disdain by the hard-core players for anything designed for the mass market. (These gamers may well deny their attraction to the game, but more often than not, they are in the world, adventuring right alongside us and having a great time.) True, *World of Warcraft*, like its ancestor *Warcraft: Orcs and Humans*™ and subsequent descendents, may not turn over many new leaves in terms of innovative and never-before-seen game mechanics, but it does something more important: it provides players with a visually pleasing, consistently satisfying experience that incorporates the best elements that Blizzard had perfected and it presents this to the player in a way that is polished, intuitive and downright fun. It is precisely this "polish" that has players around the world returning to *World of Warcraft* day after day and night after night—some to go questing and some, like Claemor, just to go Fishing.

Scott Cuthbertson has been a video-game producer and writer since 1990, having worked for several of the world's largest game publishers and studios, including Nintendo, AOL, Disney, Universal and Warner

Bros. In his ongoing quest to push for the Q, he founded Northlake Studios, LLC, a creative development company based out of the Los Angeles area, specializing in writing and design for games, film, television and graphic novels.

Underworld
of Warcraft

James John Bell

Like an Irishman who falls asleep on the beach, there is a burnt-red dark side to the economy of World of Warcraft. *Somewhere in the orient, often coordinated in Canada or Europe, are locations where people make a living playing WoW twelve hours a day. In fact, they make a better living than most of the people in their area. They do this by accumulating gold and other items to sell for gold. Then this gold is resold to other players for actual money. In a country such as China (outside the coastal enclaves) the approximate $10–15 for 100 gold is about twice what they would earn working at a local office. So is this good? Is WoW helping those less fortunate? Good for those selling the gold perhaps, but for the bulk of the players, this can be a real problem. The threat, as Alan Greenspan has often explained, is inflation. The introduction of so much money and so many blue and even epic (purple) items raises the cost of everything, for all players. This has to worry Blizzard since it means that new players, and the bulk of the players who do not buy gold, find it harder to play the game. It also means that those players willing to spend fifty dollars for a purple magic item can, effectively, buy success in the game. The problem is more apparent in companies that combine harvesting gold with leveling characters for pay—real-world money payments, that is. So while you can spend a week getting a new Shaman to Level 25, Ralph Big Pockets can pay someone $250 to do it for him and never click a mouse. As you will see in the following essay, the economy, Auc-*

*tion House, rarity of items, etc. is supposed to be a delicately bal-
anced mechanism. Gold selling upsets this balance. It devalues the
reward of getting 70 silver off a tough monster when you can buy
100 gold with one click on an eBay image. That silver or gold is no
longer much of an incentive. Inflation has become a real problem on
some servers (including the one I am on, I have to admit). On other
servers this is not as much of a concern. The difference between the
two servers for a rare epic sword can be a cost of 400 gold versus
2,000–3,000 gold. This difference makes playing on the inflated
economy servers harder, less fun and creates a rich/poor disparity
in the real world that chases younger and less solvent players off
the game. Then again, that fella in China spending six days a week
playing WoW from morning until late at night needs the money. It's
a tough grind… hey, wait, I do that anyhow.…*

*In this insightful article James John Bell gives a good look at how
Blizzard deals with this problem. Including one major way they intrude "for our own good" that makes most of us very nervous, if
not irate.*

```
Character found to be using an automated client
program that allowed the user to complete actions
in-game without any direct input from the user.
```

The hacker Rdartua awoke to his *World of Warcraft* account closure notice in his e-mail box. While he slept his Priest character had been grinding along farming gold and loot in the Barrens. Something had gone terribly wrong, so he ran the debug on his bot program *WoW!*Inmate.[1]

> 9/2/2005 5:25:51 A.M.| Major teleport detected, the player moved 6,344.02 units in 8,546.88 ms.

"It looks like I was teleported by GM from Barrens to Ogrimmar. - unbelievable. - and then he started chatting with me."

> [05:27:02][06][WHISPER]<GM> [xxxxx]: Greetings. This is Game Master xxxxx. May I have a moment of your time please?

> [05:29:38][06][WHISPER]<GM> [xxxxx]: Greetings. This is Game Master xxxxx. May I have a moment of your time please?

> [05:29:47][06][WHISPER]<GM> [xxxxx]: Your account is being suspended at this time. I will be sending you an e-mail explaining your suspension. Please make sure you check your registered e-mail. Thank you.

Over the next couple of days in early September 2005, more than a thousand such hackers and gold farmers running third-party bot programs from sites like wowglider.com and wowsharp.net were permanently banned by Blizzard. Tens of thousands of accounts have been banned since launch, many for scam-related and third-party exploit offenses.[2]

---

[1] Blizzard forbids players to use *WoW!*Inmate and monitors players to detect if they're using the software. At http://www.WoWGlider.com and http://www.WoWSharp.net you can download third-party software developed to help players hack *World of Warcraft*.

[2] Many of these players were banned for hacking violations. For example, IGN reported at http://vnboards.ign.com/forums/b1/84605313 that hundreds of player accounts were banned for using a teleportation hack.

Blizzard's December 21, 2005 announcement was a Christmas greeting to *WoW* hackers everywhere, "In keeping with Blizzard's aggressive stance against cheating in *World of Warcraft*, we have permanently closed more than 18,000 accounts over the past three months for participating in activities that violate the game's Terms of Use. A majority of these accounts were found to be using third-party programs to farm gold and items."[3]

How did Blizzard beat back the hackers? In late August 2005, as part of a routine patch Blizzard unleashed the Warden, a controversial spybot program that daily enters the computers of the more than five million *World of Warcraft* players globally.

Before the Warden came on the scene, Game Masters had to literally catch players running bots, which meant discovering if a character was being run by a human player at the keyboard or an automation program—a task somewhat like Deckard's in the science fiction film *Blade Runner* where he is trying to determine who is human and who is a replicant, making many a hacker's close call with a Game Master similar to beating Blizzard's version of the Voight-Kampff test.

It was easy to spot gold-farming bots in Azeroth before Blizzard cracked down on the bot'ers. Bots would work as a Hunter and Priest team, with the Priest bot healing the Hunter bot as they went along farming mobs oblivious to actual human controlled characters. The bot crackdown and the Warden changed all that.

"This WardenClient has put the *World of Warcraft* hacking on its knees with only a few utilities surviving the initial onslaught," explains *WoWSharp* team member Da_Teach. "Like the third-party utilities, the WardenClient has been evolving and gaining detection abilities previously not shown in any other game. For example, the code for this detection routine is not present in *WoW* but it is downloaded each time you login your account."[4]

Blizzard's WardenClient looks at other programs on a player's computer, from their e-mail application to any other program running in an open window, and if it detects anything that Blizzard deems sus-

[3] On December 21, 2005, Blizzard reports 18,000 account closers in only three months—http://www.worldofwarcraft.com/news/wow-news-12-2005.html.

[4] *WoWSharp* Team Member Da_Teach's complete rant on the impact of the Warden on *WoW* hackers can be found at WoWSharp.net, look for the September 29, 2005 post "*WoWSharp* going open-source."

pect it notifies a Game Master. How does it work? The Warden converts the programs and data it monitors into lots of numbers and bits, called a hash, and compares it to a violation list. If it finds a match, then you make Azeroth's most wanted list. Naturally this caused a wave of panic among tech types concerned about their privacy.

Blizzard's response was not very revealing to those with concerns: "...our reluctance to discuss this issue is because in order to stay one step ahead of hackers, we have to be extremely careful in regard to what information we reveal about our security measures. Otherwise, we run the risk of revealing too much information and the hackers then being able to circumvent these security measures....Legally speaking, the scans are not a violation of rights. Understandably, that's beside the point for the people who are concerned about our security measures....We'd like to make it clear that the scan does not review or retrieve anything that's personally identifiable....Again, we can't get into what specifically it does look at, but we can say that all it tells us is whether a computer is hacking *World of Warcraft*."[5]

Blizzard 1, Hackers 0

The January 2006 issue of *Computer Gaming* magazine reported that hackers had quickly developed an ingenious yet simple defense against the controversial Warden—listening to the CD *12 Songs* by Neil Diamond. Unbelievable as it sounds, all they had to do was lay a Sony BMG copy-protected CD released in 2005 on their computer, not hard to do since there are tens of thousands of them in circulation.[6]

Sony BMG copy-protected CDs prompt you the first time you try to play them on your computer if you agree to the installation of a little program. This program, publicly known as Extended Copy Protection (XCP), then burrows itself into your hard drive and hides on

[5] Blizzard's official response to criticism surrounding the release of the Warden was located at http://forums.worldofwarcraft.com/thread.aspx?fn=blizzard-archive&t=33&p=1&tmp=1#post33 but was removed. The full text of the official post is copied at http://wow.catacombs.com/forum.cfm?ThreadKey=47994&DefMessage=1161117&forum=WOWMainForum.

[6] At http://cp.sonybmg.com/xcp/english/titles.html you will find a complete listing of Sony BMG CDs released in 2005 with the controversial XCP rootkit.

your system like those nasty worms and viruses, altering your Windows Registry files. If you then try and copy the CD it will disable your burner, which sucks for music pirates. XCP's powerful defensive system however, is a boon to game hackers.

The detection-avoidance capabilities of XCP, called a "rootkit," makes it impossible for *World of Warcraft's* Warden to detect if a bot program is controlling a character. In fact, the Warden cannot see *any* files that are hidden with XCP. Thus all a gamer has to do is play any XCP copy-protected CD, and then add the prefix "sys" to file names that you don't want Blizzard to have access to, like your e-mail program. You'll need to check the used CD bins though to get a hold of an XCP-encoded CD as Sony in response to widespread criticism stopped using XCP in November 2005 and recalled all CDs that contained the controversial software.[7]

Blizzard 1, Hackers 1

To understand why hackers go through such lengths to get ahead in *World of Warcraft* is to enter into a much larger underworld where the boundary between virtual worlds and the real world blurs.

WTB/WTS—The Virtual Gold Rush

If only you could make money playing video games. Well now you can, if you don't mind violating the End User License Agreement. According to *Synthetic Worlds* author Edward Castronova, black-market gold from some Massive Multiplayer Online Role-Playing Games (MMORPGs) is valued higher on eBay than the Japanese yen and the currencies of third-world countries.[8] So, neither gold-farming start-up companies nor individual gamers are willing to let the End User License Agreement stop them from cashing in. The first gamers to turn someone else's intellectual property into real money discovered their boon while playing the first popular MMORPG *Ultima Online*™, released in 1997.

---

[7] The entire saga of the rise and fall of XCP can be found on Wikipedia at http://en.wikipedia.org/wiki/2005_Sony_CD_copy_protection_controversy.

[8] Castronova, Edward "Synthetic Worlds—The Business and Culture of Online Games," University of Chicago Press, 2005.

Ultima Online™ players started selling their game gold on eBay and sparked a worldwide gold rush into the new virtual-gaming worlds, filling the population with gold farmers. By 1999 gold farming was firmly established by these 99'ers in games like *Everquest*®, which made the late 2004 record breaking a half-million player-launch of *WoW* equivalent to the announcement of gold being discovered at Sutter's Mill in 1848.

In 1849 innovative and sometimes criminal entrepreneurs got rich off the gold rush by supplying the gold miners with much-needed supplies and services. Today the entrepreneurs are the bot-scripting hackers and the "middlemen" who run Web sites and companies that sell farmed gold to players. These black marketeers are making some serious cash, while the gold farmers, much like their historic counterparts, get the raw end of the deal.

Just how many gold farmers are there in this underworld? And how big an underground market is it? In December 2005 the *New York Times* published the investigative article "Ogre to Slay—Outsource it to China" by David Barboza in which he estimated that there are more than 100,000 gold farmers in China alone. "It's unimaginable how big this is," exclaimed a Chinese gold-farming operation owner, "in some of these popular games, forty or fifty percent of the players are actually Chinese farmers." These "Chinese farmers" are working for thousands of gold harvesting operations set up most often in old warehouses that take advantage of the cheap labor to be found on mainland China. Barboza reported that most of these workers earn less than twenty-five cents an hour, and many sleep in makeshift dorms on the premises. Utilizing cheap sweatshop labor from China and elsewhere, gold farming is globally estimated to be more than a $500 million plus black market.[9]

IGE.com, the largest and best known of the Chinese gold-farming operations, is based in Hong Kong with a shell office in New York. Blizzard and most other MMORPGs forbid the practice of selling any of their gold since it is technically their intellectual property. Com-

---

[9] Barboza, David, "Ogre to Slay—Outsource it to China," the *New York Times*, December 9, 2005, Late Edition—Final, Section A, Page 1, Column 2, 1686 words.

panies like IGE.com are violating the End User Licensing Agreement of most games, and they're getting away with it by because they are located outside of America. IGE.com even boasts that gold farming actually earns more than the online games themselves. The *New York Times* reported that the online gaming industry is generating $3.6 billion a year—that's a lot of gold.[10]

While many small transnational corporations run gold-farming warehouses in China, many individual gamers farm for personal gain in the West. One famous early bot hacker and gold farmer is American Rich Thurman, a man who, from 2002–2004, farmed nine billion gold in *Ultima Online*™ and hawked it all on eBay. He said he made over $109,000—his piece of the *Ultima Online*™ gold-farming black market that he estimated to be generating $4.3 million annually. Journalist Julian Dibbell more recently supported himself for a year playing *Ultima Online*™ and wrote a book on his experience entitled *Play Money*.

A Chinaman's Chance in Azeroth

By far, most gold-farming operations are based in China, where the minimal cost of labor realizes the maximum profit. When you meet a Chinese farmer-in-game you are probably meeting a real person, as opposed to the Western farmer who is probably a wageless bot. In China there is less need for bots because the labor is cheap and sweatshop conditions exist under the radar of human-rights advocates. While sweatshops account for some of the gold mining, a few operations appear more reputable.

"We consider the gold gathered from bots 'black gold,'" explains "Tim" the founder of a Chinese-worker gold-farming operation in Azeroth. "The gold gathered that way, is just like if Blizzard can produce their own gold with a click of a button. There is no work or effort put into it."

Tim founded the "bot-less" gold-farming company www.ItemBay. ca with two of his friends "Chris" and "Jerry"—all three are Chinese

---

[10] The *New York Times* figure of $3.6 billion in online game subscriptions was provided by DFC Intelligence. You can view the December 9, 2005 video news report "Farming for Virtual Gold" put together by the *New York Times* at http://www.nytimes.com/packages/khtml/2005/12/09/business/20051209_GAME2_FEATURE.html.

with Canadian citizenship. "Chris graduated from the University of Toronto, I graduated from the University of British Columbia and Jerry graduated from Simon Fraser University."

Finding out about ItemBay.ca wasn't too difficult. While beating back a raid on Tarren Mill a Level 1 Orc whis*pamm*ed me[11]—"Hi, plz visit http://www.itembay.ca Cheapest gold $8.99=100G $34.99=500G $76.99=1000G." A whisper and some e-mails later put me in contact with Tim, who asks to keep his character name secret. He plays a Level 60 Human Warlock in *World of Warcraft* with demonology and affliction specializations. He carries a Staff of Dominance, and loves his four in-game pets.

All three of the Itembay.ca founders, he tells me, also play *Lineage I®*, *Lineage II®*, *EQ2* and *Everquest®*. "This company started when a group of friends who loves to play MMORPGs got together and saw the potentials in the continual growth of the gaming industry," Tim explains "With ideas of our own, and with a little guidance from companies who already dipped their foots into this industry. Item-bay.ca was created.

"How players buy gold through our service is very simple, much like all the other companies out there. They [customer] provide us with information like server name, character name, faction and the amount of gold they wish to purchase. Then our customers pay via PayPal. When we received a completed transaction, we will then process the order. And when the gold is gathered, we will send it to the players." The "when the gold is gathered" part means that buying gold in amounts of more than 200 could mean a few hours' to a few days' wait depending on your server.[12] The gold comes in small amounts of usually 100 or 200, possibly to avoid detection by Blizzard's 1.9 patch mail-system upgrade, sort of like the "small bills" sought after by criminals in the movies. The gold arrives in your character's mailbox from "players" with Chinese names like Xiaoxin or Haitao—the same names of Level 1 characters hawking Level 60

---

[11] The author, James John Bell, plays WoW on the Burning Legion server. He has an Undead Rogue named Auntywar, an Orc tank called Howitzer and Wisunt, a Tauren Druid. He runs the pagan guild Skyclad.

[12] Players who purchased gold from ItemBay.ca reported great customer service and a two- to eight-hour wait for their gold.

items in general chat. None seem to go out of their way to hide their Chinese farmer identity.

"The term 'Chinese farmers' may have a bad reputation for some of the MMORPG out there," Tim states defensively, "But honestly, I don't believe farming for gold destroys the playing experience for most of the players. Most of the gold farming is done in China because, for one, China has the biggest population in the world, which means, they've got the people to handle the mass production of gold. And secondly, the cost of labor and living standard is lower compared to other places, which makes China the ideal place to host these operations... and like most industries, there are good ones and there are bad ones. I must admit, there are gold-farming companies out there that work just like a sweatshop, where people work in twelve hours + shifts. However, my take of it is that it is very normal and it occurs for all different types of industries."

Itembay.ca—these three owners argue—is *not* a sweatshop. The company's main offices are located in Canada while their "game shop"—as they call it—is set up in China. The game shop contains more than 200 computers and employs more than 400 "gamers" around the clock. Tim insists that it is a place "where players can come in and earn money at their own pace." These gamers range in age from seventeen- to twenty-five-year-olds. They are mostly men. "It's like 93% men, and 7% women.

"Like I said, the gamer work for their own timetable. They come into the game room, and play and sell us what they earn while playing. We only provide the PC and an environment for them to play in. What they make is all up to them. I can honestly say they love what they do, because they are making money from playing a great game. I remember when I was there this summer, I always hear them laugh and scream when the opposite faction attacked them. Then they will call for help to assist them in fighting. Sometimes when they don't feel like 'farming,' they enjoy going to Battle Grounds... and have fun there."

The three businessmen introduced me to some of their gold farmers. We met up with Xiao Qiao Li's Level 60 Human Rogue (combat spec) on the Mannorth server. He sported a full set of Shadowcraft armor. Xiao prefers to keep his character's name secret. He is probably one of the few Level 60s who is not in a guild.

Xiao is an eighteen-year-old high-school graduate. "I play *World of Warcraft* since it's published. I play twelve hours a day normally; but sometimes if I have something urgent to do, I will not play. I guess I play fifty hours a week. I do not really consider this as my job. In the first place, I play *WoW* with my friends for fun. . . . However, I found out I can earn my living from *WoW* golds. I could not resist the 'job' that can give you the fun and living. I can make enough gold to support my living in China. Before playing *World of Warcraft*, I work for a factory, the monthly salary is 600 RMB. After I sell gold, I earn around 1200 RMB per month."

Chinese money is called renminbi (RMB), which means "the People's Currency." The popular unit of RMB is the yuan. One hundred dollars in American currency equals about 820 RMB, thus Xiao makes roughly $150 a month; that's about seventy-five cents an hour if he works 200 hours a month earning 1200 RMB.[13]

"I do not have many in-game friends. I quest alone. I tried to be friends with American players; however, they treat me bad since I do not know English well enough. They keep calling me farmer, China dog and such. I do not have any problems with other players except American players, they non-stop racist me. My favorite place to farm gold is in Eastern Plaguelands killing elite monsters. The worst experience I had was hunting the elite there. Two alliance players came and keep calling me name. After that, they ask their horde friends to keep killing me for hours. I could not do anything. The alliance did not help me at all except calling me names."

The next gold farmer we met was Cai Lan Mak. She introduced herself as a twenty-year-old college graduate. Cai has a Level 60 Paladin with holy specialization. She asks to keep her character's name secret. "I play *WoW* for over a year. I play ten hours per day and sixty hours each week. I never consider this as my job. I love the playing style in *WoW*. I can fish, herbs and engineering. It's fun and cool. I worked at an office which I get paid for 850 RMB per month. After I sell gold, I can get 1400 RMB per month.

---

[13] The $100 U.S. currency to 820 RMB exchange rate is based on the Bank of China's RMB exchange rates, http://www.china.org.cn/english/MATERIAL/43805.htm.

"I have a few American players as friend since I graduated from college, so I can communicate with them. I do quest with some American players too. The most fun group experience is we run BRD. We wiped many times since we have no experience for BRD. But we finish it after seven hours of trying. My favorite place to farm is Western Plaguelands. I kill those Level 58 monster which will drop an enchanting recipe—crusader. The recipe can sell 350G around but rare."

Like Xiao, Cai related having problems with some American players. "Since they know I am Chinese with broken English they laugh at me and call me bad names. The worst experience in game is one of the American players whispers me saying 'I am a bitch, I should go to hell, China dog farmer.' I report him, and he has been banned. My best experience in game is running MC with my guild; and they give me one epic item which is really nice. I love my guild and friends."

The bi-faction race-based attacks that Xaio experienced and described above are similar to what has happened on multiple servers. Blizzard can and does punish players for racist attacks, but Blizzard has another problem to contend with—players complaining about gold-farming ninja looters. The all-out attack on such farmers usually occurs in places where a rare drop can be found, like the mining of rich thorium veins in dangerous zones, like Winterspring, for arcane crystal drops. If there are only two or three total veins in the zone, a farmer will ride around and continuously farm the vein. Thus the farmer controls all of the veins in a particular zone, not allowing anyone else to mine. The farmer then also controls the market for the arcane crystals in the auction house, so you'll pay twenty-five gold instead of ten to fifteen gold for a crystal. A post on thottbot.com under "arcane crystal" illustrates the problem:

> "Bliz talks a lot about fair play but making these [arcane crystals] so rare is killing the game for high-level players. We have several 'farmers' on our server that simply spend all day farming the rich veins for the crystals. If you happen to be there they will happily ninja loot your vein right in front of you if you are unlucky enough to be mobbed when mining it. We have three Level 60 miners who have (after four to five weeks of Level 60 mining) managed to acquire eleven arcane crystals between us. We have high end crafters in the guild screaming out for the bars but we just can't get enough of the crystals to even get one arcanite reaper. Sure I

guess if we camped the RTV's at two to six A.M. we might have more luck, but seriously that's not what I thought WoW was about."[14]

The farming, ninja looting and racism will continue as long as the black gold market is open for business. For the Chinese farmers who work for operations like Itembay.ca, *WoW* offers them a chance to earn a marginally better living while playing a game they love. But the farmers and the bots represent a minority of the characters you meet in Azeroth. *WoW* offers a vibrant alternative life to many players who come online to socialize, protest and create art while lvling and earning honor points.

World of Warcraft Is a Feeling

You look good in high-res
You've got uber chat skills
Won't you grind quests with me—endlessly
Tanking mobs is my role
I maintain aggro
But the rogue doesn't know, he's not MT [main tank] tonight

World of Warcraft *is a feeling*
Who needs a social life
I can't wait to log in,
Hop on a griffin

Stockades, gnomer, SM
Won't you join me, on an instance farming run
Let me hit the vendor, free up some bag space
Once I repair, I'll be good to go

World of Warcraft *is a feeling*
Who needs a social life
Stratholme, Scholo and UBRS
He just dropped my valor helm
How could I roll a 6?
Grats to my guildmate, but I can't believe this shit

---

[14] The price of arcane crystals is a good test of the state of inflation on a particular server, since they're an integral component of many high-level crafted items. The full discussion on arcane crystals and farming is located at http://www.thottbot.com/?i=5924.

This is the best game
This is the best game I've ever played
This is the greatest game
World of Warcraft *you're the greatest game*

World of Warcraft *you're the greatest game*
The best game I've ever played
Woah
I can't wait to log on
Hop on griffin
World of Warcraft, *a* World of Warcraft
A reality.

—Lyrics by purepwnage.com from the music video Episode Six—
World of Warcraft Is a Feeling.[15]

Purepwnage.com caused a stir among many *WoW* veterans when they released Episode Six "*World of Warcraft* Is a Feeling" of their *webisode* (Web video series). They tapped into the deep archetypal sarcasm inherent in the over-the-top love that players everywhere have for *WoW*. They reached into the souls of not just the gamers but Blizzard as well. Blizzard in a recap of the major 2005 *WoW* events on the first anniversary of the game gave a big rowdy shout out to purepwnage, directing players to the video.[16]

This video is just one of *thousands* of fan-made *WoW* videos that can be found on sites like warcraftmovies.com, with titles like "Mary & Jane—The Story about a Hunter and his Pet" and "(5) Rogues vs (1) Ironforge." This artistic medium of "machine cinema" is known as machinima—and is an example of emergent gameplay where the 3D game engines of popular games and a player's characters are used to create a movie. There are *hundreds* of hours' worth of *WoW* movies alone, from PvP and gold-farming videos to bug exploits and dra-

---

[15] Pure Pwnage (pronounced "Pure Ownage") is a *webisode* series by ROFLMAO Productions featuring a Canadian professional video-game player named Jeremy. Download Episode Six "*World of Warcraft* Is a Feeling" at http://www.purepwnage.com or http://media.putfile.com/PurePwnage-WoWisafeeling.

[16] You can see Blizzard's first-year recap of great fan moments at http://www.worldofwarcraft.com/community/anniversaries/year1timeline.html.

matic storylines, stuff that only a *WoW* player would truly appreciate. Many of the best videos out there are guild recruitment videos, like the one found at CraftingWorlds.com made by Tristan Pope for the guild Timeless on Lightning's Blade.

Tristan's *World of Warcraft* machinima has become hugely popular, winning a number of machinima awards and, interestingly enough, getting seen by many outside of the *WoW*verse. "I play a Troll Rogue," explains Tristan, "Originally I started out playing the Alliance but I decided that the Horde was more my flavor. It seems as though the Horde in *WoW* has a tighter sense of community as there are usually less players. Plus, I am less likely to be distracted by female armor models that look like bikinis...."

Tristan explains that making a machinima-based film in an MMO is very much like a theatre production. "You need to guide your players in the same way as actors, but you also have the film aspect in which you can re-shoot the shot, as long as the player can stay logged on and someone does not come up and gank you. I play on a PvP server so it makes the situations even harder to contain. Very often, as in theatre, I am forced to do my shots in *one* take and move on."

His machinima *Not Just Another Love Story* exploits every potential in-game sex position, and is quickly becoming the *Kama Sutra* of Azeroth. As a result just this one video has had over a million downloads.[17] Brilliantly, Tristan combines both Alliance and Horde characters in a man-woman-woman love triangle that should do wonders for Troll machismo across the realms. "In my movie *Not Just Another Love Story* the leading lady was played by a male character who in real life was actually trying to pretend to be a girl.... All I know is that I thought *it* was female so when I was on my teamspeak server trying to guide her (him) into some of the more 'entangling' situations I think my character in-game even blushed."

Being on a PvP server made shooting the many scenes that featured Horde and Alliance factions together extremely difficult for Tristan, like in the Ashenvale nightclub scene for *Not Just Another*

---

[17] Download the controversial video *Not Just Another Love Story* at http://www.craftingworlds.com/studio/?p=10.

Love Story. "I had over twenty-five Alliance players there and I was one out of three Horde. The other two were the bouncers (Tauren in tuxes). While I was filming different shots walking around blind because of my camera angle, they would fight off the spawning guards and when I would turn around there would be a pile of corpses everywhere! They took crowd control to a new level, although they couldn't save me from my own 'special effects.' All the sparkles and cool looking things on film were spells. And since I play on a PvP server, it would take my life down. At one point while I was shooting I realized I couldn't walk anymore. When I turned my UI (user interface) on, I saw I was dead. . . ."

Tristan's probably most notorious for his "Save the Murlocs" campaign that was impossible to miss by anyone who attended Blizzcon. The idea for the film first came to Tristan while he was working on a movie at E3 that was sponsored by Fileplanet. At E3 he used a Murloc puppet, but later at Blizzcon he became a Murloc by wearing a costume that his grandma made. Since Blizzard was planning to give away baby Murlocs, he dreamed up the protest idea and wandered the streets of Anaheim outside the convention center yelling "You call it quests, I call it genocide."

"I remember walking through the Marriot hotel and people were wondering if I was a Disneyland character or just some nut. If I saw a *World of Warcraft* fan there for Blizzcon I usually got bombarded with flashes of cameras, cheers and very often hugs, oh yeah . . . and the occasional, 'I need your eyes for a quest!'"

"The highlight of Blizzcon for me was the Q/A. I saw that there were two lines leading up to two microphones where people asked Blizzard Devs questions about the game. I then realized, 'Oh My God, they are also being broadcast on two *huge* screens above the audience.' Well, the lines were huge and I knew I would never make it to the mikes, so I quietly asked everyone in the lines if I could jump ahead of them. Finally, thanks to the graces of everyone in that line, I was *next*! I had no clue what I was going to say, or how to say it, I had a million thoughts running through my head, and the heat from that costume probably didn't help . . . so I started off with 'Can you hold my son' and handed my plush Murloc puppet to the guy holding the mike."

From that point forward the whole "Save the Murlocs" campaign blossomed exponentially and now you too can join the cause to stop the innocent slaughter of Murlocs and the forced slavery of their young. Get involved at www.craftingworlds.com/savemurlocs/ and don't forget to sign the petition.

What Would Cenarius Do?

When movies, sex and politics arrive on the scene, religion can't be too far behind. While Tristan is off campaigning to save the Murlocs, some guilds are organizing to literally save your soul. Heath Summerlin, from Cheraw, South Carolina, runs ChristianGamer.org "a Christian gaming Web site dedicated to sharing Jesus with the gaming community." Heath has two main characters on the Stonemaul server, Alhana, a Level 60 female Human Shadow Priest, and Gnimish, a male Gnome Arcane Mage. Alhana and Gnimish belong to the largest Christian guild amongst the realms for the Alliance, called Redeemed.[18]

"We have approximately 100 players and over 200 characters in the guild," explains Heath "We have many different players on the Alliance, from every race and class type. Every Friday night we have Bible Study; we also plan and routinely run the upper instances, Scholomance, Stratholme, Dire Maul. We also do lower instances to offer help for new characters and players.

"We do have some evangelism and outreach groups....One night we were just finishing up Bible Study in Stormwind Park when someone came by and asked, 'What's going on here?' He was quite baffled, but after a few moments he sat down and actually listened to the rest of our study. He didn't say much except 'interesting' when we finished and went on."

The Christian evangelism that goes on across the realms varies from server to server, and players have been reportedly suspended by Blizzard when they are reported for putting down another player's religious affiliation. Blizzard doesn't openly accept religious evange-

---

[18] The Christian Alliance guild Redeemed is on the Stonemaul server, and the Christian Horde guild Mustard Seed Conspiracy is on the Cenarius server; both share the guild Web site http://www.toj.cc/wow. In addition there are the Christian guilds HIS on Emerald Dream and The Omnipotent Hand on Medivh.

lism, and such players face the same risks of suspension as the hackers and gold farmers of *WoW*'s underworld.

Evangelism can be extreme, because if someone doesn't accept the word of the Lord you can always use force like in the old days and challenge the player to a duel or attack if they're of another faction. Such occurrences of evangelism in *WoW* sparked a satirical essay on the spoof site LandoverBaptist.org that pokes fun at the practice: "'It is such a rush to kill other players who refuse to accept Jesus Christ as Lord,' says one gamer. 'I feel like I can really practice my faith the way God intended it. It is like I'm fighting alongside Christians of old....'"[19] Heath doesn't agree with such extreme player evangelism: "I personally believe you don't have to beat a person with the Word to get them saved. Our job is to make it available to them and if they refuse to hear then we go on."

While Heath doesn't kill non-believers, he along with both factions vanquishes a great number of demon NPCs, like those found in Desolace. It was during a quest through this dead zone that Heath realized that even in the hi-rez land of Azeroth the Lord can speak through the virtual dead: "As I was riding through the Kodo Graveyard in Desolace, the bones brought to mind Ezekiel 37, which later resulted in a message I preached at a location and used this reference to the valley of dry bones. I eventually used it as a Bible Study one Friday night in the guild as well."

Underworld—Need or Greed?

IRL [In Real Life] it is a rare, almost impossible, moment to find yourself traveling through a valley of giant dry bones and dying dinosaur-like creatures. *World of Warcraft*, and the other MMORPGs out there, provide many such sublime moments. These moments tap into a player's deepest desires and fulfill many a heroic fantasy. In this sense *WoW* is truly *needed*, even loved, by many of its five million players. The boundary of the computer game narrative quickly gives way to a rich underworld where *WoW* players continue to test the limits of injecting their human needs into this virtual universe. A

---

[19] The Landover Baptist essay "Winning Souls to Christ in *World of Warcraft*" can be found at http://www.landoverbaptist.org/news0105/wow.html.

player's assumptions, privileges, political ideals even religious beliefs quite naturally flow into their characters and out across the realms of Azeroth.

It's important to keep in mind that *World of Warcraft* is but one world in a growing virtual universe where many of the characters that you meet will roam. The ninja player that scammed you in Azeroth is likely known by a similar name on a dozen virtual worlds from *EQ2* to *Star Wars Galaxies*™. The goblins are, or perhaps should be, the patron saints of these gold farmers and ninja looters. The giant statue of a goblin with outstretched arms on the island outside of Booty Bay reminds players that the entire world ultimately exists to make money for Blizzard—"I've got what you need!"

Greed is the blood of Azeroth; we kill in its name, clicking more often than not on the little gold coin time and time again. It is greed that most definitely drives the gold farmers in the West and the owners of the gold-farming sweatshops in China. They're in many ways like the goblin trade princes in Undermine who control rings of trade, mining, deforestation, slave rings and poaching throughout Azeroth. As we know from many a quest the goblins will stop at nothing to amass their wealth and power, whether through legal means or via underworld markets and treachery.

The goblins have, we find, the most similarity to Blizzard and the underworld of black-market gold farmers. If you listen closely you can hear *both* of these *factions* echoed in the goblin refrain, "Hurry back!"

James John Bell left ABC News for a career in advocacy communications, co-founding *smart*Meme.com and becoming an award-winning writer, producer and director. He manages advertising campaigns for critical environmental and social issues for national nonprofits, like Greenpeace and the Breast Cancer Fund, as well as smaller grassroots organizations. An avid gamer, hacker and writer, James writes regularly on issues of narrative theory, social-change, technology and cultural analysis, recently authoring the afterword to the eco-SF classic *The Sheep Look Up* by John Brunner. His work has appeared in publications like the *New York Times Magazine*, the *Washington Post*, *USA Today* and *Communication Arts*. His personal Web site is LastWizards.com, which explores the eclectic mix of emerging science, postmodern media, occult philosophy, mythography and political-change theory.

WORLD OF WARCRAFT:
Timesink of the Gods

JUSTINA ROBSON

Here is a very common scenario: it is 3 A.M., and you can barely focus on the keys. In five hours you have to leave for work. Your Paladin requires only 1500 experience points to reach the next level. The rest of the team you are adventuring with needs your healing ability. There is not even a question as to what to do. Sleep, you quickly decide, is optional.

The first computer game that most people acknowledged as being so addictive that they missed sleep was Sid Meier's Civilization™, though Populous™ was a contender before that. Like World of Warcraft, Civilization™ provided a constant stream of accomplishments and milestones that were just about to be finished. In Civilization™, these consisted of buildings, conquests, tech levels and a dozen other sundry advances. The urge to hang on until your pyramid or tank units were completed was overwhelming. I remember passing that game to the owner of the largest game store in Chicago. He called me from in front of his computer at 6 A.M. and made some very personal comments. He stayed up playing until 2 A.M. on three hours of sleep the next night as well. World of Warcraft has been constructed to accomplish the same result. And it does so in a similar way. WoW is chock-full of rewards, and this not only keeps you playing for hours on end, which pleases Blizzard, but it also keeps those monthly fees coming in, which makes Vivendi even happier.

Pavlov was a scientist who early in the study of psychology defined the role of stimulus and response, often rephrased as action and reward, to sound more applicable to humans. The key aspects

that make WoW addictive are not only the many excellent game elements or social interactions, but also a game system that provides
a constant stream of rewards while you are playing. Now, this is not
some sinister plot. Rewards are good and make you feel good. They
help make any game work and fun to play. They are good game
design. The real advantage WoW has is that—I have to assume they
did this by choice at some level—the game tends to give you some
form of a success and rewards you for it every few minutes. Then it
compounds those rewards with others over a longer period. The result is that there is always something more to look forward to happening in the next minutes or hours. Something you have to keep
playing just to accomplish. When tied to other elements like a wide
range of possible activities, broad scope, strong community interaction and a hierarchal structure (that's the fancy term for when you
are playing a higher-level character who gives you status and acceptance with the other players), this reward system helps set WoW
apart and explains its appeal to non-regular gamers.

   Some of these rewards are common to all successful RPGs, a few
unique to WoW. The most obvious example is gaining experience
points. Experience is the direct and most obvious reward for completing a task. This includes slaying a monster, solving a puzzle or
completing a quest. Experience as a reward also demonstrates another key requirement for the reinforcement to be effective. The reward has to have a real meaning in the game. It has to provide a
real benefit. Experience, for example, eventually allows your character to gain levels and the ability to adventure in a wider range of
areas and find new challenges. One superhero game—set up well
with rewards—has "badges" intended to act as rewards for tasks
such as killing Sorcerers and the like. But they arouse little interest
among the players because the value of the badges is very limited in
terms of their having any real effect on the game as you play it.

   The next most obvious, if delayed, reward you get for playing
WoW is gaining a level. Leveling is a goal and to the goal-orient-
ed it is so addictive that "I'm leveling a character" is a commonly
heard phrase. This, along with letting you defeat bigger monsters,
gives your character new spells and powers.

   The value of levels as a reward and reinforcement of the desire to

*play is shown dramatically by how levels are timed when a play-
er starts a new character. The first hour or two of play is when a
new user decides if he or she likes the game or not. So to encourage satisfaction and keep interest, the first five—even ten—levels
go by very swiftly and are easy to accomplish. This rewards new
players with a feeling of success. It also has the additional benefit of rewarding experienced players who create a new character
to play (keeps them subscriptions coming!) with ease in getting a
new character started. Money, items, titles, new spells, quest rewards and the sounds and graphics you see when something is accomplished are all added to the list of things that helps to give
the player a feeling of success. Like the good game it is,* World of
Warcraft *has taken the elements that challenge the player and has
found ways to constantly and relevantly reward players when they
meet those challenges. The effects of this reinforcement are clearly
evident in Ms. Robson's tale of her own adventures in Azeroth and
their effect on her real-world life.*

WHEN I STARTED PLAYING *World of Warcraft* in March
2005 I wasn't much of a game player at all. I once
beat a computer at chess but it was set on easy level
and to be honest, I don't really know how I did it. I
am a science fiction and fantasy writer by trade, dedicated, from an
early age, to the art of making stuff up. Role-playing comes as standard with the job but it wasn't something I did with other people.
The only RP game I had ever played was a round of *Call of Cthulhu*™
and it stood out in my mind because I managed to attack an Elder
God instead of appeasing it just as the party was right on the verge
of victory, concluding our lengthy adventure with an impressively
swift wipeout.

I started playing this game as something to do during a period of
burnout after writing two novels back to back. I was curious to dis-

cover if there could be more to such things than first-person-shooter boredom or tedious strategy games, which were the only things I'd seen before. I expected the story of the world to be a bit lame and the fantasy to be full of the clichés that people of my disposition (so-called "literary" writers) are meant to despise. But by the time the cinema intro had played out on my screen I was in love with the place. The dramatic scenes and the beautiful artistic rendering of the landscape and characters of each of the races filled me with the kind of sentimental attachment most people reserve for charismatic religions. I hardly dared hope the actual game could live up to its magic-carpet promises of an experience of living in the kinds of worlds previously only available in storybooks—and storybooks, as you know, are an individual and received experience which you participate in as an enthusiastic passenger. By contrast *World of Warcraft* claimed it was going to be like living in Middle-earth plus most of the other fantasy worlds that literature had ever painted—it was a big promise to make to people, like me, whose favorite method of escapism was traveling into such universes and after we'd been there with *a lot* of talented creators.

I entered the game with many other hopes and curiosities too. First of all, because I had been invited to consider scripting for games such as this one in the past and had no idea how they worked, I wanted to find out how they were built and how the story was worked into the game. I was curious about the depth and richness of world-building made possible in this kind of environment and how real or dramatic each player's inclusion in the world was likely to become. I wondered what it would be like to play with hundreds of others from all over Europe,[1] who shared the same universe[2]—one of my long-standing obsessions as a writer has been the investigation between the real and the fantastic, how imagination is constantly be-

---

[1] Play is divided by region, so U.S. players play with others in the geographical area which Blizzard Entertainment has decided will fit onto a particular set of servers. In Europe, play is further divided into language zones, so you can choose which language you will play in from German, English or French. It is a good way to improve skills fast.

[2] The idea was really exciting, as I like meeting people, particularly ones from far away who have different views on life. I have always been rather shy too, and the chance to meet people from the safe position of my own house and secured behind a mask seemed like a great gift. As hermit crabs do, I need only crawl out of my shell if I really want to....

ing processed into reality and vice versa. I've written a lot about cyber-worlds and virtual experiences and how they inform the person involved, and now I wanted to actually have one for myself.

In particular the opportunities for exploration of the self offered by the twin features of wearing a mask (designing characters to play) and role-playing (creating a character to be any kind of person and to make the experience as *real* as possible in a place where they'd be interacting with other participants) seemed almost endless. The environment of the game is a kind of safe theater for play which, at least in the adult world, is otherwise all but nonexistent.[3] Adults don't play like this (outside the RP world, gamers and also certain sex clubs)—they've usually learned to take themselves far too seriously by the time they hit twenty. They have also had to accept the social and economic contracts[4] that require them to invest much of their time and energy into creating a single character (themselves) with defined and certified roles, most of which are often not particularly exciting.[5] I attempted to escape the life sentence into Life (what I considered to be a mundane existence in which I was largely powerless, which just goes to show how much I was not really paying attention) by becoming a writer and spending large amounts of time dropping out into worlds of my own making.

The important part of play itself is, of course, that it allows you a safe rehearsal for moves (physical or psychological) you might not be sure of making in a more important situation where you feel the stakes are higher. It's also a place to learn skills that are hard to master, most notably social skills which are central to our experience and enjoyment of life. Computer games have never previously had much to offer on these scores. They're frequently viewed as

---

[3] This is a disingenuous statement. Almost any arena formalized by some rules could count, technically, as a play zone; international finance, for example, or dating. In fact, there is very little of adult life not demarcated like this, and knowing the rules and choosing what to do with them is the root of creativity in our experience. But it is unusual, outside of sports, for adults to play together when all they are doing is playing pretend. Most of their roles are done "for real."

[4] Not all of these are a bad thing and many cannot be avoided. We must all support ourselves and get along with our fellows to survive.

[5] It is necessary to do what is needed to navigate through our cultures and societies but we do not have to accept the features of any role into our core identity. It is all too easy to fall into this trap but every time we do this we limit ourselves and our experiences, so it is important to remember that all roles are temporary illusions, not only the ones we might create in games.

the solitary pastime of the most socially unskilled members of society who use them as an excuse to avoid contact with others or
those who become increasingly isolated in reality because of the
time they spend sunken in this solitary world. I think this, together with rapid task-orientated play, has made computer games particularly attractive to men and unattractive to women as a general
rule, but World of Warcraft, with its massive multiplayer status, is
quite different.

The first thing that a player encounters is a choice of server. The
server determines what kind of a game you are going to have and
what sort of play you can expect from others. Although every server has exactly the same game world running on it, they operate with
slightly different rules. World of Warcraft offers (at present) four
choices: Normal or Player vs Environment (PvE), Player vs Player
(PvP), RolePlay (RP) and RolePlay Player vs Player (RPPvP). There
are two major things to consider here—whether or not you will RP
and whether or not you want to engage with hostile players at whim
in contested territories.

In the most gentle version of the game you can safely wander the
world without fear of assault from other players—only the monsters and NPCs will be able to do you damage. This is a PvE setting
where you have to deliberately reset your status to PvP in-game if
you fancy fighting a player. Even on a PvP server, it is still (in my
view) foolishly restricted so that you may only fight players of the
hostile faction. This seriously limits the possible RP, since no unscrupulous Rogues or tormented Warriors from your allies are able
to mug you, pick your pocket or smack you up in a barroom fight.[6]
You can have the bar fight, but only in the form of a duel. Duels can
only be played out in certain non-residential areas and their formality robs the actions of much of their spontaneity. It is charming
to believe that all allies are utterly trustworthy but it is one of the
game's least lifelike features.

Aside from conflict issues the other notable difference in server

---

[6] I have seen a good Rogue player do a pocket pick on a friendly target thus: "Slinky sneaks up and takes a look in Ebony's coin purse.... She takes some silver. The coins make a clink...." At which point Slinky runs off. Although no money can be stolen from another player this way, it was nice to see rogues doing their thing.

choice is the RP element. Even on RP servers people have chat policies whereby they do their serious RP in public chat and emote,[7]
as they would if acting in a film. In private and party chat people
are usually not RPing very hard, in my experience, and in guild and
trade chat channels they usually aren't either. In the General Chat
channel there is no RP. Careful RP players always signal what they
are doing by using the acronym OOC (Out Of Character) if they
want to speak just as their playing selves. As you can see, this adds
a layer of complication to an already complex world of chats going on, many of which seem to rely on an unmentioned telepathic
ability. Real RPers may attempt to avoid using telepathic chat as it
is not justified in the world frame, but most don't mind it and it is
very hard to play the game without using any of the long-distance
chat options, such as Looking For Group, where you need to find
buddies fast.

On non-RP servers there is, of course, no role-playing so people simply chat freely about everyday things whilst playing at monster killing.
I always found this utterly bizarre but it is what most people prefer,
especially those who got used to using *Skype*™ and other multifriend
options while involved in other games like multiplayer *Doom*™. From
now on, however, I'm only talking of my own experience and I play
RP, so all the wonderful moments where I could have been discussing
what happened in *Lost* last night whilst running around trying to slay
gurgling fish monsters have been...lost. This is probably not the place
for an in-depth discussion of chat rooms but it could easily be, because
World of Warcraft is a genius combination of compelling gameplay and
chat room all in one. For adventurous touch typists with good reflexes, entertainment doesn't get much better. All the benefits and dangers
of chat rooms are present, of course, hence the recent introduction of
parental controls to limit play time and the inbuilt filtering that attempts to curtail use of "bad" language.

A word on the filtering. Whilst I can't say **** or **** or variations
thereof, the filters are not as ham-handed as the idiot settings on certain
Disney games where you can't even type "love" without being silenced

---

[7] An emote is a chat line in a special color where you can give your character appropriate actions,
e. g., "Marian swipes at her runny nose with a piece of linen and spits into the gutter." You are only
limited by your typing speed.

as a potential pedophile.[8] *WoW* also monitors chat, which is processed and deleted on a five-minute turnaround. However, given all the channels and number of players, the chances of catching some illegal activity (such as harassment) or activity outside the agreed licensed Terms of Play (cybersex, depending on your place of residence), even using bots to search, seem pretty slim to me. Just like the real world, all life is there.[9] But they make an effort.

NPCs

So, having chosen that setup, the next thing to do is play. At first, because I didn't know anyone yet, I concentrated on how good the NPCs were as combatants, masters, friends and socialites. The fact is that games' so-called AIs are still nothing more than Finite State Machines.[10] In fact, it is much easier and faster to make something up like an NPC than it is to get an AI to react and respond to input through real learning. Real AI chooses the blue pill or the red pill, if it is able to access the outside world, can see color and has been given some kind of stimulus to cause a preference to evolve. Real AI does not stand up slowly from a seat by the fire in a tavern, stare into the flames, throw its tankard onto the logs and stalk toward you, muttering curses as it draws a glowing Blade of The Innocents out of a fold of its ragged cloak.

Since one of my incarnations is a proud geek girl, I've never had any problems navigating through wriggling oceans of Boy Cooties[11] in or-

---

[8] I'm not sure if this is true but I heard it so I'm including it in that unjustified way I have of including things for the sake of making an interesting point. There are certainly many limits in place on chat rooms used by school-age people to try and protect them (right intention), however badly thought out they may be.

[9] For a great little article on this see http://www.pointlesswasteoftime.com/games/wowworld.html. And in answer to your wondering, yes, there are prostitutes in *WoW*. Everything is in *WoW*. Would your child be exposed to them? It is possible, just as in the rest of the universe. And yes, that kind of thing is outside the terms of the License Agreement, I think, but it exists. The sex definitely exists and some of it is good. I once materialized (logged in) in the middle of a couple having sex (inn rooms with lockable doors and silence zoning desperately needed), so I know.

[10] There is probably some mileage to be made over the possibility that human beings are nothing more than Finite State Machines made out of meat.

[11] See Debra Doyle's article, "The Girl Cooties Theory of Literature" at http://www.sff.net/paradise/girlcooties.htm, in which she explains the allergy of some men and boys to any of the softer elements of life that might be found in SF involving "mushy stuff." Boy Cooties are obviously the opposite and infest all technological and masculine enterprises ruled by the two paradigms of Hardness and Rigor. *Grand Theft Auto*™ simply crawls with Boy Cooties whilst *The Legend of Zelda: Ocarina of Time*®, in spite of being a computer game, is almost Boy Cootieless.

der to get to SF goodies, but in severe cases involving the kind of mi-
sogyny usually reserved for institutionalized religions I will sometimes
pass. Attracting women, especially those of us who are of *uncertain
age* (the Mom demographic), has long been a problem for the computer games industry, not aided by the appearance of cyber-babes like
Lara Croft.[12] Its related industries (in the U.S./European sector), comic
books and literary SF, have also traditionally been the preserve of teenage boys and men.[13] It has often been perceived by the external world's
mature women as not only infested with Boy Cooties (irrelevant and
annoying in their lives) but Nerdy Boy Cooties (the kind that never
leave home where they have set up a laboratory-cum-bedroom in the
garage, and dress as though they are always twelve or else forty-seven).
However, because games are made up of State Machines, the actions
they are good at producing in NPCs include fighting, trading, fighting
and…er…what they don't do is talk well. They recite prepared scripts
from a randomized table of five possible scripts, rather like a certain
kind of male partner stereotyped in sitcoms.

> Input: Anything the woman says.
> Output 1: You look lovely as you are.
> Output 2: Let's stay in tonight and watch the telly.
> Output 3: Fries, please.
> Output 4: Shh, the match is on.
> Output 5: What's for lunch?

The above kind of behavior would be reasonable grounds for divorce, so no NPC is ever going to win over a woman's debit card,
even if it is the age of the nerd and geeks are temporarily fashionable.
But in WoW there are some genuinely softer and more feminine moments worked into the game architecture. For instance, you might
go about capturing rabid bears for humane treatment in Darkshore
(mercy mission, kind to animals, good for the environment, quest-

---

[12] I think Lara has a lot in common with her sisters from the zeitgeist, Buffy the Vampire Slayer and
other supergirls. They all owe a lot to their foremother, Wonder Woman, and they are all inven-
tions of the male mind as it wrestles with aspects of the feminine…but that's another essay.

[13] SF itself has come to be identified along such gender lines because of the historical prevalence of
male protagonists and female-as-accessory features.

giver is a tragic hunk with a heart…go go go Girl Cooties!) but also find someone to talk with about fashion in Ironforge and who's dating who in your guild.[14]

Well, with all that in place the heady potentials went right to my head. I thought this would be an ideal setting to discover any real truth (as opposed to a wish-fulfillment fantasy intended to console) in the Beauty and the Beast ideal; we are often fooled into making untrue assumptions about each other by outward appearances; underneath our exterior disguises we are all lost creatures of Heaven, looking for love. I was hoping to create a character who more truly reflected the inner me than my actual physical self. I also thought maybe some interesting things might happen in a universe where the masks people wore (their characters) were gendered but where there was no power difference between the genders or races, none *at all*. Giving everyone a level start would surely be like stripping off the unfair social and genetic handicaps and advantages. Maybe some kind of new society would emerge? I also thought it would be a safe play area since if bad things happened it wouldn't matter, because it wasn't quite real….[15]

Of course there are gendered power differences in *WoW*, once you get away from the game stats. If there weren't, why would so many players play the "pretty" races of Night Elves and Humans and almost universally choose the most attractive faces for their character: the one with the biggest eyes, slight smile and smooth features? In the Alliance faction there are two pretty races—Night Elves and Humans—and on the Horde side you can manufacture a reasonable Troll or Tauren quite easily. Even the Undead have a pretty face for the girl variety. However, people who want to look fierce and scary are mostly teenage boys (by my estimate anyway) and everyone else seems to want to be cute—unsurprising, given that outer beauty is the Universal Lubricant for all social situations. For true beauty you have to choose a female character, as none of the male characters are

---

[14] I stereotype female interests here in the cause of equal opportunities and to shore up my point.

[15] IMPORTANT NOTE—unless you are a practiced psychopath, never assume that anything you do in any sphere is unreal in the sense that it will not have an effect on you because you are distanced by a role or physical space. I should have known this after twenty years of writing but it's funny how clueless one can be on such matters.

quite lovely. Many male players must have done so and it was an additional interesting game to play inside the world, attempting to spot who was playing an opposed gender to their own. Detecting some kinds of information about players is impossible without their consent, of course, but all the important things you need to know about people are reasonably transparent, even in this interface.[16] I found that after a couple of weeks I could tell a lot just by the way people navigated the landscape.

There are people who move out of the way of a toppling ogre and people who don't. The ogre won't squash you flat in the game. In fact, when it comes to being squashed flat by dead tonnage there's nothing in Azeroth that'll do it to you, so there's no need to get out of the way. You end up transecting the thing and looking like you grew out of its stomach. But some people dance aside and some don't. Some people have perfected the running loot because it looks cool, and some loot with deliberate care. Some people hesitate at the fringe of battle. Some people have no concentration and are slow to the fight. Some people are on the situation before you notice it. Some people just aren't with it at all. You can pick this up just from the way their character moves, and how well they execute their most common actions. Like in reality. Some people have weight and character and presence and some…don't. There is significant weight of psychological evidence to demonstrate that mostly you invest other people with powers or abilities you feel you lack, or else come to detest them for features you most detest about yourself, but the triggers that cause you to place such importance on one person rather than another, whatever they are, emerge here as surely as they do in real life. I'd take bets that in an RPG like this one with its limited interface you can tell a great deal about someone before you even use the chat pane.

However the interesting question about role-play is how closely the character resembles the real player behind it. My character was a free version of me, and most people were playing varieties of this

---

[16] Your success rate at detecting these things will not be greater than your real-life success rate, of course, so if you habitually miss the obvious in social moments the lack of information here will not help. I would also add that trust violation issues in RP situations—where a player chooses to reveal themselves but lies about who they are and their life story in order to garner sympathy or attract an attachment—is common enough to warrant a significant cautionary moment here.

with some additional storyline dramatizing their background, as far as I could tell. Only really practiced RPers seemed able to do characters with less reference to themselves. My curiosity about this is based in the longing to discover that no matter what shape or age we find ourselves, whatever our outer form, underneath we are equal— *so* equal that if you gave us all the same frontage we'd be free in the way that God intended, not blinded by our superficial (yes, perhaps genetically driven) biases.

In fact, I think that the MMORPG environment does provide a high degree of this and that's why the people who are in the position of playing themselves are often liberated and forthcoming when it comes to talking with others. The interface seems less guarded than an ordinary meeting. It's a fabulous moment when you realize nobody knows you're the one that was always picked last for netball, and they need *never* know…because now you're a rip-snorting Tauren Shaman called Wildmane. Protected by such beauty and anonymity…who would not dare? What a relief to be free of one's old form!

And by beauty I don't just mean those voluptuous Human women with their Vidal Sassoon hair and double-D chests[17] (yeah, you'd *run* everywhere with those). Everything in *World of Warcraft* is strangely beautiful in an epic, fantastical way. This is such a determining factor in the way that the populations distribute that on the coming upgrade the Horde is getting its own "pretty" race—Blood Elves—for all the people who want to be as gorgeous as Orlando Bloom but also eeeevil to the core. For the most part, nobody chooses the savage faces for their characters and the NPCs are all glamorous in that way of actors on a big stage, even horrible creations like Stitches, Abercrombie's Undead Frankenmonster, who lumbers eternally through Darkshire on the hunt for the living. In fact, the other major mitigating factor against the deadly Boy Cooties of the game type is *World of Warcraft*'s audiovisual crafting.

The division of the races follows a fantasy standard that reach-

---

[17] My RP buddy insists that they are nowhere near as bloke-oriented as the women in *Prince of Persia*™ but it remains something of a mystery when the more powerful an item of clothing gets on a female character, the smaller and flimsier it looks. Sadly for lecherous types of all ages, you can't take off the doll underwear.

es down from stereotype immemorial. The Dwarves are all Scottish (!) and drink. The Gnomes are perky and bonkers. The Night Elves are snooty and sexy and the Humans are regular down-home types. The Tauren are noble and deep, the Trolls cool and mystic, the Orcs are…Orcs and the Undead are romantically ruined Byronesque figures. Their native lands fit them in the way that 100,000 books and movies from *She* to *Aliens* have suggested they always would, so that the world feels "right" and real even though you know it's a load of storybook hokey and the regions have a way of changing that is geographically looney. It's a stereotype taken to an art form. The snow outside Ironforge is crisp and the sky is blue. Thunder Bluff is awesome and fine. Everything is the way you longed for it to be, flagons of mead at mighty halls or rotting shacks full of crazy voodoo priests lost in the backwoods. Little mysteries and mighty legends abound. There are dragons and there are hosts of other creatures from every fable you ever heard about. And it looks and sounds beautiful. I love the footprints you leave in the snow, the way sand kicks up, the changing music of the places which is good enough to listen to as ambient on its own…and the color palettes of the changing skies are just gorgeous. Sure, other games are graphically better in some ways but artistically, *WoW* has the edge. Look at *Doom*™—what a grim old place. Needs a bit of nice goblin wallpaper with pineapples on it.

Wiser MMORPG players may laugh here. I went in like Flynn. I thought I'd be done in three weeks but time moves differently in other worlds, as you know, and by the time I woke up, seven months had passed. In the time I spent in Azeroth I could have written a novel and I should have been doing just that. Instead I lived another lifetime—two lifetimes actually. I made friends, found a sister, fell in love, broke hearts, fought demons, put down dangerous religious cults, faced madmen in the jungle, fought dragons in sunken temples and rescued cute pets from horrible fates. I made money and joined a guild and became a trade master. I went from being a lowly Level 1 player to a Level 60, able to swank about with the best of them. It would take books to tell you everything that happened and about the people I met.

But shouldn't I have been working? Oh, yes. In my case I was running away from two years of non-stop work pressure, illness and the sudden explosion of unwelcome domesticity and social vacuum that new motherhood brought. I made friends easily and soon gained a level of intimacy, due to the chat interface and the game structure, which I rarely reached in real encounters. I soon knew players better than I knew my own neighbors.

The thing is, although all the game-playing stats are fundamentally something anyone can get, given enough hours, what's true in real life is true in *World of Warcraft*—social skills are everything, and on an RP server they are often much more entertaining than anything the actual game world can throw at you. The game is also designed to encourage social activities. Most quests go faster with a party of buddies and many of them are almost impossible without a variety of characters helping one another. Thus, in sharp contrast to the passivity of television and the isolation of single person shooter games or mysteries, *World of Warcraft* demands interaction and lots of it. As my time in the game progressed I came to realize more and more what a huge difference this made. I had never lasted more than a few weeks at any game before, but in this world the possibilities seemed infinitely more exciting. There is always someone else around, and for the most part people are helpful and once you've made a few friends whose company you enjoy the experience can be wonderful. Suit up, we're off to have some *fun*!

There are also gentler and less competitive activities on offer in Azeroth, compared to other MMORPGs' dedications to fighting and trading, many of which make the game utterly charming. The long list of ready-made emotes is one such thing,[18] and individual players' skills in dishing out occasional custom emote actions can bring a smile that lasts a long time . . . as, for instance, the Gnome I saw aboard one of the ships sailing from Menethil to Darkshore.[19] The Gnome walked aboard the boat and climbed up toward the wheel, where *he tests the play of the wheel then gets out a spanner and makes his little adjustments. . . .* In *World of Warcraft* characters can also dance, make rude gestures, tell jokes (Blizzard really needs to work on the Elf

---

[18] http://www.worldofwarcraft.com/info/basics/emotes.html.

[19] This was after the demise of the much-loved Captain Placeholder, who used to teleport players back and forth. There is a commemorative song dedicated to this charming NPC here: http://en.wikipedia.org/wiki/Captain_Placeholder.

jokes...), laugh, cry and do many other things quite charmingly. Of the non-animated emotes I particularly like /golfclap [You clap half-heartedly, clearly unimpressed] and /shindig [You raise a drink in the air before chugging it down. Cheers!] but there are many more, and you can create your own actions as fast as you can type. Animated emotes also provide almost the only communications (bar fighting) possible between the warring factions of the game. Thus it is that you can come across parties of Horde and Alliance players dancing with each other on the road instead of fighting.

And there is no need to fight if you don't want to. There are other things to pass the time pleasantly, such as Fishing. I always thought it strange that you can do something like Fishing in this universe—accumulating fish, of course, and possibly treasure maps and old boots—but you can't play chess with someone, or cards...surely there must be a market for combining net poker and online RPGs.

I know that in the U.S. version of the game you can order take-out food from a shop in-game and it comes to your real house. Anyway, the lack of certain objects in the universe doesn't stop the most inventive minds. Empty shops and taverns in the major cities such as Stormwind attract entrepreneurs, hence the players who stay put as innkeeper, his steward and waitress instead of heading off into the wilderness for adventure and mayhem.

When I first came across this I was baffled—you log on for hours to work in a virtual bar? But yes. They cook real food (which requires cooking skill). And the drinks make you drunk: if you have a couple of stiff ones the screen goes blurry and you can't walk straight, if you are sitting down the room seems to go wobbly and when you talk your words appear slurred. These are delightful programmed touches, and there are other humorous and lifelike features in the world that add great moments to a lot of ordinary play. One of my favorites is the unreliability of the Engineering skill, which produces items such as EZ-Thro Dynamite, an item which has the cheerful label on it "hardly ever goes off in your hand." Not to mention the teleport device which sometimes takes you to the wrong town, or materializes you 200 meters above ground, resulting in unplanned and gruesome death. There are further joys and jokes everywhere, from things you eat that change you (such as Savory Deviate De-

light, which turns you into a pirate or a rogue) to minor spells like
Rat Nova ([you turn into a rat]...you need cheese!).

Besides the humor of various items, there are too many pop-culture
references embedded in this universe to list but here are a couple. Why
do the gorillas in Stranglethorn drop empty barrels?...because of *Donkey Kong* of course. Why is there a character called Hemet Nesingwary
looking for the pages of his book Green Hills of Stranglethorn?...be-
cause of Ernest Hemingway. He also teaches Fishing, in a slightly
different guise down in Booty Bay. Bishop LaVey gives quests from
Stormwind Cathedral—whilst the real world counterpart Anton La
Vey founded the church of Satan...which makes me wonder about all
those Paladins and their so-called devotion to the Light.

And if you don't care for or know any of these wry jokes you can
always amuse yourself by going to a wedding, say, which will have
been organized and catered for by one of the player-built businesses
that do everything from find a Priest to get the dress made. Speaking
of Tailoring, I think fondly of the fashion show that was organized at
a beautiful spot in Duskwood.[20]

Players turned up in outfits they had culled together from many
hours checking the Auction House—and this was before Blizzard
wisely put in the Wardrobe function, which sadly does not take you
to a wintery land ruled by a big lion but shows you what items look
like on your character. The Horde champion even turned up in his
casuals. It was *that* civilized (until some fool killed Dorc, the Orc
from the newspaper comic strip,[21] and it got a bit nasty).

And pets—you can have entire menageries of pets—not only
Hunters have pets they partner up with for life that fight for them.
There's good money in cats, by the way. Cats are as popular in Azeroth as anywhere, and if you know where to get cats you can make
a tidy profit from people who don't. This brings me to the problems
of the economy. As the populations are aging the inflation rate has
become so horrific that it's much harder, financially, to be a low-level
player than it used to be.

The issue of corporate cash farming, where players create charac-

---

[20] Where there is now a Raid Dragon stationed, but at the time it was just a pretty portal and a ramp.
[21] Read all about it at http://www.theallianceherald.co.uk/, our server's player-produced tabloid.

ters to collect money and items, then make profits by selling them out of game for real-world cash, has almost closed off the rare and epic armor/weapons market to anyone not in the gold-for-cash loop. Since MMORPG trades in the real world are worth the GDP of a minor nation these days it seems like the deepest pocket is going to win. Unless you don't care about all that stuff and realize there is no victory condition coming your way in any case. Me, I didn't care about my relatively crappy gear. I wasn't the only one, but I was reasonably rare. Most people get to Level 60 and set to grinding dungeons for "their" epic armor sets and "their" perfect weapons. It's duller than watching paint dry to return to an instance[22] fifty times and, for me, one of the game's biggest drawbacks. Coupled with the fact that higher-level dungeons tend to be larger and take many hours to play, it is by far the worst feature of the world. Even with additional regions and quests coming into line for Level 60 players, I think that most of the fun to be had is down around the 20 to 35 level mark. After that point most people tend to get a bit serious because of the major purchases and efforts that lie ahead (buying a mount for a huge sum of money, then going into harder instances and in bigger groups, eventually needing to join raid guilds with additional online time outside the game if you want to be really serious about getting all that "essential" gear). To my mind, this is more like being on the management staff of a demanding but tedious corporation than it is fun, and considering you get no pay it is time better spent using the same skills in a real job.

High-level dungeons and dungeons in general, as well as suffering from relatively unrealistic NPC behavior,[23] suffer from the World State problem. The persistence of the World State is a feature that a low-fantasy game like *World of Warcraft* can't really avoid. No matter what a player does during their quests or battles, it is not possible for them to either alter the World State or to alter the high-fantasy storyline which provides the backdrop. Added to this is the respawn issue, necessary to keep the world populated with enough monsters for all in general use areas, but meaning that you can kill the "same" bear every ten

---

[22] A nice feature which allows groups to participate in their unique version of each dungeon.

[23] The aggro ranges mean that NPCs act as though deaf and blind to battle well within their range, making them seem stupid and unreal.

minutes. This results in players being forced to suspend their disbelief a great deal as they see others repeat tasks and quests they have already done within an unchanging landscape, and in particular when
they must repeatedly enter dungeons to kill bosses they killed the day
before...and the day before that, too. This mostly causes significant
trouble to RPers who hoped to realistically integrate their lives with
the world's high-fantasy story, but it undeniably spoils the effect, as do
some of the other features of *World of Warcraft*, such as the ridiculous
aggro ranges and hit scores on their general area wildlife. Players with
high-level characters can still be unhorsed or damaged by creatures
that are orders of magnitude lower in strength. Realistically, such con-
trasts of power should provoke fleeing in the NPCs as much as the reverse situation produces fleeing in the player.[24]

There are games which do not have static World States, such as
the MUD Achaea. For this to work, however, the players need to
be able to rise to positions of power in various hierarchies and to
determine some story arcs of their own in the natural way. Since
any changes of World State in a game like *World of Warcraft* would
require implementation by programmers of a truly evolving world,
they would entail continual updates of a significant proportion of the
world map and NPCs, an ongoing development far in excess of most
abilities. Some progress might be made by employing real players to
sit behind the major NPCs in the game, employees who had Game
Master powers to alter the world order, but again, it's hard to see how
this might be implemented when it could easily require significant
alterations on a daily basis.

The way that Blizzard addressed the stagnation issue of a static
world is a reasonable compromise—it chose to issue regular patches with small updates, continually responding to various changes
in server populations and player comments, and releasing various
dungeons, landmasses and races at key stages in population matu-
rity so that as many people reach the higher levels, more activities
become open to them. There were also many seasonal touches of

---

[24] Leeroys excepted. Leeroy is a name for stupid group-play that has passed into general gaming
talk after the spread of a video shot in a WoW instance where a player of that name jumps up and
pulls all the monsters in a dungeon into the patiently waiting and well-organized party with devil-
ish delight...because he is stoned.

fun, such as the Halloween celebrations and the Darkmoon Faire to add interest. Sadly, however, my personal long-term goal of locating Malfurion Stormrage and getting him to pitch that irritating tosspot Fandral Staghelm off the top of his tree looks like it will never be fulfilled. In my Machiavellian dreams I wonder what it would be like if World States were allowed to evolve...every server a different parallel universe...ah, the horror for Developers....Oh, if only AI really worked![25]

But it doesn't, though it will one day, thanks to this game and others and the fact that they are slowly carving out their own real-world economic power. *World of Warcraft* is a very Phil Dickian artifact. Like all MMORPGs, it is a curious timeslip phenomenon—one of those things which is both Real and Science Fictional at the same time. To have reached the point where people would kill one another over ownership of a virtual sword—why, I almost feel the same chill of future shock as I do when I contemplate Neil Armstrong's footstep on the moon. But I am sad that the moment is such a tragic one. Many people reacted to the incident itself with a sad shake of the head—my goodness, the thing isn't even *real*! Those poor, deluded saps in that game-world, they can't tell the difference between reality and a game. We have a way to go before we are all willing to realize how much of reality is just something we make up, too.

Meanwhile the MMORPGs offer anyone the opportunity to be a hero, but not one who can change their world. They seem to provide an arena in which we can escape various shackles, and make spiritual journeys of self discovery, as well as entertain us. As I played I often thought of a comment written by Philip K. Dick on a character he had developed called Perky Pat. Pat is the ideal woman, living the ideal life in a metaverse accessed through taking a mind-altering drug. When you take CAN-D and observe the paperdoll world of the metaverse you become Pat, if you are a woman, and her boyfriend if you are a man (he only specified about heterosexuals). Anyway, Dick wrote a story about Perky Pat, and then a book featuring her world and how it could be used, called *The Three Stigmata of Palmer El-*

---

[25] It doesn't, but when you can rent roomfuls of telesales operators, why not roomfuls of professional players? If gaming is to move on I can't see another way of getting more realistic interactions...maybe much bigger state machines...hmm...perhaps that is the way to AI, after all?

dritch. It was a book that made him so frightened that he was unable to proofread it—it was an expression, he thought, of the greatest evil, and the evil in question is that of determining reality for others and making them slaves. Pat, the perfection of escape, was the character he would have most liked to meet. Palmer Eldritch, the manipulator behind the scenes, was the one he was afraid of. He met neither in the end, but he said,

> *"I guess that is the story of life: what you most fear never happens, but what you most yearn for never happens either. This is the difference between life and fiction. I suppose it's a good trade-off. But I'm not sure. {PKD 1979}"*[26]

In fiction, especially fantasy fiction such as those that *WoW* is based on, we like to express our fears and desires in their strongest forms. I am not sure there is a trade-off. We give form to those fears and desires in our imaginations and now we render them into metaverses of their own. Fantasy literature and other media are the most psychologically raw of those forms and that is why their stories are so often driven on what seem very unsophisticated and morally distinct principles—things are good or bad, frightening or lovely, desirable or hateful. Fantasy is the language before thought, where analysis of our lives really takes place. It populates our dreams and fills our waking lives with fears, small and large, and desires, which are fears in other guises. In my opinion, Pat is the nice face of slavery (the slavery to the pursuit of love and self acceptance, for everyone compares themselves to Pat and feels wanting) and Palmer is the truth behind it (Palmer will trade the eternal illusion of being Pat in exchange for your life—a first-order Faustian bargain). The ubiquity of the formats in High Fantasy stories is the grammar of the subconscious and the situation on offer, of becoming some kind of Pat figure, the hero of a lifetime, is a heady lure that takes you out of your own life. This is heavily present in *WoW*, much more than any other game I have come across so far.

---

[26] Taken from this site: http://www.philipkdickfans.com/pkdweb/The%20Days%20Of%20Perky%20Pat.htm.

However, though this lure offers certain freedoms, as I mentioned earlier—to get out of oneself, to live other lives—it does so within the confines of a generic and comforting fiction operated by secure rules and limits far in excess of any safety you might encounter in the reality of your physical world or the workings of your own mind. *Warcraft*, in particular, is a very safe world. You cannot really die. Nobody can harm you (even on PvP servers, players who exist simply to harass and kill other players are rare and there are measures in place to discourage or bar them from play). The only danger to you lies in the emotional situations you may create with other players, or the physical problems you might develop as a result of spending hours sitting very still at a PC.[27] For me, however, Dick's aforementioned quote rings true. One goes out to the game world in the hopes of finding your fictional perfect love, or your great adventure, the things you wish for but can't get in reality, even if it's only to blow off steam killing monsters. If this weren't true, why would people love the place so much? It's so full of innocence, safety and hope, little achievements and virtuous effort. It is morally, physically and politically easy to understand. Goodness[28] is rewarded (with game rewards, XP, money, skill points and friendship) and badness (griefing players) is punished with ostracism and tough solo times or even excommunication. Welcome to a Just Universe, sanitized for your comfort and protection.[29]

The above few sentences represent reasonably well why Fantasy in general has great appeal for many people and why some people hate it so very, very much. It's because of the War of Realities issue. There is a moral question surrounding the recreational use of Fantasy which is deeply embedded in Western society. I can't speak for the regions of the earth where MMORPGs and fantasy gaming are most popular (Korea, China and so forth) but here there has been

---

[27] Speaking as a fitness instructor, I must tell you that this is not an insignificant threat to your well-being. I spent too much time at the computer and have back problems, despite sitting on my very expensive no-back-problems orthopedic seat. MMORPGs are bad news for your real body if you don't look after it well each day. More on this later.

[28] I don't mean "light vs. dark" goodness in the high moral sense of Azeroth's politics, I mean goodness in the sense of a player doing as they are asked to by quest givers and assisting others in whatever their goals are.

[29] If you, reader, believe that the world in which we live is a Just World, because of religion or because you haven't been paying attention, you have my condolences.

a strong sense for a long time that immersion in the fantastic weakens character and only by facing up to Reality (by which the people making this statement mean the "world as I see it") can we acquire and demonstrate the kind of backbone-in-the-face-of-frightful-chaos from which civilization is built.

This is a mistaken complaint, put at the wrong door. People who hate Fantasy for its allegedly *easy* moral universes hate it because they see it as promoting a (mistaken) black-and-white moral worldview with overly simplified solutions. They do not see it as a necessary and welcome relief from the infinitely muddy and highly pressured world of complex human relationships that we inhabit in our daily lives. However, although the mistake is to think that Fantasy fosters ridiculously simple notions of reality,[30] it is not a mistake to note that escapism in general does not do anyone much good in the long run, since it only addresses the symptoms and not the causes of whatever is being escaped from.

I mention this with regard to *WoW* because, like all entertainments, it serves this purpose of escapism very nicely, allowing people to vent all kinds of frustration and explore unmet needs. As long as they are doing that (even if it causes them to lose their jobs or whatever else) they are not out and about questioning the government or asserting their rights or meddling with institutions of power or creating better lives for themselves or anything crazy like that. As some wise person once remarked (I paraphrase since I can't recall the quote exactly), "Jailers don't mind escapism. It's escape they don't like." It is no surprise to me that the people most in need of escape are those whose daily lives are most circumvented by institutional and social pressures to conform with fairly hefty punishments (economic or otherwise) doled out for failure to do so. The Chinese government must have thought long and hard before they put a three-hour upper limit on the playing of MMORPGs—the loss of all those working hours against the release of so much positive energy which might otherwise have leaked into some other kind of action. . . . It's a tough call.

---

[30] I think it expresses a longing for life to be simple and relatively easily sorted out, rather than promoting that as a worldview—it's very hard to pitch good vs. evil with any conviction these days, in fact it's so difficult that it mostly only occurs now within major reality-denying systems of thought . . . no prizes for spotting religious fundamentalism in that group but you can have 1100XP and a 100XP bonus for every ideology you wanted to add.

The devotion of time and effort to lives other than the one you are physically living can go two ways, of course—positive changes that bring benefits to you and your relationships, or negative changes that spoil those things. One negative that is difficult to mitigate against is the loss of contact with people you know in your real life, unless they are prepared to play with you.

In the world of physical reality our bodies are in continuous contact, if not with other bodies, then with everything around us. The virtual worlds of any kind that we encounter where contact is very limited by interface issues create a peculiar arena in which there can be great intimacy—in a conversation for example—but at the same time this enormous sense of a gap which, under ordinary circumstances, you would have a great deal of contact with another, through eyes, sharing and reading of body language, expressions and direct touches. At the same time this community of friends, or even lovers, might comfort you, the degree to which you feel connected to those people, players or characters becomes tinged with the loneliness of all long-distance relationships, particularly when you have to log off. At the same time the game provides a fresh environment in which to meet and know others, its nature almost guarantees that you will be separated from them.

Many people go on to meet in real life or form friendships outside of these games. Some get married and live separate lives in the game with players they will never meet in reality. Some people leave home forever to live with friends they met in the metaverse. On the plus side, one would hope that being able to make lasting relationships with people you never see would be a good thing, for if you see them perhaps inhibitions about their appearance (yours, as well as theirs) might mean you never would start what will turn out to be a great friendship or even love. On the other hand, without the physical world and its masses of additional information, you are vulnerable to being conned by unscrupulous others more than usual.

The abandonment of the body for the rarefied world of pure mental existence is a staple fantasy of science fiction which has leaked steadily into real scientific explorations of consciousness. The dream of being downloaded and living in some kind of digital format inside a computer is something people actually work on today. In most cases, where this makes the news or feature columns, there is not much sense that anything great is going to be lost in this transaction. Perhaps this is because such science fiction is all written by boffins who play MMORPGs in their spare time.[31] It goes along with a general sense of the physical and sensual world as a frightening and degrading thing, a notion that arrived with the spread of various religions around the world shortly after the height of the Roman Empire and one which was consolidated by further stages of philosophical and Christian thought into the division of the human into highly demarcated segments with accompanying social and moral attributes: body (yucky and sinful), soul/spirit (pure but vulnerable), mind (place of true knowledge, route to purity, susceptible to corruption), emotions (frightening, spontaneous, leading to problems in most forms).

As a result of this Cartesian divorce, our concepts of how we were became fragmented and our experiences became fragmentary also. Because we have to speak about them in this divided way, because this has become the language of knowledge and the accepted form of thought, it has also become the way in which we experience our "selves." This is so prevalent that now to speak of experiences as holistic is exceptional and to encounter ourselves in a holistic way requires dedicated attention to the present and to every part of our beings, as in the practice of yoga. It's no longer our natural state.[32] It really does seem as if the mind might be separated from the physical world, like cream from milk. Freed of the demands of the body and the so-called "irrational" pestering of the emotions, our mind and spirit will be able to escape, goes the story, which is nothing more than a life-after-death scenario rewritten into material terms. During the absorption of play in an MMORPG, as in any other immersing task, it really seems so.

This may seem like an overly deep kind of thought to bother with—World of Warcraft is only a game, right? But while the personality adventures, the body is under enormous stress through lack of movement, poor support and frequently having its demands to eat, drink and excrete postponed or denied due to the timesink fea-

---

[31] I say this rather jokingly, but it's not as untrue as I wish it were.

[32] Although it is for animals, because they aren't hampered by language which necessitates division and demarcation.

tures built into the game that produce the "just five more minutes" factor[33] which makes us sit and play in spite of other needs. The timesinks and the very variety of possibilities within the game make it particularly difficult to create clear firewalls around tasks so that a player can acquire definite break points where they feel content to stop playing. If you complete a quest, then you need to hand it in, at which point you often acquire another. If you finish anyway, it's time to sell your loot or check the Auction House or gather some herbs or help someone who just called for aid in a two-minute job or put five points on your Fishing skill....[34] The list of potentially useful and self-advancing actions is almost endless. What has that to do with contact and the division of experience? I think that it is an extension of the way in which we already perceive our lives and their purpose taken to an extreme expression and yielding extreme results (that are also extremely bad for your health). I'm sad about it because I love the game but I can't deny the horrible effect my compulsive play has had on my health.

Nobody living in the corporate-driven worlds that produce the most players of MMORPGs can fail to have noticed that the cocktail of social pressures to achieve and, uniquely in this century, to "improve" oneself to levels of physical, mental and social good requires that one needs to be working hard at all times, even working at play, to reach the lifestyle goals that our culture endorses so heavily as good. *Warcraft*, like other games, is fun, but it is also as demanding and stressful as work, requiring devoted attention for long periods. Since many of us spend our working lives at computers instead of striding about doing physical work, it means even more hours locked into physical stagnation and isolation. Your character may run a marathon during play time but you haven't moved an inch except for your mouse finger and a few keystrokes. You have not been aware of any of your physical senses. I felt divorced from the world on my return to it and

---

[33] Five more minutes in game terms always turns out to be half an hour and you can scale up temporal estimates on the same ratio, I have found.

[34] I still think that math should be taught on a quest-and-reward system like the *Warcraft* one. Instead of killing trolls one could complete equations or solve problems. Then, when one delivers a paper, one receives a great new item or cash for one's character…entertaining AND educational, all in one. I'd have a degree by now if it worked like that.

ratty and aggravated for no reason. It's because of the lack of movement. We were made to move, to run, leap and work hard with our bodies, to make all kinds of contact all the time. In an MMORPG world we don't do any of that, but it gives the illusion that we are. It's all of the work and none of the health benefits, sadly.

To that end, the next great leap forward in game terms must be the full physical response gear that means that when I have to make the trail run from Theramore to Thousand Needles, I'll be running every step of the way myself. When I need food, I'll be eating it and drinks ditto—bought in-game, taken in reality. The dizzy dream of Neo in *The Matrix*—"I know kung fu!"—will become true. If I want to fight and beat people, I'd better get fit enough to move well enough that my character can do it. I can go to the athletics stadium in Elwynn Forest and win the Azeroth Olympiad....

Of course, then there will be people writing essays about those dying of physical exhaustion whilst running and jumping around in unreal worlds, forgetting to stop and sleep and rest, but at least in that scenario there is a natural incentive to cease play when you're losing due to undeniable tiredness, and the animal requirements to live in the world and pump various endocrines through your system will ensure that your cellular body gets some of the rewards.

However, my main point about contact is that lack of it produces stressed, unhealthy and lonely people. While these games give a strong kind of mental contact, they deprive you of all the rest, just as you can be socially deprived by a life that is solely perceived in the game terms of Task-Execute-Reward repeated *ad infinitum* because in life and in *World of Warcraft* there is no Endgame and no ultimate Victory Condition.

The joy of playing and living is the playing and living, not the pitiful handouts of a quest reward system. But you can easily forget this because in *WoW*, particularly, you are hit by a reward approximately every five minutes and the constant reinforcement and rapid success rate gives a heady sense of progress. As someone who likes to achieve a lot I felt that this factor played heavily into my (then) lack of self-worth that meant I saw achievements as stars on the board of my self-justification (for play or for life), so I got hooked into the "just five more minutes" thing very hard. In the end I was unable to manage my time playing and make it part of a more rounded day-to-day life, so my only choice was to uninstall. I made a decision that when I returned to *World of Warcraft* (if I did) I could only go back when I was fit and had restored my life to a sane balance. And written another novel or two.

Of course, I do want to go back because, even with all the drawbacks, it was such hellish good fun in so many ways, not least discovering all the creative delight that had gone into creating such a rich and charming environment. I didn't expect to encounter people who would challenge my beliefs about myself and my life either, but that's what I found. I went in as a curious adventurer, not knowing my real quest (to find self-acceptance, actually) or that relationships I began in *WoW* with other players would overlap into my real life as heavily as they did. For my known and unknown online friends, I would like to return to Azeroth, the community that exists only in a machine but is as lively as reality, and find out how they are all doing. I'd also like to thank them for all constantly affirming that Real Life was more important than the game, even though they didn't always manage to apply that wisdom to their own lives.

After leaving Azeroth, I am close to completing my personal quest at last. The reward is epic, and it was well worth all the trials, which in my earlier life I had never been able to resolve but which came to conclusion through the agency of this fantastic metaverse and the people I met there. For reasons I still don't understand, it was easier there than in reality to address things which bothered me too deeply to dwell on. It has something to do with dressing up and hiding, just enough, to be free of some fear, something you can't do in face-to-face RP games because…everyone knows you. And it's easy to talk to people not connected to your life about what really bothers you. I soon came to view it as therapy and, at £10 a month, it's really cheap compared to the other kind.

Justina Robson lives in Yorkshire. She once won a literary prize (the amazon.co.uk Writers' Bursary 2000), and two of her books have been shortlisted for the Arthur C. Clarke Award. Her third book, *Natural History*, was runner-up in the John W. Campbell Award. At time of writing she has two novels shortlisted for the Philip K. Dick Award and one for the Best Novel, British Science Fiction Association. She likes going out to coffee shops and writing. Sometimes she does yoga but not as often as she ought to. She is writing a book about a half robot girl detective. She plays *Warcraft* far, far too much.

LFG...
AND A LITTLE MORE

NANCY BERMAN

There is no question that World of Warcraft *is one of the most so-cial role-playing games ever developed. In many cases it has more player-to-player interaction than even* The Sims™. *The reason for this is actually quite simple. From the beginning of the game, there are many rewards for cooperating and communicating with other players. Once communication has begun, things tend to grow from there. The bonuses gained from fighting as a team virtually man-date your joining one regularly. Communication is then forced be-tween formerly unknown players. The guilds also provide a simple method of establishing a small peer group in a larger-than-life en-vironment and that adds to the interaction. Perhaps the greatest incentive for players to chat is simply that the game is interesting. There is a lot within playing WoW to talk about. Once the conver-sation gets going, anything seems to be discussed. Needless to say, with a game that has many male and female players, some conver-sations are not limited to the best way that you can gut an Orc or Dwarf.*

WANTED: Single experienced (Lvl 40+) F Tauren Shaman seeking M Tauren Warrior for grp vs. uber mobs & Alliance; will also grind for gold[1]

N OT THE MOST ROMANTIC personal ad you've ever seen? If you're an MMORPG[2] player, it's actually full of promise. It immediately tells you that the poster, probably (hopefully) a real girl, knows the difference between social and serious play and is looking for someone to hook up with, at the very least for some gaming. (If you're not an online gamer, "grind for gold" doesn't mean the same thing outside of online gaming.)

In the ten years since *Ultima Online*™ debuted, MMORPGs have made some huge technology advances that increase the (generic) "wow" factor of these games. However, whether players want to admit it or not, a significant driving force behind this genre is the desire for social interaction, which can mean anything from taunting people to duel outside Ironforge to finding the love of one's life in the moonlight on Teldrassil. In addition to the joy of hitting things with swords and spells, and finding cool stuff, MMORPGs provide a one-stop social shop—a huge chat room, a virtual introduction and online dating service and a host of networking opportunities—without ever having to leave the computer.

Because interpersonal relationships in online games are part of what encourages persistent play, wise Developers and Publishers pay

---

[1] LFG = Looking for group; grp = group; uber mobs = high level creatures and enemies; grind = to perform boring, repetitive actions.

[2] MMORPG = Massive Multiplayer Online Role-Playing Game.

attention to this non-quantifiable element. Blizzard is certainly not blind to the romantic possibilities in *World of Warcraft*, as evidenced by their 2005 "first official *World of Warcraft* Wallpaper Contest" themed for Valentine's Day in Azeroth. Again, in 2006, elaborate arrangements for Valentine's Day included the ability to gift other players with Peddlefeet, little winged goblins that followed avatars around like tiny green cupids. While they served no real purpose, they were incredibly cute. Romance is woven into Azeroth's back-story, resulting in a number of quests for both Horde and Alliance characters that involve delivering love letters and flowers, returning jewelry or helping scorned lovers exact revenge on faithless partners. There has been some recent online discussion about how Blizzard would handle "official" in-game marriages, including shared bank accounts, children and even divorce, so that will be an interesting development to watch.

Despite the fantasy elements, online worlds like Azeroth are de-signed to feel incredibly real. The upside is that players have the freedom to express themselves and experience things that would probably never occur in the real world (unless, of course, your job requires you to work closely with Orcs and Trolls). The downside is the strong possibility that players could become so immersed in the game world that they lose sight of what's real and what's fantasy. In-teraction in MMORPGs can take on seriously dramatic urgency and deep emotional relevance, sometimes even more so than in real life. Such is the allure of this genre (especially in fantasy worlds), that romances sometimes entice some players to give up (or lose) every-thing—job, house, even marriage—to pursue the virtual relation-ship.

I was curious to see what kinds of romantic experiences fellow players have had, and whether they regard MMORPGs as a viable hunting ground for romance and possibly marriage. While nowhere near as exhaustive as Nick Yee's five-year-old, 35,000+-response Dae-dalus Project (http://www.nickyee.com/daedalus), I created a short survey and solicited responses from thirty friends who play a variety of games (mostly *EverQuest*®, *City of Heroes/Villains*® and, of course, *World of Warcraft*). Twenty-eight responded, thirteen male and fif-teen female, ranging in age from mid-twenty to mid-fifty, and spread geographically from Australia, east across the U.S., from California to New Jersey and across the Pond to the U.K. For the most part, all the respondents are involved in the computer, gaming and/or entertainment industries in some capacity. All attended at least some college, and several have graduate degrees. Fourteen are married, two are divorced, and twelve are single. Among the married players, four are married to non-players. Seven of the respondents were heavily involved in MUD/MUSH[3] games prior to the advent of graphic MMORPGs, while the rest have played only online games with graphics.

I wanted to know how players interacted socially in the game and whether they regarded MMORPGs as a place to meet a potential life partner. The questionnaire ranged from asking about motivating factors for avatar choices to whether players were actually married both in- and out-of-game.

In an MMORPG, you can choose what you look like, alter your online age/gender/marital status, and participate in a community where real-world appearances and successes don't compare to what level you are and how much high-end equipment you have, whether it's armor or computers! Surprisingly (at least to me), more male than female players admitted that physical appearance was a major factor in character choice. *World of Warcraft* Gnomes were definitely chosen for their appearance rather than any statistical benefits, as one player noted, "flash over substance." In my case, I chose Gnome females because they have big eyes and the option to have cotton-candy pink hair. It took me a long time to play a Horde character and even longer to play an Undead because they are so creepy. (Those blue-skinned Dark Elves on *EverQuest*® were another matter entirely....)

There is an interesting phenomenon in MMORPGs that male players will offer gifts of money and items to female avatars whether they know them or not. Several male respondents to the questionnaire have female avatars but none admitted creating one with the con-

---

[3] MUSH = Originally, "Multi-User Shared Hallucination." "A MUSH is an online, interactive, text-based role-playing game, where the object is to create a character that fits within the theme of that game and then act out that character's experiences. In many ways, MUSHing is like being inside a book, where the readers—or players—can take an active role in the plot and interact with the other characters" (http://realms.demoe.com/).

scious intent to cash in on these Random Acts of Kindness toward Well-Endowed Females. One player in the U.K. (we'll call him "Rak") expressed surprise that there are those who would do such a thing, but he's a writer and a game designer, so his response ("They do that? Really?") probably belies more than a little actual firsthand experience. He has had a number of unique gaming experiences: "Nobody even liked my avatar. (I played a MUD for a while about twelve years ago, but quit when it cut into my roleplaying. So the information you get will be based on my character, the awesome Stodjkin Ironpants, and my Troll character, the Curmudgeonly Weisshaupt.)"

One of the most obvious factors that affects online social encounters (and represents a source of deep concern among male players) is whether the player with whom they are having a romantic encounter is male or female. Most of the respondents said that they had never resorted to lying about their actual real-life gender to avoid being stalked or hustled in-game. This is possibly due in part to the ability to put another player on Ignore, a particularly valuable game aid when visiting capital cities in Azeroth. (While we are accustomed to hearing girls screaming and yelling on the schoolyard, it is unclear what motivates male players to shout when they are in public places like Ironforge or Stormwind.) One female player recalled, "When I was young and MUSHed, I just hid from annoying people who only wanted to have tinysex[4] (or cyber, as it's become known). Now that I'm older and playing MMORPGs, I just don't go on the servers where that's more prevalent, or else [I] hide from the areas where it goes on the most."

Another female player responded:

> "I've never played a male character (except briefly as a temp character for the purpose of doing a storyline while I was staffing MUSHes). I've never had to change my avatar name or design to avoid being hit on in-game. In fact, except for a one-time incident where a player wanted to 'show me their katana' (and the incident that proceeded it) I've never had a problem playing as a female in any game I've played, nor do I remember any time getting any special advantage either." (To clarify, in *City of Heroes*®, this female player had been getting some unwanted attention

---

[4] Tinysex is the MUSH/MUD term for engaging in text conversations about and descriptions of sexual encounters.

from an apparently male player so she had shut off incoming messages. I really DID want to show her my character's cool katana and had to phone her to let her know it was me!)

On the other hand, several players (including yours truly) have claimed to be married to avoid being stalked. Rak replied, "I get stalked all the time in online games anyway, but usually by snipers. Would saying I'm married get them to leave me alone?" (I told him that I didn't think it would make a significant difference.)

Flirting is a major component of in-game encounters and in some cases, is actually programmed into the game through "emotes" which usually can be accessed by typing "/" plus a command. In *World of Warcraft,* targeting another player and typing /blush produces the following onscreen text "You are so bashful...too bashful to get (Target's) attention." You can blow kisses, hit people on the head (regarded as a way of expressing interest among some age groups), and produce a number of bodily functions, the least offensive of which is the ability to burp at someone. You can cuddle (or ask to be cuddled), flirt, gaze eagerly at someone, massage someone's shoulders (or ask for a massage), point, poke, purr at, slap, tickle, whistle at, smile, smirk and grin wickedly. If nothing on the list suits your mood, you can always describe your actions or thoughts by typing "/em" followed by a description of what you want to do or appear to be doing. *World of Warcraft* has also thoughtfully provided animations of avatars dancing everything from the electric slide to an Irish step dance (particularly fetching when done by a large bovine avatar) to a startlingly accurate rendition of Michael Jackson grabbing at various parts of his anatomy. All of these are apparently designed to assist players in their social interactions online. Two of the respondents who flirted in-game ended up marrying the object of their attention, but did not have a romantic relationship in-game. Most of the respondents have flirted in-game—except Rak, who said, "Nope. I knew a guy who did. The character he flirted with was played by a big beardy bloke called G* who lived in a basement in Dundee."

At some point in their lives, most girls spend at least a few moments (yes, I'm being sarcastic) planning their wedding. In *EverQuest*® you could get a wedding dress, a cake (players with the Baking trade skill could make one) and an officiant (one of the server GMs) who could provide fireworks at the end of the ceremony. I asked whether anyone's avatar had ever been married to another avatar in-game, and if so, whether they had an in-game wedding. Male responses were *significantly* negative about in-game marriages. Maybe they should read Nick Yee's positive approach to in-game weddings:

> "...*a virtual wedding is a combination of social entertainment, extensive role-playing and sometimes political intrigue. Instead of thinking of a virtual wedding as the corrupt bastard child of a real-world contractual agreement, the virtual wedding should be considered as an elaborate form of collaborative digital story-telling—a ritual of its own right that fulfills a completely different purpose.*"[5]

When I was playing *EverQuest*®, I attended several weddings. I was a bridesmaid in one that was held atop the tower in Lake Rathe, presided over by Helena, the lead GM on Rodcet Nife. It was a lovely affair, marred only by the persistent presence of aggressive aviaks and the fact that in order to make room on the platform, I stepped backward a bit too far and crashed to my death on the rocks below. Fortunately, we had an adorable little Gnome cleric who resurrected me and the wedding proceeded without further incident.

One couple, both of whom are involved in the gaming industry as players, game masters and freelance writers, wrote about their in-game wedding which occurred at "Callahanian Army of Light," a Web site devoted to collaborative fiction of mixed genres "from superheroes to dragons to techno-mages." They are part of the growing phenomenon of people who meet online and marry in real-life. Their relationship progressed from online correspondence to the telephone and then to an in-person meeting (he is a Californian, she is from Connecticut.) Their in-game characters and Society for Creative Anachronism personae mirror their real-world relationship, and today all three "couples" are happily married.

Three other couples who responded to this survey also met online and are now married in real life, but only one couple had an in-game wedding. The husband in one of the couples declined to wed

---

[5] The Daedalus Project, http://www.nickyee.com.

his wife's avatar, despite my...I mean her, subtle and not-so-subtle hints in both *EverQuest*® and *World of Warcraft.*

A few of the specific responses to the question of whether real-life married couples are also married in-game:

"My friend and I were married in game once. It was a hoot. I am female in RL and play a male char, and he is male in RL and plays a female char, so that role playing was fun."

"I married my boyfriend online in 1999 and we were married in reality in 2001. The wedding was held in a special chapel in the game and a 'Seer' preformed the ceremony, with much pomp and circumstance. We received specially engraved wedding rings which are blessed and cannot be lost should our characters die."

"My real life wife and I took very seriously our in-game wedding. During my time as a counselor in Ultima Online™*, I observed many weddings. While some were for intrigue or RP purposes, many of them were an online representation of a real-life attraction between characters.... Weddings were serious enough business in* Ultima Online™ *that several counselors specialized in performing weddings and weddings were considered an office part of support."*

"I've been married twice....The vows were strange, because normally people don't think of a pair of Dark Elf Shadow Knights to be all happy happy love love. But you know, it was your normal evil wedding with vows about walking the path of darkness with each other and slaying the innocent, etc. LOL. Followed by a drunken guild fight in the arena."

"Yes I have been married three times, the first two times just a role-play arrangement. The first wedding my husband got drunk and fell in some water and drowned. The second was supposed to be in my favorite place in Lesser Fay fairy ring, sadly before I arrived the whole wedding party was wiped out by the corrupted horse so the venue had to be changed. But the most meaningful was the third time because I had truly fell in love and now am married to this man in many different lives."

"My first wedding was very special....On a specific date, our friends and guild members met us by being summoned and a gm friend who was a cler-

ic 'married' us. Afterwards, we had wedding cake and lots of ale etc. We had no unruly nor unexpected guests. It was a very nice experience. My second wedding was several years later after my first virtual husband had left the game. It was very romantic. He asked me to marry him at sunset on the Oasis beach."[6]

Just as in real life, there is a dark side to in-game romances. One of my former *EQ* Guildmasters recalls, "I think that in-game weddings could have the potential to ruin outside-of-game relationships. As a guild leader in *EQ*, I saw this happen." In that guild, we saw one particularly spectacular marital conflagration that ended with divorce, shattered friendships and almost required Verant's intervention to deal with a stalking incident. Between the two *EQ* guilds I played with over the course of five years, this was the most dramatic occurrence, but there were probably another half dozen or so that resulted in people leaving the guild and leaving each other in real life as a direct consequence of the in-game romance-based hostilities.

The intense interactions and high levels of competition in MMOR-PGs tend to focus a sort of virtual death-ray at the weakest spot in a relationship and cause it to shatter. While MMORPGs are frequently accused of perpetrating a host of evils on society, the fact remains that broken relationships almost always have a deep flaw that would have been revealed sooner or later anyhow, although it is convenient to blame the game rather than the gamers.

On the positive side of relationships, where one might expect to see in-game society reflect real-world society, there seems to be a more relaxed and adventurous approach to virtual marriage. Of the respondents who are married in-game, most are not married to their real-life spouses (either because the spouse doesn't play or because the spouse is married to someone else's avatar). In most cases, the respondents either have unmarried avatars or spouses who do not play MMORPGs.

Some approach the in-game marriage situation very practically: "He knows, doesn't care. It's a game, and is IC[7]. We are not our char-

---

[6] The Daedalus Project, http://www.nickyee.com.

[7] IC = in character, referring to a player's avatar, rather than the player him/herself.

acters, and our characters are not us." Others seem a little vague about it, giving the impression that as long as they don't ask, it's safe for them to assume that their spouse is more or less okay with it: "My wife is certainly aware that I've had characters that were married before they were to hers [but] I'm not sure how she'd feel about it now. It would probably depend on how she felt about the player of the other character." If little warning bells aren't going off in this player's head about his in-game marriage(s), he should probably have a serious talk with himself and then have one with his real-world wife. "You didn't tell me—you didn't ask" is more often than not a prelude to disaster. A wiser player responded:

> "I guess the RP marriage can get a bit sticky when one or both players have a RL relationship that potentially can create conflict. I ran into this situation when a friend of mine announced he was marrying a girl [in-game] in a neighboring city close to our guild. He had a RL fiancé and to me, I saw it as an issue....For me, it's something I wouldn't have done."[8]

So, what about other kinds of social interaction? One of the things MMORPGs offer is a chance to act in ways that are either totally unacceptable (or impossible) in the real world, contrary to a person's real-world behavior, and/or too dangerous to try for real. (We're not talking about killing all sorts of giant magical creatures—we're talking about things like running across a continent "naked" or trying to have a physically intimate moment on one of the swaying bridges in Thunder Bluff.)

The questions about whether players have ever cybered[9] elicited responses from just about everyone, which wasn't surprising because this issue is one of the most controversial aspects of online relationships, be it chat room, MUD/MUSH, or MMORPG. When asked whether players had ever cybered or described suggestive behavior in public or local say/chat, all the respondents answered.

---

[8] The Daedalus Project, http://www.nickyee.com.

[9] Cybered = engaging in sexual situations in an online setting, either through text messaging and/or physical movement between avatars.

"I have been cyber-sexing since before there were mu*s. E-mail, forums, chat rooms. . . . The only place where I /don't/ hotchat[10] is City of Heroes® (and soon, City of Villains®). That's just dorky, in a graphic environ."

"All-text, sure. Graphics? Nah."

"We discussed everything in chat rooms, and I'm amazed our phones didn't melt. <g> [There was] also some very suggestive e-mail."

"Yeah, but I only got to first base so it really doesn't count."

"Gentlemen don't speak of these things."

On the other hand, thanks to the movies, art imitates art, as noted in the following example. A thread on a *World of Warcraft* board last year displayed a series of screen captures of an extremely personal and explicit text encounter in public chat rather than tells between two avatars on the Deeprun Tram connecting Ironforge and Stormwind. When the third party (the person who took the screenshots) tried to involve himself in the encounter, the other two players were insulted—and when he posted the screen shots online, one of them got absolutely irate. The couple seemed to believe that because they were in a relatively empty area, no one could see or hear them. Uh-huh. I am reminded of the old adage my mother taught me, that a person who is walking down the street naked should not be offended when people laugh and point. This applies as much in the real world as it does to Naked Gnomes running across Norrath or unclad Night Elves cavorting in the Moonglade during the Lunar Festival on Azeroth.

Rolling back to a somewhat less controversial subject, I asked whether anyone had ever joined a guild expressly to find online and/or real-world romance. The answers were again surprising. One respondent felt it was okay for members of different guilds to suggest activities (i.e., raids, market days, language clinics) with other guilds for "online romantic purposes," but everyone else answered no. Rak was honest about his motivation for joining a guild, which, not sur-

---

[10] Hotchat = in-game text conversation of a sexual nature.

prisingly, had nothing to do with romance: "I joined my guild because the guy who ran it said he would give me a magic axe if I did. He gave me a magic club instead, which I actually preferred."

From this limited sample, it seems that guilds are viewed as appropriate venues for non-romantic socializing and mutual achievement of game goals (like levels and treasure), but not intrinsically as a potential real-world partner pool. I suspect that online romantic relationships grow out of MMORPG play, in part, because people have an instant base of commonality and a chance to talk about things in a socially non-threatening environment. (There is always the distinct possibility that on any given Saturday night, the players behind the two incredibly well-endowed and well-equipped avatars are sitting at their computers dressed in their jammies and fuzzy bunny slippers and snacking on a bag of chips or a quart of ice cream, but that's a reality they can avoid confronting for quite a while.)

When taking encounters from virtual to real-time, most of the respondents who have attended game-based conventions weren't going specifically to find romance, but Rak (who is happily married) related a friend's experience: "I know someone who did. That's how he knew his 'girlfriend' was a guy." This is, of course, the thing that male players seem to dread the most, as noted above, that another male player is playing the object of their affection.

A more realistically serious concern among players is that they might be carrying on a relationship with someone who is significantly younger and possibly underage. Sign-in deterrents that strive to keep the thirteen-and-under crowd out of the game appear to be laughably unenforceable. If you are concerned about the age and gender of someone you encounter online, here are a couple of helpful tests:

It's probably a male player if:

- The spelling is atrocious.
- The language is almost exclusively l33t 5p34k[11] (odds are the male player is fairly young).

---

[11] "L33t 5p34k" refers to a coded language used in online games (http://en.wikipedia.org/wiki/Leet) where symbols replace letters to create verbal shorthand like d00d (dude) and lewt (loot = valuable items).

- The avatar greets you with "Can you hook me up?" (which means they've been in the game about ten minutes and want handouts of good equipment) or "Got any (spare) gold?"
- The avatar challenges you to a duel and persists in the challenge despite polite refusals (I got so tired of this I created a macro for all my Horde characters that admonishes the challenger to kill enemies not allies. Most of the time, the challenger laughs . . . and then challenges someone else).
- The avatar persists in shouting in public areas and/or taunts other players with a variety of (frequently misspelled) pejoratives, usually questioning sexual orientation.

To be fair, the player is possibly a mature (older than sixteen) male player if the avatar greets you with well-crafted role-playing speech, bows and thank-yous for buffs.

Most of the respondents denied ever having a romantic encounter with a younger and/or same-gender player. One veteran online gamer recalled,

"Not so much younger as to actually be an issue. Never the same gender, to my knowledge. Then again, this was back during the MUSH days, and there was a pretty close-knit community. We all knew someone who knew someone who knew the person on the other end. Not to say there weren't surprises, but you could figure out things RL about other people if you tried hard and did your homework."

And another said,

"With regards to your survey, in the long ago days when I was mushing I engaged in cybering with a guy (though we called it tinysex back then). I was pretty new to online gaming and hadn't been introduced to the fade-to-black concept. I thought at the time it [tinysex] was something you had to do as part of role-play. I certainly didn't think it was much fun and after I learned that one didn't need to do it, I never did again (especially after I find out my in-game 'partner' was a high-school student. He turned out to be a very nice kid and we exchanged a few letters back and forth and a few phone calls)."

It's interesting that there appears to be less concern about having a virtual romantic relationship with someone who neglected to mention that they are married in real life. I asked respondents if they consider in-game flirting or marrying equivalent to cheating on their real-world partner. Most of the respondents appear to have established boundaries for their behavior that enable them to flirt without guilt.

> "No, not unless you get really into it to the point that it is a distraction and drain on your real-life relationship. If it passes beyond the point of being an amusement and into something you'd rather do than be with the person you're with real-life, then...yeah, it could be. Not in and of itself, though."

> "No. We both have alternate characters who flirt with other PCs."

> "No. It's just a game."

> "Depends how serious it is. Mostly no, but there are things that would take it over the line."

> "As long as it doesn't interfere with my relationship w/ my real-world partner, no, I don't. Flirting is just fun and harmless, and in-game marriage is a part of the game."

> "No, but then, simple flirting I don't consider such in real life (though I try to be considerate of my wife in that regard, since she has admitted green-eyed tendencies)."

The normally flippant Rak replied,

> "I would frown greatly on such behavior. Seriously."

Most respondents seemed to feel that forming non-romantic friendships is part of the positive social benefit that MMORPGs provide, but taking it beyond that was less desirable. One person said, "I have guild friendships with people that have developed into real life friends. Never had anything that went 'beyond' that." Rak recalled his introduction into online gaming:

"I only got dragged into MUDs by my friend, and he was still my friend when I packed it in. So we didn't fall out over me accidentally losing all his magic stuff when he died and I had to lug his corpse around for a bit till he got resurrected.... I was more brought in as someone [my friend] could trust to hoover up his stuff when he died. He didn't really figure on me being incompetent."

In-game friendships seem to thrive outside the game, probably due to the ease of communication provided by in-game and outside e-mail. Only three respondents use in-game private messaging to send romantic notes, while the rest who use private messaging rely on it for communication about game and guild-related activities. Only one of the respondents does not conduct out-of-game correspondence with in-game friends. Some also post on in-game friends' blogs, although most of the players who started in the MUD/MUSH era tend not to use blogs.

In response to whether any players had exchanged photos with in-game friends, other than as a submission to a general photo page on a guild or server forum:

"No. That's creepy."

"Only when they didn't believe I really do dress up in armor and beat people in RL when I'm not in game." (This is in reference to being a member of the Society for Creative Anachronism.)

"I have friends in game that have sent me their picture and pictures of their family. I've also sent them pictures of me and my family."

Rak noted that he "wasn't good enough at ASCII art. This was, after all, 1993 we're talking about." (He has since then mastered the art of sending jpegs.)

As previously mentioned, the downside to developing an in-game relationship with someone other than one's real-life partner is the very real risk that the virtual will supplant the actual. None of the respondents had ever cancelled a real-world romantic date to meet up with someone in-game, but several noted that they have skipped real-world parties to go on raids and have scheduled real-world activities around online raids. Rak expressed the hope that he has "grown a lot from the days when I used to cancel dates to play the Playstation or watch *Frasier* or role-play." (Being married and the father of two young children undoubtedly helps keep him focused on what's real in his life.)

We hear stories all the time about people who run off with people they meet on the Internet (not the youngsters who are lured by predators, but adults who feel compelled to leave partners and even families). I knew that none of the respondents had ever done this, so I did a little more digging and found "Metavisual," who tells a poignant story about almost ruining his marriage to run off with a woman he met on an MMORPG.

"Metavisual"

"Suzy and I started to get close. We spent a lot of time together playing, which eventually carried over to e-mail, Instant Messaging and then phone conversations. For some reason, Internet time seems to travel a lot faster than regular time. After knowing somebody for a few weeks, you get a feeling that you've known him or her forever, and your judgment seems to get very cloudy. 'I've known her forever, she's like my best friend' is not an uncommon thing to hear after knowing somebody online for only a month or so, whereas in 'real life' they would fall into the 'acquaintance' category. So begins the problem. . . ."

He got as far as buying the plane ticket to meet Suzy in real life, but his wife intervened.

"Tickets were purchased, on the intent of me just going somewhere. Let's say a ' personal trip,' I mean, I couldn't tell my wife the truth, could I? I could turn it around on her, and make her think I just needed to get away; to sort my feelings out about her and our marriage, and then worry about the consequences later. She blew it off until the time came around for me to actually leave. And then all Hell broke loose. My wife, smart woman that she is, made it IMPOSSIBLE for me to leave the house. She grabbed her shoes and ran out right before I was supposed to leave, thus making it impossible to leave, as she knows I would never leave my children all alone."

It's a sobering lesson that could have been avoided, as a sadder but (hopefully) wiser Metavisual now realizes.[12]

Five of the respondents know someone firsthand whose marriage ended in divorce over an online relationship. I personally know four couples who split because of an MMORPG and several more where a spouse abandoned a family to run off with someone initially encountered online. A female gamer relayed that she started playing *EQ* with her live-in boyfriend but he "grew jealous of my online friends. Ultimately the game that I had started playing to spend time with him became a huge downfall in our relationship. He began to accuse me of spending more time with my *EQ* buddies than with him, that I cared more about them, etc."[13]

Before we devolve into utter depression over online relationships, let's flip over to the positive stories with happy endings. Sixteen of the respondents said they would consider marrying someone in real life whom they had met on an MMORPG.

"I play MMO's with my fiancée. I'm a graduate student on the west coast, and he lives on the east coast. It's a way for us to do things together. In game, we were much the same as out of game. I think it helped the relationship, because it was more 'personal' contact than through phone calls, e-mail, or some sort of instant messaging program."

"I believe I am a lucky man, as I married a woman who also has a great love of gaming. We met from different countries in an online-gaming guild, played together and eventually fell in love."

"I play almost ever day with my real-life boyfriend (soon to be husband). We work very well together in game and it makes for a great playing experience. . . . No in-game experiences have changed our relationship, if anything we are closer because we share something together that we both enjoy."[14]

---

[12] http://www.kuro5hin.org/story/2005/11/3/115030/460.

[13] The Daedalus Project, http://www.nickyee.com.

[14] The Daedalus Project, http://www.nickyee.com.

This would seem to indicate that meeting in the virtual world first is no deterrent to forming serious and successful romantic relationships in the real world. (One person noted that that there are odder ways to meet people.)

> *"My fiancé and I met on an online game, struck up a conversation and became fascinated with each other. He helped me through some rough times, and we fell in love, then met in person, and it was fireworks."*

> *"Our game was/is* Dark Ages of Camelot®. *Something about a knight in shining armor protecting a lady that just gives it that romantic flair, I guess."*

> *"I met my husband through an online game called* Everquest® *about years ago.... It was a bit unusual to meet someone from thousands of miles away, but we had been such great friends online we just had to meet!"*[15]

I had my own share of romance while playing *EverQuest*® for five years. In my first guild, there was this Wood Elf Bard, totally cool guy and a musician in real life, so I created a female Wood Elf Ranger and flirted pretty blatantly with him in hopes that he would propose to her. I wasn't interested in a real-time romance (he was younger and struggling to establish his career). He was sweet and even flirted back a little, but as far as he was concerned, we would never be more than friends, so in (mock) despair, my poor Ranger committed suicide by flinging herself off the highest platform in Kelethin. A couple of months later, the Bard had an in-game marriage with a mid-level (30s) female High Elf Cleric who pretty much took him for a lot of his lewt and then dumped him. (I confess to a moment or two of gloating when I heard the news.)

It's a good thing that Bard didn't marry my avatar, because there was this other guy. He was a high-level Wood Elf Druid/High Elf Cleric, I was a low-level Dark Elf Shadow Knight and it could have been oh so dramatic and romantic, but he was into things like pathing and risk-ratio reward, while I was into socializing. He eventually converted me to his way of thinking and I almost made it to Level 60.

---

[15] TravelForum, http://www.thetravelforum.com.

We quit playing *EverQuest*®, got married in real life, and now we play *World of Warcraft* but none of our avatars are romantically linked because he still doesn't approve of in-game marriages.

Nancy Berman is a freelance writer and editor with production and writing credits on forty computer and video games and more than twenty role-playing sourcebooks including *Los Angeles by Night* (*Vampire: The Masquerade*) and Alderac Entertainment's *7th Sea/Swashbuckling Adventures* line. She has co-authored several novellas for Microsoft's *Crimson Skies*, one of which was the prequel for the Xbox game *Crimson Skies: High Road to Revenge* released in 2004. She recently completed work on a role-playing book based on the works of noted fantasy author Katherine Kurtz. Nancy is also a contributing writer for a Web site designed to help preteen and teenage girls maintain a positive attitude about themselves. She received a B.A. in English from U.C. Santa Barbara and has completed graduate coursework in English literature, costume design and folklore and mythology at UCLA. She is also a member of the Writers Guild of America-West. Nancy and her husband, John, are amateur chefs and avid sports fans who currently live in Reseda, California, and actively support the Horde's ongoing struggle against Alliance oppression of the Tauren people.

Reframed Relationships:
MMORPGs and Societies

Mel White

The best and most concise definition of a role-playing game I have heard can be attributed to Darwin Bromley, the founder of Mayfair Games, which was one of the pioneer companies in doing D&D modules. He defined RPGs as "quantitized, interactive storytelling." World of Warcraft Online and other computer games have since began to put emphasis on the "quantitized" since this is what computers do best, crunch data. The storytelling was added by the designers and includes a few good examples: Lord British with Ultima™ and Jon Van Canegham with World of Xeen. It was the case, until just the last few years, that the interactive part was the weakest. Mostly you interacted with the environment. Soloing and/or playing in groups gave a nearly identical experience. Over the last decade, beginning with EverQuest® and Asheron's Call 1™, the games finally achieved enough sophistication that the interaction among players actually meant more in terms of game results than just additional firepower. Now in WoW, guilds and teams are an important element of play. This means, though, that now players, with lives, opinions and feelings, interact with real people, not just NPCs with a few preset responses. Actual people interact and cultures develop. Even in the highly abnormal (to non-gamers, anyhow) environment of World of Warcraft, this is true. Here an anthropologist, who just happens to be a cartoonist, artist, game and fantasy writer, as well, takes an in-depth look at the cultures and subcultures of World of Warcraft. Every once in a while when reading this, feel free to pause and realize "Hey, I do that."

Introduction

HERE IS A WORLD inside and outside of this world, where things that could be are things that become real. It is a world of masks and masquerades, where things that have no real value can be bought and sold. It is the world of the pay-to-play Massive Multiplayer Online Role-Playing Games (MMORPGs), where identities are assumed and heroes are created and some of the most fascinating social structures ever to cross an anthropologist's path come to life. With richly textured storylines, quests, characters, landscapes, inventively scored mood music and sounds for any environment, MMORPGs have made the transition from a game fit only for those with powerful computer systems to one of the most popular forms of entertainment in today's world. And, arguably, few have done it better than Blizzard Entertainment with their MMORPG *World of Warcraft*.

Unlike other MMORPGs such as *EverQuest II®* or *Horizons*, which have been designed for the serious gamers and the highest-end computers, *World of Warcraft* has been designed for a more casual user and a less-advanced computer system, a strategy that led to its phenomenal success. Since its launch on November 23, 2004, *World of Warcraft* has broken records in the online gaming industry. On the day of its launch, more than 200,000 people bought the software and created accounts. A check of population showed that 100,000 people were playing at any given time, and the number of online members has grown astonishingly since then. Blizzard Entertainment added servers and resources as more players signed up. By the middle of

March 2005, 1.5 million players had registered for the game. As the company added special language interfaces, a broader market developed. By September 2005, there were 4 million registered users, with 1 million of those living in North America, 1.5 million in China and (at the time of this writing) eighty-eight servers to host everyone.

So who are all these people playing *WoW*? The answer may surprise you.

There's a social perception that online gamers are an odd bunch—pizza-munching teenagers with no social skills; sloppy, sullen introverts who grow increasingly violent as they become more involved in their fantasy worlds or "slacker" college students who are gradually dropping out of life. It's a common analysis, based on the belief that fantasy gaming (except for fantasy sports games) is something appropriate only for children and any adult who plays these games must have some serious psychological problems. Unfortunately, this attitude was reinforced by academic papers about individuals who were having social and psychological problems—people who also played games. The psychologists and academics who reported that gamers were a dysfunctional group never considered game playing as an appropriate activity for themselves, and a sort of "us versus them" mentality arose. "They" were role-playing depressives whose inability to get along with others was reinforced by fantasy game playing—and the "us" was a "normal society" as defined by the gatekeepers of normality. They viewed themselves as healers who could help bring those unhappy and dysfunctional gamers back into the social mainstream along with the rest of "us" and felt that the emotional and social problems they saw in this small group of people would be found in every other gamer.

This attitude was bewildering to the vast majority of gamers, who thought of themselves as creative, rational and well-adjusted people who fit into society as well as any other group.

It wasn't until the mid 1990s that the picture began to change, thanks to researchers like Sherry Turkle, Edward Castronova and Nick Yee. Rather than observing the game, they joined MUDs and other cyber-worlds as players, immersing themselves into the games in an attempt to understand why people found cyber-realities so appealing and to find out how these societies worked. Yee, a long-time gamer himself, took a data-oriented approach and began surveying players on several popular MMORPGs where he also played. After the surveys were finished, he compiled the data and published the results in a blog. This opened the data up for discussion and feedback from other gamers, which provided richer insights into what the data presented.

What they discovered was what gamers knew all along—that yes, overall, they are a pretty normal bunch and they're not particularly violent or aggressive. Gamers have a great deal of creativity, many interests and have a wide social circle that includes not only people local to them, but people who may live on the other side of the world. They are part of a global culture, sharing experiences and friendships with people whom it would be impossible to meet under ordinary circumstances. They are avid socialites with strong friendships both on and offline. And researchers also discovered a misconception regarding what their age group was thought to originally be. People from ages ten to seventy and older play and enjoy these games—and not all of them are male. One of Yee's recent surveys revealed that nearly seventeen percent of players are women, a number that undoubtedly will continue to grow.

There are other similarities in this group as well. Most gamers are people with reasonably good user-level computer skills and an interest in technology. Most hold full-time jobs, and many are actually involved in the computer industry as Web designers, coders and support staff. Although there are a large number of people playing *Warcraft* who have not played other MMORPGs before, the bulk of the population has had some sort of experience with online gaming.

It's not unusual to find people who are related to each other playing the game together. Last week, I encountered two players on U.S.-based servers who were the real-life mothers of other players on *Warcraft* and they occasionally team up with their own children to do dungeon areas. Sibling and cousin teams also exist. Married and engaged couples play together, as do lesbian and gay couples. In the *World of Warcraft* community, kinship bonds and friendship exist.

The *Warcraft* clientele is also a group that is not blindly loyal to one particular brand, and Blizzard Entertainment seems to be aware of this. MMORPG customers are picky, and pay-to-play customers are even more demanding. In order to keep interest in the game, cyber-worlds have to continually upgrade with new quests and monsters and to make a system of merited achievements, like leveling, that is not overly time consuming. This is also an audience who demands top-notch resources for the game. Innovation and humor are important, but they will leave the cyber-realm if the servers are too jammed or if the computing resources are poorly allocated; they will drop their subscriptions and join another MMORPG.

The World behind *Warcraft*

The players' view of *World of Warcraft* is made up of the game world, their own characters and the people who play on their servers and other servers. It's a model based on how they see stand-alone games—the world is an autonomous thing, set into motion by a company, and the player is free to do as they like. Nothing could be further from the truth. In addition to the "visible world" of these elements, there exists another "hidden world" that affects how the game is played and how the society within the game works as a whole.

At the top of the "hidden world" is the company, Blizzard Entertainment, which establishes the policies and rules of play, buys the hardware and directs the vision for the world. Players don't interact much with this area. While their opinions may be solicited by the game company, individuals have little direct impact on this level of the game hierarchy. For all intents and purposes, what goes on behind closed doors at the corporate office is not revealed to the public until the company issues a press release.

The technical staff of Blizzard Entertainment is the second level of an invisible hierarchy that affects the gameplay. This group includes game coders and the designers who work for them, as well as the hardware administrators and technicians who keep the servers running and the database engines and game engines online. While their functions are mainly invisible to the gamers, it is this group that has the most impact on the gaming environment. Computer code is the invisible heart at the core of MMORPG society, but the programs that make up the game system do more than just run a game world. They also act as regulators that enforce how a community behaves. Many

of the company's Terms of Usage policies are implemented directly in
the game itself, with programmers tweaking the code to allow or prevent players from doing certain things. For instance, *World of Warcraft* has added a profanity filter to help alleviate parents' concerns
about their children encountering inappropriate language.

Sometimes the rush to get a new module into the game has unexpected consequences. In September 2005, an error in the Zul'Gurub
dungeon code created a plague that spread across servers and caused
chaos and confusion in a few areas. Inside the dungeon was a monster called Hakkar, the God of Blood. Players who fought him were
hit by a spell called Corrupted Blood that killed lower-level players and could be transmitted to nearby players. While the original
intent was that the plague would only affect those in the dungeon,
an error in the code turned the surviving players into "plague carriers." Those who survived the dungeon and returned to their home
cities brought the plague to their home areas. Player reactions were
strongly polarized. Some griped and stayed away until the code was
fixed, while others treated the plague as a scenario in the game. Coders scrambled to patch the error and confine the plague to the dungeon as originally intended, and the incident was officially closed
within a week.

In the visible realm of the game itself, Blizzard Entertainment is
represented by the most powerful player group—the GMs (Game
Masters). GMs are part of the service staff of the company and are
online helpers whose job is to monitor the game and resolve issues
as quickly as possible. They deal with player complaints, pass along
notes to the coding staff about erratic behavior in monsters and
game areas and they help explain commands and functions to players. They form their own social structure in a closed society that is
composed of Game Masters, Senior Game Masters and Lead Game
Masters. They are not recruited from the rank of players, though
players can apply to become a GM when there's a job opening at Blizzard Entertainment.

The most visible segment of the game's hierarchy is composed of
the customers that the company works to please—the players themselves. This is the community that is most commonly studied by
MMORPG researchers. It is a complex society, formed of individuals

and groups of individuals in social structures similar to a "tribelet." These tribelets generally tend to be egalitarian and informal, made up of a player and their friends or family members with whom they have strong trust and friendship bonds. Players and player tribelets may also belong to guilds, larger social cooperative structures with weak friendship bonds and strong trust bonds that establish rules of behavior and serve as a resource pool for exchanges. Guild members generally have relationships of trust rather than of friendship, though relationships in guilds can become much stronger as players interact with each other.

The Reality of Cyber-Reality

What makes *World of Warcraft* such an appealing environment to explore? Part of the reason is that it creates its own sense of reality, a reality that players can control or re-script to make the story more appealing. A number of studies show that humans seem to have an inherent need to create world replicas in the form of daydreams or mental images. The most common examples of how we create alternate realities is the act of "losing yourself" in a book or a piece of music, where the text or sound evokes a world that has its own type of reality, no matter how brief. This immersion is the reason why we experience powerful emotional reactions to books, movies and music. In *World of Warcraft*, rich visual detail and well-timed audio cues help create depth to this alternate reality and immerse players into the game in much the same way that a good book or movie draws us into its world. Players form strong bonds to images in the *WoW* realities just as we form strong bonds to characters in plays, books and movies. Although this can have some negative psychological consequences for players, it also has some strong social and psychological positive effects. Bonding with a character in a book, movie or game allows the viewer to feel a sense of empowerment when the protagonist overcomes obstacles. A kinship is formed with this unreality as players see aspects of themselves in the protagonist. This is the same sort of bonding that occurs between a player and their character. The character becomes the player, though the player does not always become them.

There are other, and more subtle, psychological reasons why these online realities are so appealing. *World of Warcraft* and similar MMORPGs are societies where advancement comes from merit. The players rise in rank and reputation by killing difficult monsters, by fighting honorable battles with other players and by solving quests—not from who they know or how much money their family has. Rank and merit can't be stolen, nor can it be exchanged. It can only be earned.

In cyber-worlds there is an added sense of power to the experience because the storyline is not necessarily immutable. Players can set limitations outside their normal boundaries and explore alternate versions of "what if" in a safe situation, where they become immersed in a fictional world. "What if that Horde Warrior didn't kill us?" "What if we managed to sneak past that one higher level Kobold?" *WoW* allows players to tinker with personal storylines so that they can play and replay scenarios. Death is not an ending but an inconvenience. The option to do it all again in a graphically rich environment is a reward for their playtime and a reinforcement of the cyberspace world-dreams. The only permanent "death" the players' characters endure is deletion from the server.

Who Are You in the Online Space?

As with other cyber-worlds, *World of Warcraft* allows the player to experience other people in a way that is divorced from normally contexted reality. In this strange borderland between reality and unreality, the player sees others as avatars instead of the person at the computer keyboard. They can't reject them because they're too old or too fat or because they're the wrong race or gender. They don't see the face of the real person playing the character. They see only the mask of the avatar image—and they see only the avatar. They are free to explore other identities... playing non-human characters or playing a character of a different gender. Many people find this oddly liberating and create a variety of characters to explore different options in the game. Because the *WoW* society has learned to judge other players on their words and actions rather than on their appearance, *World of Warcraft's* social bonds cross barriers of age, race, religion, gender, sexual orientation and social class in ways that are not possible in real life.

In this new reality, language cues and styles form the basis of social bonding. Players judge how alike others are by grammar and spelling, style, slang, use of abbreviation and other subtle signals such as the length of time it takes to type messages. They assume the person at the other end of the keyboard looks like them and shares similar values if the way they use language is similar to the way they use language.

Language also provides cues about how familiar the player is with MMORPGs in general and in specific with *WoW*. Newcomers to the *World of Warcraft* game find the chat channels are full of cryptic-looking messages, codes in the language of the community that plays the game. While shorthand texts such as "LFG SM PST" appear to be gibberish to the novice, the experienced player understands that the sequence of codes translates into a message that a certain player is looking for a group to go to Scarlet Monastery and is asking interested parties to please contact them via the in-game "tell" system.

But judging people by their use of language isn't an entirely foolproof system. As gamers are well aware, someone who's sixty can use game acronyms and "leetspeek" as easily as any eighteen-year-old. And character gender is no real clue to what or who the player really is.

Researcher Nick Yee has estimated that half the people playing female characters are actually men. In a current survey, he found that only three percent of women in *WoW* are playing male characters, a social marker that shows just how much online social behavior has changed since 1990. In early MUDs, many women preferred to play male characters to avoid being harassed by almost constant messages pressuring them for sexual chat exchanges. Pressure on communities by women who wanted to play female characters without being subjected to this kind of harassment caused changes in MUD and MMOR-PG policies. Gender-based harassment is fairly uncommon now, and players who violate these rules on *WoW* can be booted out of guilds and find themselves developing a very negative reputation throughout the community. Those who persist in this behavior will be reported to the Game Masters and will be banned from the game.

There's no single, simple explanation for why people play characters of a gender different than their own. Some are exploring different aspects of their own personality with this choice while others are making an aesthetic decision. One player told me that she liked to play male characters because if she was going to invest her online time in staring at some avatar's backside, she would rather spend her time staring at a male butt than a female butt. Oddly enough, one casual survey of players showed that this was one of the common reasons for playing a differently gendered character.

A Valued and Valuable Society

In a pay-to-play MMORPG, characters and accounts have value, in terms of the money spent and the time invested in creating the character. In addition to emotional value of avatars and equipment, there's also an economic worth attached to these virtual artifacts. MMORPG game companies originally followed the kind of economic system found on MUDs, where players could barter equipment, leave it in guilds for other players, donate equipment to less well-armed players or sell at shops. But in an environment where people wanted to acquire goods and gold and were paying to play the game, many liked the idea of taking shortcuts. Eventually someone got the bright idea of selling characters, equipment and game gold on eBay and a black market in virtual objects began to flourish.

This practice, referred to as "farming," is controversial and disruptive in a society that assumes players have achieved high rank by their own merit and by fairly earning the gold that they use to purchase equipment and other artifacts. MMORPGs reacted to this underground economy by changing their Terms of Service to ban the practice. Most gamers will report suspected farmers to the DMs, but in spite of active policing by the *Warcraft* players, the practice still continues to flourish. In some of the Asian countries, an industry exists where gamers sit at the computer and acquire gold and objects that they will later sell for more money than most of their countrymen will make in a year.

There's a great deal of social and economic risk for those who decide to take this option. It's against the Blizzard Entertainment Terms of Service, and the player risks having their account banned. Even those players who successfully manage to cheat often end up at a high-power rank with no social bonds, no available groups open to them and little idea how to use the skills that they've acquired. No obligation exchanges are conducted, and they have no social or group resources. Experienced players can spot those who have "bought" their rank and generally avoid them or sneer at them.

Within the game itself, the commercial value of artifacts that involve time and game gold to acquire foster a system of exchanges that can reinforce social bonds and give the player prestige within their city or group. These exchanges can be economically based— someone allowing another player to buy an artifact from them—or they can be a form of gifting; but whatever form they take, they are acts that reinforce the sense of community and make the game more enjoyable. It's not unusual for a healer to trot by a place where another character is having trouble with a monster and heal the player so that they don't die during that round. These random and altruistic gifts of combat healing, shielding for low-level players, monster damage or potions are common in many realms and confer some prestige on the gifter. On a communal level, guild members are also likely to freely exchange resources and materials to help a member achieve a certain goal or purchase a piece of equipment they need.

Just as prestige can be won in a community, it can also be lost. Players who "ninja loot"—who take valued items instead of sharing them in accordance to the group's agreed-upon rules—are usually ostracized and their reputation as a looter is broadcast on channels and boards. Begging for gold, although not very common, is something that many players and guilds disapprove of because the player is trying to achieve advancement not by merit within the game, but by circumventing the logic of the game itself. Players who habitually beg for gold find that their reputation drops. Guilds will reject their membership application and other players will avoid inviting them into groups.

Groups and Guilds and Societies

Guilds are a popular form of grouping. Guilds provide players with social interactions and with a way to share important resources and skills. They also provide a pool of available people to explore the more difficult dungeon areas. On many cyber-realms, guilds are based on character race or profession. This means that the number of guilds is fairly small and the number of guild members is much larger. But Blizzard Entertainment followed in the footsteps of Sony Online's *EverQuest*® and put no such restriction on *World of Warcraft*. Anyone who's played a character long enough to reach Level 10 can start a guild. As a result, there's a large number of guilds available for players to join.

Allegiance to a guild is not very strong—some players will change guilds every five or ten levels. This guild-hopping and membership swapping results in a preponderance of very small guilds on *WoW* of two to eight players. Some of these can merge with larger guilds as the players desire the kind of prestige or combat assistance that a smaller guild cannot provide, but many continue to exist as a small cadre of friends who team together in their realm.

Guilds form when a player manages to recruit a group of nine other players who agree to form a new guild. While there's no particular advantage to belonging to a guild if your character is under Level 10, once a character level enters the teen levels, belonging to a guild offers them a very distinct advantage. Players can take advantage of others' skills and form reciprocal gift exchanges based on what skills they know. In *World of Warcraft*, the player can learn certain specialized trades and create trade goods to sell or exchange. For instance, someone who has a character with Alchemy skills can team up with another player who has Herbalism skills. The herbalist can locate plant material that the alchemist needs and the alchemist can create special potions for the herbalist. Both can sell their wares to vendors, other players, or offer them for sale in the civic Auction Houses on Azeroth. Players with no guild have to buy potions and armor from merchants, paying the going price.

Groups, in contrast to guilds, aren't formal chartered organizations. They are loose associations of players who may or may not be acquainted with one another, who team up to explore certain areas. Within *World of Warcraft* there is a specific channel called "LFG," where players who want to join a group can ask for interested people to contact them. In addition to the chat channel, there are also "meeting stones" at dungeons and other playing zones where teams can form. However, as many have found out, mobs of random players can be difficult to organize into an efficient raid.

Guild raids are usually better-organized affairs, when someone announces they want to raid a particular area and recruits party members from the group to show up at a specific time and location and commit to a certain amount of time. In the loosely formed mob there is no such arrangement. Players may have significantly less commitment to the raid and may not stay for the full duration of the battle. Issues of leadership of the group and of certain teams within the group arise in loosely organized mobs, and conflicts over ownership of loot and unique items can arise. If the mob of players is formed from members of one or more guilds, some sort of social order will be established. Raid planning becomes more streamlined and the raids themselves are more effective.

Guilds are responsible for policing social regulations. Players who have managed to annoy guild members by breaking social rules will be ejected from the guild group. Sometimes these outcasts try to form their own guilds or hop from one guild to another to avoid the consequences of their bad reputation. But gossip is an efficient way of spreading information. While there may be no direct slander of the player, word usually spreads via community bulletin board and chat to avoid inviting them into any groups and to avoid associating with them. They aren't prevented from playing the game, but they are denied the benefits of friendship and society.

The Darker Side of Gameplay

One of the more irritating and disruptive social elements in MMOR-PGs is the "griefer"—a person (sometimes a group of people) who prefer stalking and killing a target player as many times as they can during one day's play. This social misbehavior first appeared on MUDs in the early 1990s, and Wizards soon noticed that when newbie areas were haunted by a pack of griefers that the MUD would start to die. Without new members, the game stagnates and devolves into chat or random player-killing mode. Older members will stop logging on when they've solved most of the quests that they were interested in and the world eventually becomes a fairly deserted realm. It was enough of a problem on free games that many MUDs dealt with it by patching the code so that players could not be killed without their consent.

While this practice is annoying on a free MUD, it is a serious, real problem in pay-to-play MMORPGs like *WoW*. The victims, who are subscribers to the game, find that they are being prevented from playing the game by a Hunter or pack of Hunters whose sole purpose seems to be to find the character and to resurrect or kill the character again and again and again. Protests, threats and attempts to negotiate with griefers never work. Griefers don't feel any particular need to justify their choice of victims. Social punishment doesn't work— they find enough pleasure in upsetting others that even the threat of being banned from the game doesn't control their behavior. Their patterns of attack can have components of obsessive behavior. It's rumored that one player was continually harassed by a griefer for two consecutive days every time he/she logged in.

In dealing with griefers, Blizzard Entertainment took the same course that most cyber-games did—by patching the game code so that a player had to give permission in order to be attacked by another player. Griefers responded by changing their disruptive behaviors. They generally issue a challenge and then harass their target until the other person responds. Their victims are ususaly new to the game— very few experienced players will take the bait. If the victim is a member of a guild or has strong social ties, a "posse" may gang up on the offender, killing him and driving him away from the area. Many will simply report the player to a DM, sending screenshots to confirm the complaint so that the griefer can be banned from the game.

On a less serious level, some players run into trouble by breaking other unwritten rules. One of the more common reasons for shunning a character is if the player violates the rules of sharing loot within a group. Although altruism isn't an outright command, the system of exchanges in *WoW* works by people who are willing to share resources to enhance others' enjoyment of the game. Selfish players find themselves shunned by players and guilds as their reputation spreads in chat and on message boards. Help and resources will simply not be available to them. This behavior isn't enough cause for banning, though. They have broken social rules but not server or game rules, so the situation is resolved within the community rather than by Blizzard Entertainment's coding. Social punishment usually causes these players to repent their actions and prevents others from trying the same sort of tactic in group situations.

A Last Word

One of the many things that has changed throughout our human existence is the way we approach recreation. MMORPGs represent a new form of entertainment for people: a type of diversion where one is not simply a passive viewer but can participate in the surrounding community and world. They offer stress relief and escapism, as well as the opportunity to form strong social support mechanisms. Players bond through play, and learn through exploring different "what-if" concepts.

Detailed alternate realities like *World of Warcraft* offer us broadly constructed societies to explore, societies with a framework of relationships that mirror those we experience in everyday life. While this form of recreation isn't appealing to everyone, those who enjoy being immersed in a cyber-reality find sources of support and creativity. If you haven't tried it yet, I strongly recommend it.

~

Science fiction cartoonist and author Mel White has recently graduated with a masters in anthropology. A long time MUDder and MUCKer, she is an avid *World of Warcraft* player and can be found on the Durotan server, geeking about buffs, drops, mob and Hunter pet stats.

THE ECONOMY OF
WORLD OF WARCRAFT

JERRY JACKSON

Two main ways in which a player is rewarded, for even small successes, in World of Warcraft *are with gold and magic items. This action-and-reward pattern is designed to reflect the scale of the risk and effort. With gold, the money of the virtual world, this scaling is easy. The bigger the risk, the larger the total. In items, greater risk is reflected not only in the greater bonuses of an item gained, but also made apparent by the color coding. The best items are purple and epic, and blue items rank below them. Simply having the name of the item in purple instantly raises its value to players. Why are there colors and not just higher values? The colors are there to make acquiring the item instantly and more greatly satisfying. Once you get into playing WoW you soon realize that the blue and purple items do sell at a premium, and mere sight of those colors raises your greed factor, and with it the expectation of getting a larger sell-off price.*

The economy is such a vital part of the reward system and gameplay, and it is one of the reasons those running World of Warcraft *are concerned with farmers and cheaters. Jerry Jackson now takes a more detailed look at how a game economy is built. He has to play the game every day in the real world, handling not only Game-design ideas, but also worrying about the real-world finances of a new RPG company.*

ECONOMIES IN MASSIVE MULTIPLAYER Online Role-Playing Games (MMORPGs) are fickle things. The ability to have an economy that works and one that encourages players to accumulate wealth has developed slowly. Take *Asheron's Call*™ (AC1), which was one of the first games where gold (platinum, mithril, etc) actually meant something. At first it was simply hard to get rich. In the early RPGs gold had weight, and gold is heavy. To lighten your load you had to buy notes. They were great but cost you ten percent of your money. Later, they made coins weightless, but they still took up room, so people stuck to buying the larger 10,000 and 20,000 credit notes. A part of the problem was there was nothing to spend money on except for food (which was cheap), armor and weapons (but quested and dropped items were always better). But, if you were at the right vendor at the right time, you could buy an item, like the Ice Heaume of Frore, that someone had just sold. By Level 30 you had more money than you could spend and being at higher levels, where characters sold off good items, was much more important than the cost. Economies are a natural extension of wealth, though. In *AC1* they just missed what constituted wealth. At higher levels, Strong Iron Keys, needed to open chests containing powerful items, replaced gold as the basis for trading between players. I suppose this is not stranger than the giant stone-wheel money found in Pacific Oceania. But I wonder if it surprised the designers.

The games that followed didn't always learn from the experiences of the games that preceded them. *Star Wars Galaxies*™ (SWG) became an example of an economy gone wild. Because of trade skills, and the player-based economy, merchants became extremely rich. Also, people could get a group, go to high-level planets and blast away at 40,000 credit animal dwellings. People became rich doing the same thing repeatedly. There were people who had trillions of credits. When you get a house, you pay maintenance, which is X number of credits per hour, depending on the size. 100 credits would last a few days; 1000 credits would last about a month. But when you have a few million credits, it wasn't unusual to see someone paying off their houses in years, rather than the weeks the designers obviously planned on. (I wonder if wealthy players tended to favor the Imperials... sort of the game version of the Republicans.)

Some games marginalize their economies and what little trade occurs is simple barter. There were several of these, most of them having failed or faded. This reinforces the importance of having a viable economy to add to the level of social interaction.

Now comes *World of Warcraft*, which has a much better balanced economy. It is possible to earn inordinate amounts of money, but it takes either a long time or cheating. Money is relevant in the game; the player-run economy works well. Overall it's the most balanced economy going.

How is the *WoW* economy like the real world? In simple economic terms, they have created an excellent supply and demand situation, a chase for capital, scarcity and division of labor. These elements work because there are things you can only get from merchants, things you can only get from players, and where there is crossover, the player wins. Money is hard to come by in this game. Most missions net only a few coins. So something else has to be done to earn a living.

What makes *WoW* work is that the economy has several parts and each part contributes.

In looking at an economy, one of the most important things to remember is the chase for capital and scarcity. In order to make your finished goods, be it a sword, armor or potion of healing, you have to literally chase after resources. You have to skin the animals for Skinning, find veins for Mining, find plants for Alchemy and so does everyone else. So don't be surprised when you see the blip on your radar saying a copper vein is near and, as you run to it, see it disappear and someone running away. Fortunately, spawn points are abundant enough that given time you will find what you need... if all the spots are not camped by a farmer.

Now that you have your initial capital, which is your raw materials, you have to do something with it. No matter what, whether you sell the materials directly or keep them, they will ultimately become a finished good, unless you sell them to a vendor where they go out of the economy and you are paid below what they are worth. Finished goods are the key to the economy. Once you mine that ore, you have to smelt it. Now that it is a bar, you have to smith it into something useable and then you can sell it for much more than the base ore.

Another source of the economy is the items found as loot. This is likely the largest part and also the most random. The most expensive and best items are generally found this way. Even where some purple items can be crafted, the ingredients needed are such a hassle to gather that it often discourages their manufacture except in rare instances, usually after the buyer has found or bought the rare and costly ingredients for you.

A third part of the *WoW* economic picture is the sale of services. A few of the professions have the ability to make items used during play, such as the best arrows, bullets or potions. There are also a few functions, the alchemist's ability to create certain metals needed by the smiths, that allow the higher-level players to make some gold by providing a service. And then there are the enchanters, who can make everything you have better and more fun to use.

Okay, we have found or made an item. As in any good economy, we sell it for a profit. The best place to do this is the Auction House (AH). The primary purpose of the AH is to sell items without wasting much of your play time. Also, because they are located in major cities, you don't have to run all over the place. This is the heart of the economy. This is where it truly plays out, where supply meets demand, where capital is raised and exchanged, where scarcity is realized as you discover you don't have enough money to bid for what you want. All of the dynamics of a real economy can be found in the AH. You can sell to the vendors found all over the maps as well, but any real items are worth ten times as much at auction as when sold to a vendor.

As you noticed in the example at the start of this article, just accumulating wealth loses meaning fast if you can't use it. In fact, it loses meaning fast unless you *have* to use it. Fortunately there is a lot of built-in demand that makes your character need to spend all those shiny coins. Okay, so you make the "purple sword of salacious greed" and sell it for a bundle. Why do you want all that gold? The obvious answer is: to buy other items you need, such as the mace of grinning greed which has several bonuses when used. But that is not the only way that the *WoW* economy keeps wealth moving.

Certain NPC vendors, smith and weapon makers, also offer a needed service. Armor gets damaged, weapons wear out. If you want to keep your armor and weapons in top condition, vendors are the only way to go. Going to certain vendors allows you to repair your items, for a slight fee. Your items are always wearing down, so this maintenance is an ongoing concern.

There is another expense to move money around, and that is training. All of the great skills that make each character class unique cost money, and the only way to obtain them is by purchasing them from NPCs. As you reach higher levels, the cost of the skills goes from a few copper pieces, to several silver pieces, to several gold pieces. This is a stark contrast from *SWG*, where players can train you for whatever they want, which is usually free since they receive experience for training people. This is also different from *AC1*, where skills increase as you use them or spend experience points for them but have no cost in gold.

These all help keep the economy flowing, make sure that the PC has an advantage, and help to remove money from the economy, but it still is in stark contrast to a real economy. No matter what, *WoW*'s virtual economy is not akin to the real-world economy.

There are several differences between real and virtual economies such as unemployment, banks and governments. In a virtual economy, everyone works and everyone can find money comparatively easily. Need some quick cash and can't complete a mission? Just kill a few things, loot them and sell the loot to a vendor. The vendor is always open and will always buy what you have to sell. This doesn't happen in the real world. First of all, no one is painfully poor or starves in *WoW*. The game is meant to be a positive experience so the penalties for poverty are just a lack of gaining benefit, not the loss of something important.

The biggest difference between the *WoW* economy and that of the real world is the flow of money. Because there are no governments and banks, money flows like water in a virtual game.

A quick economy lesson: the flow of money in the economy is controlled by the government through the bond market. To tighten cash flow, the government issues bonds, taking cash for them. To loosen the cash flow, the government buys bonds, releasing cash into the economy. This, combined with the Federal Reserve Bank regulating interest rates, determines the flow of money and inflation. These do not exist in a virtual economy. Eventually people will have their horse, they will be trained in everything they need, they will have bought the best of the best and they will still make money on missions and looting. Which, especially when combined with selling gold to players, leads to a major problem. A problem that has yet to be successfully dealt with in WoW, and many will say not dealt with very well in the real world, as well.

Inflation is a natural side effect of virtual economies. What usually happens, as the years go by, is the characters at higher levels pass their money down to the characters at lower levels who now buy things that, at the beginning of the game's life, players at that level could not afford. Or in the case of certain items, such as bags, they become hand-me-downs to lower levels. At the highest level of the game, maintenance is the only thing moving money out of the economy and it is rarely enough to balance things. Since new items are added when players find them, but none are lost except when characters leave the game, there is a constant growth of wealth in WoW. The result is that the items that are still rare, such as epic weapons, tend to increase in cost as the months go by.

There are two things that are happening that are having a negative effect on the economy: monopolization and farming. Monopolizing occurs when a person buys up one type of material (wool, for example), at low prices, then resells it in the AH at an outrageously high price. So wool, which might go for 10 silver for 20, now goes for 10 gold for 20. This can make for a frustrating experience for new people as well as old-timers. This practice has to be reported to the WoW officials so they can ban these grievers. The second detriment to the game is people known as Chinese farmers; they do not care about the game, only the money. They take away from the immersion, help inflate the virtual economy, and where they are located, it is hard for legitimate players to complete quests, leaving them frustrated. They get the name "Chinese farmers" because most of the people who engage in this behavior are "supposedly" from China, or Asia. It's called farming because they go to an area online and using a bot (a character that works on macros) will kill creatures and loot them. They then sell the loot to vendors to collect gold. Once they have accumulated a lot of gold, they sell the gold to a company for cash. This company in turn sells the gold online at such places as eBay. People buy this gold and get an illegal leg up in the game. While *WoW* does try to crack down on this behavior, it has yet to stop it.

But the economy of *WoW* works better than that of most third-world nations. And even the substantial inflation rate mostly affects high-level characters. So what is the ultimate secret to the economy playing out the way it does? Why, in spite of everything, does it work? It all goes back to the AH. Yes, my friends, the AH is your friend and the ticket to wealth. It is also what helps drive the player-run economy and keeps it running smoothly, in spite of the abusers. Since many things can only be created by players, those who don't have the skills to make these items have to buy them. It does not matter whether it is potions, raw materials, armor or weapons, people are always looking for better stuff, better potions to stay alive and better components to make their stuff. Now, other games tried to create a merchant class and met with less-than-successful results. You can go the way of *AC1* and *SWG* where you shout out what you are selling, spamming the airwaves. The problem is this gets annoying and makes people avoid towns, not to mention it takes away from valuable play time. *AC1* tried to solve this problem by making a marketplace where you can shout to your heart's content or where you can place bots. *SWG* allowed people to create vendors, which are placed in player-owned buildings. The problem is people create droids that go around major towns screaming the location of the vendor. It is because the AH is a central location that it works. Except for enchantments, if you don't want to spend all your time screaming "looking to sell X," you go to the AH. If you want to buy items and don't want to go around screaming "looking to buy Y," you go to the AH. It is the single point of contact for buying and selling. It brings people together better than the yellow pages, even though there are those who are currently trying to exploit it.

And there is another point which also helps to keep the economy moving along. Though it has been jumped around and talked about, it hasn't been explained. This is division of labor. Yes, Adam Smith would be proud because, no matter what, no *one* person can do everything; the labor must be divided up. But what makes the division great is that it is divided between NPCs and PCs. It forces the alchemist to buy bottles from vendors, forces the blacksmith, leather crafter and tailor to buy flux and coal, thread and dyes from vendors, leather only from PCs and colored shirts, the best weapons and armor from PCs. Enchanting can only be done by PCs. This division of labor is helped along in that a person can only have two professions. They can be complementary, such as herbalist and alchemist, a gathering type such as a skinner and a miner or a finishing good type like an alchemist and a blacksmith.

This division also helps drive supply and demand, just as in a real economy. There are many things we can't do in a real economy, so we have to get them from others; so it is in *WoW*. We can't be everything, so something has to give. When it does, we have to rely on others, and this creates the supply and demand needed to drive the economy.

All of this, the chase for capital, supply chain, supply and demand, the division of labor and even your character class combine to help drive the economy, in spite of those who exploit it for their own means. Money is taken out of play, but something is gained by the player when that happens. And that is why *WoW* has one of the best economies for any game going today. It is multileveled, interactive and creates a firm pattern of supply and demand. Alan Greenspan would be proud.

Jerry Jackson was born in Cleveland, OH, second of three boys, but raised in Decatur, Georgia, a suburb of Atlanta. In the fourth grade he won a writing contest and has loved to write ever since. At Columbia High School he first experienced using computers. He then went on to Georgia Tech on an NROTC scholarship, where he majored in management science. His love of computers and gaming flourished while there. He was an officer in the Navy and is a veteran of Operation Desert Storm/Shield.

Since then he has had various computer positions and got his MBA from Kennesaw State University. When not at his day job, he and his partners are forming a computer gaming company, Service Bay 12, where he is designated the CEO. He enjoys online gaming and has played various MMORPGs. He has been playing *World of Warcraft* since release. He lives in Kennesaw, GA, with his wife Luz. He has two stepdaughters and two grandchildren.

ANCESTORS
AND COMPETITORS

CHRIS MCCUBBIN

World of Warcraft *did not just happen. Those who designed the game and implemented that design learned many lessons from the games which came before* WoW. *Part of the success of* WoW *is that the creators did learn these lessons, and they understood the reasons behind them. In some ways* WoW's *game design doesn't break new ground, but rather it refines what has been done before and takes it to new levels. Though there is no question that some of the coding, you can bet, went where no programmer had been before.*

On the question of how to handle failure alone, there have been as many solutions as games. How do you handle death and defeat? The instant reaction of a judge or even a designer is that if the player makes a mistake, they have to pay for it. This reaction assumes that avoiding pain, or at least a pain-in-the neck penalty, is a positive solution. Psychologists have long shown the fallacy in this. You can learn to avoid pain, but you also must react by avoiding painful situations. When this is a game, and one you are paying a monthly fee to play, that can often translate into no longer playing or paying. When RPGs were run by live judges they could moderate dying to keep the gameplay going. It was, and is, no fun to sit and watch others finish an adventure you started, so a way was found to keep you busy to run the monsters, or a convenient resurrection medallion just happened to be in the next chest. The route World of Warcraft *took reflects the concept of rewarding and good play. They still have a penalty for failure and for dying, but Bliz-*

zard reduces the cost of dying to be nothing more than a short and transitory return to your corpse. In the worst cases, where you can't retrieve your body, the penalty is only being less effective in battle for five minutes. Moving, selling, bidding or training is not affected at all. They even speed your movement as a ghost to make it easier to get back to your body and work toward those positive rewards again. This fits the design philosophy to base the experience on rewarding the player's successes while minimizing the main source of annoyance—inability to play effectively. This doesn't make dying any less embarrassing, but it helps to make the frustration a small and passing thing.

FOR FANTASY FANS, a great part of the appeal of World of Warcraft is a reassuring sense of familiarity. WoW takes many well-loved conventions of fantasy gaming and blends them together into a harmonious and entertaining whole.

Okay, sure, WoW is based on the Warcraft line of strategy games. That's where we get the original form of the world, and most of the races and classes. But in this section, we won't be looking much at the fictional framework of WoW. Instead, we'll concentrate on the influences that went into the game design, and into the overall look and feel of the game.

World of Warcraft is not one of those games that try to reinvent the wheel. The creators of WoW are not out to astonish us with the daring uniqueness of their vision. If there's a stroke of genius behind the popularity of World of Warcraft, it's a genius of focus, not innovation. The designers took many elements from other well-established games and blended them together into a satisfying and unified whole, then they went back through these concepts and mercilessly deleted *anything that wasn't fun*. It didn't matter if it was something a game was "supposed" to have—heavy penalties for in-game death, a complex virtual economy for crafting and trading—if it wasn't *fun*, it was either simplified or removed. The result of this process is a game that offers us—the players—a remarkably high entertainment-to-tedium ratio.

In this chapter, we'll look at some of the classic games (computer or otherwise) in *World of Warcraft's* evolutionary tree.

What It Is

In official game-design speak, *World of Warcraft* is a graphic, persistent world, Massive Multiplayer Online Role-Playing Game. (From massive multiplayer online role-playing game we get the acronym MMORPG, and its various shorter variants—MMOG, MOG and so forth.) What, exactly, does this mean?

Graphic

This means that most of the game's story is told through pictures. You see the monster approach, you see yourself draw a weapon or prepare a spell, you watch yourself battle the monster and in the end you (hopefully) see the monster fall. This may seem so obvious as to not even need stating, but keep in mind that computer graphics are still a very new technology, and the earliest online RPGs were purely text based (and the pen-and-paper games that preceded *them* were speech based).

Persistent World

This means that the game goes on pretty much all the time (barring occasional maintenance). Things keep happening whether you're in the game or not. You can't "save" the World State of your game—much like real life, it just goes on with or without you. This is perhaps the most profound and basic difference between modern MMORPGs and their predecessors.

Massive Multiplayer

There can be lots of players in the game at the same time, at all levels of experience, and not necessarily all working on the same thing, but (at least theoretically) all able to interact with one another if they care to. The line at which an online game becomes "massive" is a fuzzy one. There are games out there that max out at a couple dozen people on a given server, or a couple hundred. In general, most of the major MMORPGs can handle a consistent load of hundreds of players live on a given server, with a theoretical max that's much higher.

Online

Played over a network connection (of course); in the specific case of MMORPGs, however, "online" has a few unspoken connotations. Specifically, these games can only be played over the Internet, and only on the game company's official servers. You can't load up a private instance of the game on your desktop that only you can access, or a server that's only accessible to you and a handful of friends via LAN. The upside is that you get game worlds that are far larger and more complex than any solo game could ever be. The downside is that you get to pay ten to twenty dollars a month for use of the company servers.

Role-Playing Game

This is a rather big term. Its exact definition has been vigorously argued for decades, and its meaning can definitely vary depending on the medium you're gaming in. For the purpose at hand, it means that you only control one character at a time (there are octopods out there who are capable of controlling two characters from two different accounts by simultaneously manipulating two computers, but let them go for the moment), and all your interactions with the world take place in the persona of this character. From a larger perspective, a role-playing game is one where you don't play to "win" a specific goal, but rather to simulate an imaginary life. Your character strives, succeeds, fails and grows. This process, and the story that your character generates along the way, is the "point" of a role-playing game, in any media.

Paper Games

Dungeons & Dragons®

Long, long ago, before the Internet, or even personal computers, people played role-playing games (RPGs) with rulebooks, pen and paper. The first, and still the most popular, RPG was *Dungeons & Dragons*® (currently published by Wizards of the Coast). *D&D* is, in a very literal way, the sun source from which all fantasy gaming, computer and otherwise, is descended.

In the early '70s, a couple of young gamers named Gary Gygax and Jeff Perrin published a thin little book called *Chainmail*, a set of rules for medieval military war games using lead miniatures. In the second edition of *Chainmail* they added a few rules for including fantasy-inspired heroes, like wizards, in these campaigns.

Much as the strategy game *Warcraft* would later spawn the *World of Warcraft* role-playing game, *Chainmail* led to the publication of *Dungeons & Dragons*, by Gygax and Dave Arneson. Gygax also created a publishing company, Tactical Studies Rules (later TSR), to distribute his new game.

The background is a mishmash of the writers' favorite fantasy authors. The Lord of the Rings is the obvious primary influence (from Tolkein, *D&D* got its basic lineup of player races—Humans, Elves, Dwarves and Halflings—a taxonomy that still holds true, with minor variations, in most modern fantasy games, including *WoW*) but there are also strong elements from the tales of Fafhrd and the Gray Mouser by Fritz Lieber, the Elric stories of Michael Morcock, Robert E. Howard's Conan the Barbarian and Poul Anderson's short-but-seminal '50s fantasy novel *Three Hearts and Three Lions*.

From the late '70s through most of the '80s, the game divided into two versions, basic *Dungeons & Dragons*® and the much larger and more complicated *Advanced Dungeons & Dragons*®. Eventually basic *D&D* went extinct, but *Advanced Dungeons & Dragons*® remained the official title of the game throughout the '90s. In 2000, TSR was acquired by an ascendant game publisher called Wizards of the Coast (WotC; best known for the *Magic: The Gathering*® card game). WotC undertook a soup-to-nuts reconstruction of the *D&D* system. Dropping "Advanced" from the title, they returned the official system name to *Dungeons & Dragons*®. This is the version of the game that's currently on the shelves.

There are dozens, maybe hundreds, of concepts that permeate modern fantasy gaming, online or off, that can be traced directly back to the early editions of *D&D*. Perhaps the most basic and pervasive, however, is the idea of character classes. The basic classes of fantasy gaming all started in *D&D*. Fighters, Mages, Thieves and Clerics were the four cardinal classes, and they subdivided into a plethora of variants and hybrids, including Paladins, Druids, Assassins, Bards and Barbarians, to name only a few. Once you pick your character's class, you're pretty much stuck (some systems, including *D&D*, have rules for class changes and hybrid classes, but that generally isn't the easy way to go), and your abilities and tactics follow directly from that fundamental choice.

You advance in the game by earning Experience Points, which are rewarded for doing things appropriate to your heroic role—most generally, for killing monsters and taking their treasure. This earned experience allows you to rise in character level. A first-level hero is a fragile thing indeed, but by Level 10 you're a force to be reckoned with. The upper levels (whatever they may be for a particular system) are truly superhuman in power.

Now, even by the standards of heroic fantasy, this is not a particularly realistic model. When you think about it, there's no logical reason why a reasonably motivated and well-connected young warrior can't learn to pick a lock, or maybe cast a quick spell or two. And classic fantasy characters like Elric and the Gray Mouser, while they certainly evolved and grew in power over the course of their sagas, displayed nothing remotely like the astronomical ascent possible in many RPGs.

As a gaming concept, however, it was brilliant. It gave even the most inexperienced a clear motivation and understanding of their character's fundamental nature, which offered role-playing guidance without being restrictive. Furthermore, the player gained a series of clear-cut, satisfying goals, each one individually achievable, all combining to create a long and open-ended role-playing experience. It made legendary heroism something that was just hard enough to be worth working toward, without being so hard as to be discouraging. This combination of simplicity and satisfaction, for many players and designers, trumps all concerns about "realistic" advancement, making the class/level model for character advancement still the most popular in fantasy gaming.

Warhammer®

Like both *Chainmail/D&D* and *Warcraft*, *Warhammer®* is a strategy game that has spawned various role-playing spin-offs. Predominantly, though, the system was, and is, a set of rules for fantasy battles pitting various armies of more-or-less exotic creatures against one another.

Warhammer® is the flagship line of Games Workshop, the predominant publisher of non-computerized fantasy games in Britain. Originally published in 1984, the system really came into its own in the '90s, with the publication of the hardbound third edition. The game is expensive, but brilliantly (some would say, ruthlessly) marketed. GW maintains ironclad control over both the rule books for the game and the miniatures required to play it. Although its popularity is not what it once was, it remains a game tailor-made to encourage obsession in its fans.

The mechanics of *Warhammer®* have much more in common with the *Warcraft* strategy game than they do with *World of Warcraft*, but the game has a unique viewpoint that has left its mark on the entire *Warcraft* franchise.

Warhammer® is violent, funny and very, very dark. While Americans tend to favor a brighter, more black-and-white view of morality (particularly when it comes to games, genre fiction and other media regarded as being particularly attractive to children and teens), the Brits are much more comfortable with a viewpoint that's...well, let's face it...evil. The Elves, Dwarves and Humans in *Warhammer®* tend to be a rather grim lot. They're not particularly likeable and they're ready to win by any means necessary. The monsters, on the other hand (orcs, lizardmen, rat-like skaven, Undead and others) are nasty, bloody and very cool.

Warcraft, it must be said, is not nearly as dark as *Warhammer®*, even on the Chaos side of the fence. We can, however, thank *War-*

hammer® for much of *Warcraft's* sense of humor...and, perhaps most importantly, for being the game that once and for all let the "monsters" come out from under the bed and play.

Multiuser Dungeons (MUDs)

It's a lucky coincidence that fantasy RPGs appeared about the same time that universities got mainframe computers for college kids to play around on. Of course, both the *D&D* game table and the computer lab appealed primarily to the same basic type of person—highly intelligent, socially suspect and drawn to fantasy adventure. Almost the second it appeared, it seems, eager computer science majors were trying to use their computers to recreate the *D&D* experience. There were utilities, like character generators, there were combat-based "dungeon crawls" where your digital character fought his way down through some nasty-infested forsaken ruin and there were the text-based adventures, which described an imaginary adventure in detail, allowing you to make choices at key points which determined your ultimate fate.

The MUD was a sophisticated attempt to combine combat gaming with text-based adventures. Most radically, the MUD included a strong social element, via the emerging science of computer networking. The first true MUDs, *MUD1* and *Scepter of Goth*, were developed independently of one another in 1978.

MUDs allowed users from all over the world to create fantasy characters and bring them together in a single virtual world to fight monsters and each other to gain treasure and fame. They picked classes, gained levels and won powerful magic weapons and armor.

The MUDs also foreshadowed the problems that still plague large online communities to this day. Not just technical frustrations like lag and inconveniently dropped carriers, but also problems like player killing, looting, kill stealing, flaming and harassment. In response, the MUDs created the first online game masters, Terms of Use and Codes of Conduct.

Ultima Online™

Fast-forward two decades. In that time computer games have come a long way. Side-scrolling maze games like *Donkey Kong*® have given way to first-person shooters like *Doom*™, and then to cinematic adventure games like *Diablo*®. A major factor in the success of both of the latter games was their ability to allow small groups of players to connect to the same game via LAN or the Internet, and to play together, as a group.

The designers at Origin Systems decided the time was right to take online gaming to the next level. Their vision was a game that would combine the real-time speed and graphic sophistication of a *Diablo*®-style adventure game, with the scale and human interaction of a MUD.

For a setting, they chose Britannia, the world of Origin's long-running, best-selling fantasy adventure series *Ultima* (at this time, the series was up to *Ultima VIII*™, plus spin-offs). Under the patronage of Richard "Lord British" Gariott, creator of the *Ultima* series and founder of Origin, the team began work on *Ultima Online*™.

They succeeded beyond their wildest dreams. *UO* was an immediate smash hit.

UO is an ambitious, complex game. Character advancement is based on skill building; there are no classes or levels. Instead, you gain skills from actually trying to use them (while *WoW* is basically a class-based game, it uses a similar experience system to build combat skills). Players can mix and match melee, magic, thief and trade skills to come up with the ideal character for them. You can choose to concentrate on one trait and become, say, the best archer in the land, or you can be a generalist, with a basic competence in several different fields.

The crafting and trade system is particularly robust. If you don't want to be a fighter or a Mage, you can specialize in being a miner, an armorer—even a cook or fisherman. A surprisingly large number of players have found they actually prefer these mercantile professions to more combat-intensive endeavors. However, there are, of course, a wide variety of weapons and armor, as well as a detailed and powerful magic system.

Animal training and player housing have both been part of the system from the very first. These are hurdles that many games that have followed *UO* have never achieved, or even tried to address. It is even possible to own and sail your own ship. Soon a player guild system was introduced, which remains the model for such systems throughout the genre today.

There have been problems as well, of course. The designers had hoped for a true virtual economy and virtual ecology, but that proved to be impractical. Player killing was, in the early days, unrestrained, and the willingness of some experienced players to prey on the newbies became discouraging to some (others, however, thrived on the intense, life-or-death competition). Problems with kill stealing and looting quickly appeared and had to be dealt with.

It has to be remembered, when talking about the early days of *UO*, that nobody had done this before. The designers had literally no way of knowing how the players would interact with each other in this new kind of virtual community. Everything had to be done on the fly. There were technical glitches—lag problems, stuck characters. A class action lawsuit was actually filed against the company based on the fact that the labeling for the game didn't warn against unscheduled downtime, of which there was plenty. All these challenges had to be met and answered.

Today, *Ultima Online*™ is still up and active. It's no longer anything like the sensation it was upon release, but it has its own stable community. The graphics have been upgraded several times, new lands and creatures have been added and safeguards have been put into place against nonconsensual player killing and other uncivil behavior... but *UO* is still the same game it's always been, and some of the characters who are still active in the world got their start when it first rolled out for public release.

EverQuest®

If *Ultima Online*™ was the Wild West of MMORPGs, it fell to the next major player out of the gate, *EverQuest*®, to civilize the territory. As popular as *UO* had been at launch, *EQ* quickly surpassed it, and it has remained the most popular American MMORPG ever since (until *WoW*).

Where *UO* had opted for complexity and depth, *EQ* (designed by Verant and published by Sony) went for simplicity and user-friendliness. *EverQuest*® returned to the class-and-level advancement system that veteran gamers knew so well, rather than a skill-based system like *UO*, with its bewildering array of options. While *UO* had only human players (a relic of the *Ultima* series it was based on), *EQ* offered several options for non-human role-playing—not just Elves (spectacularly embodied by their curvaceous, blonde cover-Mage Firiona Vie) and Dwarves, but also Ogres, Trolls and other monstrous options, for those who prefer to be bad to the bone.

Instead of *UO*'s mouse-only movement system, *EQ* adopted a mouse-and-keyboard system that was already familiar to gamers from popular games like *Diablo®*.

The real secret to *EQ*'s long-term success, however, is probably the game's focus on retaining the interest of high-level players. *EQ*'s designers realized that, once they got a little experience under their belt, most gamers could move quickly through the intermediate levels and reach the top of the game. Most of them would, of course, develop multiple characters of various types, but multiple characters only took you so far. The secret to player longevity, it was decided, was making sure the top-rank characters never ran out of things to do.

The main lure used by *EQ* to keep the uber-players interested is ultra-rare item "drops," which can give their heroes a crucial edge over other maxed-out characters. The process is set up to require skill, planning and almost infinite patience. A group has to set up "camp" at a spot where a unique enemy is known to spawn. The group waits, often in relays, for days (sometimes literally). When the chance finally comes, they face a tough fight for a chance at their desired prize. Multiple parties are often camping the same spawn, and the community soon evolved elaborate rules of precedence to make sure everyone got a fair shake.

The system is far from perfect. Most veteran *EQ* players have at least one story of camping a spawn faithfully for hours or days, only to have all their plans come to naught due to an inconveniently timed bathroom break.

Why would such a seemingly tedious system exert so much fascination over players? Even many *EQ* veterans don't seem to know. Players quickly coined the term "EverCrack," to reflect the game's weirdly addictive hold on its faithful followers.

In 2004, Sony released *EverQuest II®*, a completely revamped and updated version of the game. While *EQII* quickly surpassed the original game in popularity, both systems continue to flourish. There are also spin-off *EQ* games for console systems, and even for mobile phone gaming.

Asheron's Call™

The third major system to hit the market came from industry grand-daddy Microsoft. By the time *Asheron's Call™* appeared, *EQ* had already established dominance over the industry, so *AC* never became the major sensation that its two immediate predecessors had been. However, *AC* did find a faithful niche audience among slightly older, slightly more sophisticated gamers, who craved a gaming experience that was a bit more challenging than *EQ*, but not as Darwinian and vicious as *UO* (which at the time was at the height of its player-killing crisis).

In fact, *AC* made a major innovation in interplayer community co-operation by introducing a patronage system, whereby a powerful, established character could become the patron of a newbie character. While other systems fought to discourage "twinking" (the practice of power-leveling a new character by having an established character protect him from danger and shower him with powerful gifts), *AC* smoothly worked it into the game system. The newer hero benefited from the patron's guidance, protection and generosity, and in return the patron gained a small percentage of his vassal's earned experience. The end result of all this interdependence has been a community significantly more unified and civil than the medium had seen before.

Technologically, the game was impressive. The art was a significant step up from either *UO* or *EQ*. The landscape was thoughtfully designed and well-textured... snow on trees drifting down to snow-covered mountainlands, beautiful sunrises and sunsets, two moons, deserts filled with elements other than sand and beasts. *AC* had artists involved in the creation of the game, not just programmers with a library of textures. That overall excellence in design has certainly spilled over to the look of *WoW*. Also, earlier games had been plagued by "zoning," an annoying wait when you moved between one area of the world to another, while the game loaded the new zone. *AC* managed to eliminate this problem. Smooth zone transitions are also a hallmark of *WoW*.

AC was also the first game to mark the location of a fallen character's corpse on the radar map, making body retrieval easy. This foreshadowed *WoW*'s non-intrusive philosophy of character death.

Unfortunately, *AC* made a major misstep when it tried to release *AC2*. When *EQII* would come around a couple of years later, it would be a major success, but most fans agreed that *AC2* missed the boat, offering a dumbed-down, incomplete game that lacked much of the appeal of the original. Most fans who made the move from *AC* to *AC2* eventually moved on to other systems entirely. Still, despite the *AC2* debacle, a loyal coterie of fans continues to faithfully patronize the original *Asheron's Call*™.

Dark Age of Camelot®

The second generation of MMORPGs was defined by systems breaking off from the fantasy roots of the genre and experimenting with science fiction. Notable examples included *Anarchy Online* and *Star Wars Galaxies*™. *Dark Age of Camelot*®, however, was an exception to this rule. Instead of turning away from medieval fantasy, this game embraced it, and determined to do it right.

Based on real-world culture and legend far more than any of the other fantasy MMORPGs, *DAoC* offered characters a choice between three distinct cultures. There were the chivalrous Avalonians (based on medieval Britain), the Hibernians (based on Celtic races and legends) and the Viking-like inhabitants of Midgard. Each of the three cultures offered a complete and unique assortment of available classes and races.

Player vs. player combat was at last brought fully under control. The three realms are eternally at war, but they cannot intrude on one another's homelands (where the newbie characters dwell). Instead, they have to meet in remote wilderness zones to battle for control of massive keeps. There are also a series of strictly level-controlled "battleground" zones, where mid-level characters can meet to battle against one another without having to worry about running up against a maxed-out superman.

DAoC offers an expanded quest system (as do *Anarchy Online* and *Star Wars*) that eliminates the need for tedious camping of rare spawns. Instead, characters are offered a chance to gain a desirable prize when they are ready for it.

DAoC also introduced the concept of "Horse Routes." You can't own a horse in the game, but you can rent one, and it quickly takes you from one specific point in the game to another, saving significant travel time. This system is the immediate ancestor of *EQ2*'s and *WoW*'s system of gryphon stations.

City of Heroes®

This is the most recent game in this chapter, appearing only a few months before *WoW* made its debut. This is not an imaginary world fantasy, or a space opera. Instead, *CoH* is the first MMORPG set in a world of four-color comic book superheroes.

Although its high-flying, spandex-wearing gameplay may not seem to be related to *WoW*, in fact these games share a very similar design philosophy. Call *WoW* and *CoH* the standard bearers of the third generation of MMORPGs. This generation is dedicated to simplification and fun. Depth and complexity are no longer seen as particularly desirable traits—they only tend to put new players off. Player death is treated as a minor inconvenience, not a major setback. The idea is to get the player back into the fun stuff—adventuring—in a quick and efficient fashion without making him retrace his steps.

CoH offers an extensive mission and quest system, making extensive use of instanced zones where a solo player or group can face an array of villains specifically tailored to their individual numbers and levels.

Some would say that *CoH* takes this philosophy of fun and simplification perhaps a bit too far. As of this writing, about a year and a half after it was released, *CoH*'s subscriber base is about half of its early maximum—a very dramatic drop-off for an MMORPG, particularly one that has a whole genre all to itself. Among gamers, this rather poor rate of retention is attributed to repetitive gameplay, the lack of a player vs. player system and a certain lack of very high-level content. *WoW* must (and so far has) avoid these pitfalls on its quest for fast, fun gameplay.

Bringing It All Home

So let's review. How do the last thirty years or so of RPG evolution add up to the game we now know as *World of Warcraft*?

From **Dungeons & Dragons**® and the other paper RPGs came most of the systems still used in *WoW*—notably: character classes, experience points and experience levels—as well as many of the assumptions about fantasy races, magic and other fictional concepts that informed the design of the *Warcraft* fantasy setting.

From **Warhammer**® came the concept of large-scale fantasy battles, an extension of the concept of non-human role-playing to "evil" races and a dark and irreverent humor, all of which were central to the original *Warcraft* strategy games.

Text-based MUDs gave us the first look at a functioning persistent online world, and the unique problems that such communities would attract.

Ultima Online™ was the first true MMORPG, and pioneered many of the concepts of that genre, including crafting, pets and player guilds.

EverQuest®simplified and streamlined the fantasy MMORPG, returning in many ways to the familiar concepts of *D&D*, and creating a template for success that has not been equaled until the rise of *WoW* itself.

Asheron's Call™, **Dark Age of Camelot**® and other fantastic MMORPGs refined the look and playability of the genre still further, virtually eliminating such persistent problems as nonconsensual player killing and protracted "camping" for rare spawns.

City of Heroes® and other MMORPGs of *WoW*'s generation try to keep the action fast and fun, by eliminating or streamlining unnecessarily complex secondary systems, and by making heavy use of quest missions and instanced adventure zones to keep players' interest in the game high. The danger here is that the game might come to seem superficial, but *WoW* has avoided that pitfall more successfully than most of its peers.

Chris McCubbin has been part of Incan Monkey God Studios since it was the publications department of Origin Systems, back in the early '90s, creating documentation and game guides for all the *Ultimas*™, *Wing Commanders*™ and other games that Origin produced. A few years after Origin became part of EA, IMGS spun off and formed an independent design house. IMGS created the original guide for *Ultima Online*™, the first really massive online game, and one of its first projects post-EA was for the initial *EverQuest*® expansion, *The Ruins of Kunark*™. Since that time, IMGS has created guides for all sorts of PC and console games, but the majority of its work has covered MOGs, of all shapes and sizes. IMGS's MOG guides stand out for one reason—it has recruited a dedicated panel of game players who play the games and help IMGS write about them. IMGS doesn't try to create a guide with one or two writers—nobody can know a massive game that well—but with input from all the panelists who are playing that game. Chris and IMGS took that same approach in *The Battle for Azeroth*.

Maps and Mapping

James M. Ward

World of Warcraft *is the next level of development in Role-Playing Games. RPGs are actually a relatively new development. Board games have been found in 5,000-year-old tombs, and the human race was cheating at cards as soon as there was paper. RPGs started out as pen-and-paper products only a bit more than thirty years ago. Although this was still before the Apple II and TRS 80 were glimmers in an engineer's eye, it can be easily argued that RPGs are the greatest innovation in gaming that wasn't caused by technology in the millennia. They are common to us now, but when it all started, these games were a strange, and to some, frightening phenomenon.*

E. Gary Gygax and Dave Arneson first turned an interest in Fantasy books and the Lord of the Rings epics into playable adventures back in 1973. They started it all, as told by Gary, as a way to set up battles for their tabletop miniatures gaming that used the Chainmail miniatures war-gaming system. Someone wanted to scout out the other guy's castle so his troops could enter the table on the best side. So both players, and the judge, sat down to talk through what the spy could do to enable the judge to determine how much he found out. After that, things just got more complicated. Where you have spies, you have assassins. Next there were hidden troops, poisoned wells and traitors being bought off. Then if you have knights, why can't a Tolkein fan convert some of his figures to Rohan, or even Orcs? The next version of the Chainmail rules had a few pages in the back for fantasy figure statistics. But this new type of open and creative gameplay just kept growing. Sometimes they took weeks to get to the battle, and where they are gamers, there are disputes. Rules were written down and kept growing. Mineograph machines in schools and insurance offices churned out pages on topics that would have amazed the bosses. The result was Dungeons & Dragons® (or D&D), which ushered in an entirely new category of games: the role-playing game. Unlike board games of the time, Dungeons & Dragons® didn't use a board or have limited interaction between players. At first many D&D judges used some sort of map, but the real action took place in the imaginations of those playing and was supercharged by the constant exchange of ideas between the judge and the gamers.

As the first game where players could do anything they imagined, D&D took the world of wargaming by storm, creating its own niche and giving birth to a multitude of role-playing games. Games featuring science fiction, horror, superheroes, cartoons and westerns appeared over the next decade and a few even continue to be popular today. Perhaps a dozen new game systems appeared in hobby shops in 2005 alone. However, "fantasy role-playing," mostly D&D, continued to dominate the field.

The first edition of D&D featured a few character classes and about two dozen monsters. The three thin books were really two sets of general guidelines and what would now be called a campaign module, Blackmoor. Like the waistlines of those of us who were playing then, soon the books grew thicker. Advanced Dungeons & Dragons® greatly expanded the character classes, monsters and spells. In 1989, AD&D Second Edition was published, which revised the rules yet again, consolidating some character classes and revising the combat system slightly. Not long after this, the first computer role-playing games appeared. As the games grew more sophisticated, so did the environment—the world that you played in. James M. Ward was one of the first employees to work for TSR. He has been their head of design and president of other gaming companies for almost thirty years now. He is also an excellent fiction author. From the perspective of the man who watched it all happen from the beginning, he presents us with some insights into the maps and environments used in Role-Playing Games and how they evolved over the decades.

I T DOESN'T MATTER on which side of the computer screen or gaming table you play, having maps and making maps can greatly increase the fun and enjoyment you gain from most games. I've worked as a game designer in every form of gaming, from award-winning computer products like *Pool of Radiance*™ to best-selling role-playing games set in many different trademarked worlds, from *Greyhawk* to the *Serenity* science fiction universe, and I've had fun making maps for more than thirty years. I know the enjoyment and positive gaming experience of making maps, and I have little graphic talent myself. In playing Blizzard's *World of Warcraft* online RPG, I know from my own experience any herbalist or miner can increase their wealth and experience by noting where his herbs and mineral nodes are in the lands he explores. Even a rough map, made while playing, can help an online gamer do better in any computer game they play. In the paper-and-pencil world of gaming, the typical role-player can reap many benefits from the maps they create as they explore their world. Many players know the agony of coming back to the same four-way intersection time and time again, because of not having or using a map. I know you'll find game masters in any medium—from miniatures to role-playing to computer gaming—can have more fun by organizing their gameplay with a useful map. For the referee, maps can provide the continuity players expect in a well-run campaign situation.

Game players and game designers quickly learn there are features every map should have to allow those diagrams to become useful tools in their gameplay.

A compass point should go in the upper right-hand corner of your map. Your compass arrow should point to the top of the paper, and that becomes north. Modern mappers always place north at the top of the map, but it hasn't always been so. The ancient Romans used east as the top of maps because their empire spread out further east to west than north to south. As you're gaming with your map, you will often tell others where they are going; using the compass image allows you to explain directions of travel your players use as they move about your mapped world.

Distance scales are necessary to determine travel times between map locations. Such scales inform a map reader how large an area on the map is, from a major city to a blocking mountain range. Scales establish the scope of an encounter area. For example, if the map of a battlefield shows an entire area is less than 200 yards wide and long, you can tell someone precisely how missile weapons affected the course of a battle, as you know the maximum possible ranges for those weapons when compared to your map. Some type of distance scale is necessary to let you know that an inch equals a mile or that same inch on another map equals ten feet.

A map legend tells you what all the symbols on the map signify, so that you don't confuse swamp grass with thick woods. Map legends can also provide a world of detail you don't need cluttering up your map. You don't want to write out the words *castle*, *large city*, *forest* or *gold mine* on a map when you can do all notation with a simple and small symbol that fits in many different sections of your maps.

Most maps benefit by using graph paper to set them up. I favor the ten squares to the inch kind, but I know many others who prefer four squares to the inch. Hex paper is also available and this type of paper works well when mapping out sections of land in the outdoors. All the interesting areas of the map need their own listing, either in numbers of letters with a few words of details noting the area. Each of these listings eventually needs a brief description of what the area shows the viewer. Putting this all into practice allows players to become even more successful as they make their own maps in the games they play. For game masters, such maps can be their entire set of notes for a night's adventure or even a longer campaign. Naturally, working in pencil is a good idea as you will make mistakes and need to change the page.

When you're ready to begin to draw a map, practice always helps. It can be fun to map areas you're familiar with, and the effort sets the stage for trying to map during a game with your friends. Trying to map your house and then the block you live on can be an interesting exercise. Later on, you can use those mapped areas with your friends as places where dangerous encounters happen. Some of the most fun Halloween role-playing experiences I ever had used my town and the people in the town for background. It's remarkably easy to imagine your neighbors becoming zombies and vampires as you role-play raiding the houses you've known for years to put stakes in the hearts of Undead friends turned vampires.

Recently for the rerelease of the *Metamorphosis Alpha*™ RPG, I had to redraw the maps for the starship *Warden*. It's a big spaceship of seventeen decks, and each deck is six to eight miles long and four to five miles wide. I prepared my three-ring binder and three-hole-punched my graph paper and began to work on the levels, remembering to keep them simple. None of my players knew the naval terminology for north, south, east and west. If I would have given directions using real ship terms, such as, "You're headed toward the prow of the starship level," or "You move toward the starboard of the level," they would have been lost and confused. One of the very unusual considerations on a science fiction starship is describing weightless areas like the outside of the ship. Concepts like true north and south become very abstract, which is one of the reasons ships have a prow and a stern. Having your players make maps, even as they travel in airless space, can help them avoid confusion. In the *MA* maps I was making, I needed to continue to use north, south, east and west for every map marking down the compass point and putting in the scale of miles. The project mushroomed on me as I discovered the need to also map out the only large city on the ship. Then I needed maps for the mutant villages the player characters would encounter. I had to map out the corridors and chambers of the berthed spaceships stored in the cargo holds of the *Warden*. To make a long story short, I ended up doing thirty-four maps for the ship when I had only planned on doing seventeen. When I was done, at least I could easily take them from level to level explaining what they saw by using the information on the maps I had made. Map legends told me what each special area was on the ship without me having to go to the detailed legends describing what "A" was on the ecological level of the ship.

Bradygames has created the official *World of Warcraft Strategy Guide*, and this book is well worth having if you are a fan of the *World of Warcraft* online computer game. Although there are many

maps and these maps detail the quests and locations to be found in
the game, there is still quite a bit of information that a player can
add to these maps to help them advance quickly in the game. Although the maps list many things, they do not show the locations
of the mineral and herb deposits to be found by characters hunting
such things. I've found by taking the strategy guide maps and marking down the location of the mineral nodes and the herbs, I know
where to look night after night as I come back to these places looking for the valuable resources needed for the game. In this computer
game, the AI maps for you and you always know where north is, but
there are things like resources that you can add to increase your use
of their maps. As a player, I also like to list, on the maps I use, the locations of difficult encounters I have had. This helps me to remember what I did, and in an online game players go back many times
to the same area as they play other characters or come to a location
with new friends who haven't been there before. My book of maps is
filled with my own notations adding material to what the writers of
the book already supplied.

Gamers who role-play know the usefulness of making their own
maps. No player wants to wander in circles seeing the same ten-by-
ten cobwebbed chamber with nothing in it. New players might be
hesitant about making maps, thinking they have no artistic skills.
These players can benefit by being introduced to the concept of the
trail map. A trail map is just lines on paper reflecting the distances
and directions a player travels. Anyone can make up one with any
bit of paper and a pen or pencil. Start with a blank piece of paper
and start in the middle of the paper. Your referee is describing your
travel through some type of area. As he tells you about traveling two
hundred yards north, you make a line up toward the top of your paper with twenty little crosshatched lines through the long line letting you know you've gone two hundred yards. He tells you the path
turns east and west and you make a T with your line and draw one
hash mark left of the line and one right to show that you can go either direction. As you travel about your unknown area, you make
letters along your lines and note on the side of the paper what those
letters are, i.e. "A" is a small pool, "B" is the ruins of a large fountain,
"C" is a lair of a giant snake and so on. You don't care about carefully

detailing your course of travel. You are just making a very rough map that tells you there are killer bears if you go east along your path or that there is a dangerous guard if you go west at the T intersection.

As a game referee and a player for more than thirty years, I've set up my campaigns in almost every way possible and played in many types of games. I've designed complex maps with hundreds of notations on the map, adding pages and pages of detailed explanation on the encounters and monsters. I've written many products with detailed maps and pages of encounters on those maps. Playing in games, I've created detailed maps on other people's dungeons as well as simple trail maps to get me from place to place. Now I find that I can run many of the games I play with a very simple map and a listing of twenty different things placed on the map. If I need the text on a creature or a long listing of treasures and goodies for my players to find, I can look that up in a separate book or prepared sheet made for that purpose. In short, I'm saying the KISS system is the best way to make maps and play games, i.e., *Keep It Simple, Stupid.* When I'm trying to buy a product and there is a large selection of possibilities, I always go to the maps of the product to judge its worth. I'm looking for color maps with detailed legends. Maps that don't have a compass point or a scale of distance are products I don't buy. If they haven't taken the time to place these basic map features on their products I'm sure the rest of the product details have been skipped, as well.

Successful author and game designer since 1974, James M. Ward created the first science fiction role-playing game in *Metamorphosis Alpha*. He's written for Marvel, DC Comics, Random House, Del Rey, Bantam, Tor and Western Publishing. Voted into the Game Designer's Hall of Fame, he also received the best game of the year for *Gamma World*. His novels have been on the best-selling lists of Waldenbooks, B. Dalton and Locus. His game credits include work with: Charlie Brown Licenses, Sesame Street Licenses, He-Man Licenses, Conan Licenses, Indiana Jones Licenses, Dragon Ball Z Licenses, Marvel Licenses, DC comics Licenses, Worlds of Wonder Licenses, Robert Jordan's Wheel of Time, Josh Whedon's *Firefly* & *Buffy* and Wizards of the Coast/Hasbro Licenses. He designed the smash-hit card game *Dragonball Z*, breaking sales records since 2001. His TOR novel *Midshipwizard* is selling well in stores everywhere and the second in that series comes out in September 2006. He lives in the Midwest with his wife. His three genetically perfect sons have all moved away and have families of their own. He has five grandchildren that he happily baby-sits for upon request. He's taken up fencing and this hobby constantly pits him against younger, faster people, just like in the game business.

Should We Sell World of Warcraft by Prescription Only?

Maressa Hecht Orzack
and Deborah S. Orzack

Can you imagine killing yourself or others because of a computer game?

Can you imagine playing until you drop dead because of a computer game?

Can you imagine exploiting others to get ahead in a computer game?

Can you imagine losing your job or flunking out of school because of a computer game?

Can you imagine taking out your rage on others when forced to give up a computer game?

P EOPLE WHO EXCESSIVELY and compulsively play Massive Multiplayer Online Role-Playing Games (MMORPGs) will answer yes to these and similar questions. But when gamers are in trouble, they are often in denial and only their family or friends are left to answer yes to these questions. News stories, case histories and scientific studies show that MMORPGs draw in millions of people around the world. Most gamers relish playing these games, experiencing the roller-coaster ride, but they know when to turn it off despite the enticing qualities that draw them in. A computer game is one part of their life, not their *entire* life. However, up to approximately forty percent of these game players do not stop, do not turn off the computer at appropriate times and do not live a balanced life.[1] They crave the game, play it despite the consequences and need to play more and more to get the same feelings and effects. For these players the MMORPG is an addictive drug that needs to be regulated.

Makers of MMORPGs freely acknowledge that they design them to be never-ending games. The design lures players to finish one quest and immediately start another. Each level has its own rewards of power, wealth and connections with promised virtual thrills and pleasures waiting around the bend. What are those thrills and pleasures? In reality, the games are built on the theory of the intermittent reward, similar to gambling. The odds are stacked against gamers so that the higher the level, the more difficult the task. Not every action receives a reward, but enough actions draw people in to keep them playing the games. A major factor in drawing in players is the instant gratification of meeting people with similar interests.

Entry into the games is easy, relatively cheap and nobody knows who you are; these are known as the three A's: *Anonymity, Accessi-*

---

[1] Herz, J. C., *Joystick Nation*. New York: Little, Brown., 2005.

bility and *Affordability*.[2] Gamers can be anyone they want, choosing characters, becoming lords or monsters in alternate worlds. Characters often mirror the gamers' personalities or may be characteristic of what they have always wanted to be, do or say.[3,4] A shy, cautious individual may choose to act as a promiscuous, violent individual, scooping up women at every turn. Men pretend to be women, and young players choose characters that give them the power, control and thrills that their real life may lack. The violence within the games allows even the most peaceful player to use their character to wield power whether for good or evil, often wreaking havoc in their wake without facing any negative consequences. Many say that they "zone out" when they play, feeling their palms sweat, their heart race and their face flush depending on what their character is doing. Those whose realities are most unpleasant find it difficult to return to the real world. Overdue bills, family responsibilities, unmet school or work deadlines are ignored as gamers trek through forests, fighting and triumphing where evil is vanquished with swords and spells instead of hard labor and paperwork. Marijuana, nicotine, alcohol and other substances often increase the fantastical quality of the experience.[5] The games are a thrilling and fun place to be and it is often more exciting and entrancing than the real world. Anyone who has read a book or watched a movie has had that moment when they looked up and were surprised to see they were not back in the world of fairies, under the sea or piloting a spacecraft. However, in *World of Warcraft* and other MMORPGs, a player has *choices*. Players meet together in virtual realms where the phrase "*reach out and touch someone*" takes on a new meaning. Contact with different gamers enhances these encounters, whether by chance or at pre-arranged times.[6] Players use Internet Relay Chat (IRC) to chat with

---

[2] Cooper, A. L. and E. Griffin-Shelley, E. "Introduction—The Internet: The Next Sexual Revolution." In *Sex and the Internet: A Guidebook for Clinicians*. New York City: Bruner-Routledge, 2002.

[3] Orzack, Maressa Hecht, Andrew C. Voluse, David Wolf and J. Hennen, "Ongoing Study of Group Treatment for Men Involved in Problematic Internet Enabled Sexual Behavior," *CyberPsychology & Behavior*, August 2006.

[4] Yee, Nick, "The Demographics, Motivations and Derived Experiences of Users of Massively Multi-User Online Graphical Environments." In *Presence: Teleoperators and Virtual Environments*, June 2006.

[5] Student Interview, 2005.

[6] Yee, Nick, "The Demographics, Motivations and Derived Experiences of Users of Massively Multi-User Online Graphical Environments." In *Presence: Teleoperators and Virtual Environments*, June 2006.

each other during the games, whether they are talking in character about the game or out of character about their lives. The individual combatants also chat, increasing the sense of contact during a bout. Coalitions form, both large and small; some last for only a few sessions, others are more permanent. The players will tell you that one of the main reasons they continue playing is because of the online connections.[7,8]

So who are these players? Why are some people able to play *World of Warcraft* and other MMORPGs without losing their lives in the games? The typical gamer is male, and despite the press, the majority of gamers are adults with families and steady jobs, not just hormone-crazed teenagers.[9,10]

Jonathan is a typical gamer. At the age of twenty-eight, he has lived with his fiancée, Kara, for more than a year, and they just bought a house together. He is a car salesman and a guitar player in an alternative rock band. He plays computer games on weekends and holidays, but knows when to stop. *World of Warcraft* is a chance for Jonathan to quest, fight and assume other identities, yet he does not let it rule his life.

Contrary to public opinion, though, gamers are not all male: a small percentage is female. Many begin playing with brothers, fathers or as part of a romantic relationship.[11] Some women who play do so for the same reason as any other gamer: the escape into a fantasy world. Jonathan's fiancée, Kara, is an example. Kara began playing games because of her grandfather, Paul.

It started when Kara's father got a job in Australia. Visits to her grandfather, which used to be a run across adjoining backyards, were now restricted to bimonthly phone calls. The calls were never enough,

---

[7] Orzack, Maressa Hecht. Taken from "Online Video Games: Psychpathological or Psychotherapeutic?" In NYC Lecture, American Psychiatric Association, May 2004.

[8] Yee, Nick, "The Demographics, Motivations and Derived Experiences of Users of Massively Multi-User Online Graphical Environments." In *Presence: Teleoperators and Virtual Environments*, June 2006.

[9] Orzack, Maressa Hecht. Taken from "Online Video Games: Psychpathological or Psychotherapeutic?" In NYC Lecture, American Psychiatric Association, May 2004.

[10] Yee, Nick. "The Daedalus Project," Nick Yee Daedalus Project Home Page, January 2005, <http://www.nickyee.com/daedalus>.

[11] Yee, Nick. "The Daedalus Project," Nick Yee Daedalus Project Home Page, January 2005, <http://www.nickyee.com/daedalus>.

and Paul saw his relationship with his granddaughter breaking down. Rather than lose this connection, Paul hit on a great idea. He had been playing MMORPGs since *Dungeons & Dragons*® back in college. Paul quickly realized that Kara might be several thousand miles away, but online she was still next door. He started her off with *Dark Ages of Camelot*® because he knew she loved King Arthur. Kara was a natural, particularly good at searching out different ways to solve problems, and she loved meeting with her grandfather at specific times. Initially, Kara was playing first and leaving her homework for later. Paul heard this, making her promise always to do her schoolwork first; then and only then was she allowed to visit the game. Kara rarely missed their biweekly sessions, and they went through several games and assumed different identities. Kara came back to the U.S. for college and continued gaming. Jonathan met her because a mutual friend introduced them, figuring they would have much in common. They sometimes play as a couple, and sometimes as separate characters. Usually they form coalitions, and both agree that gaming together has made their relationship richer. They met because they are gamers and they stay together because they are gamers.

Millions of people play *World of Warcraft* and other MMORPGs, yet forty percent of the players who turn on MMORPGs get into trouble.[12] What makes them different? Years of case histories have painted pictures of the classic adult computer nerd holed up in a dark room eating dried pizza as he punches code by day and enters the computer game worlds by night. Yet Doug, a fifteen-year-old middle-school student, is a typical out-of-control gamer whose only friends are other online gamers. Convinced that nobody understands him, he has retreated to a virtual world of quests, dragons and magical powers. He plays online until three or four A.M., forgetting to do his homework and sleeping through classes. When his parents challenged him about flunking his midterm exams, he told them he had amassed several million dollars of virtual gold and was figuring out which spells were best for his latest quest. His online friends agreed that algebra and geometry are worthless in the game, so why bother

---

[12] Orzack, Maressa Hecht. Taken from "Online Video Games: Psychpathological or Psychotherapeutic?" In NYC Lecture, American Psychiatric Association, May 2004.

studying? His parents, in horror, sent him to a counselor. The counselor, not understanding the addictive properties of games, told him to join a church group or the Boy Scouts. Doug kept telling her how proud and strong he feels when his character masters a new spell enabling him to lead or even challenge his fellow guild members. He has power, control and people who understand him. Why should he give that up for school where he is miserable, bored and alone?

Compulsive adult gamers are no different. Sam, a forty-two-year-old computer technician, illustrates problems they usually face. Sam was downsized when the computer company failed after the IT boom and bust. His life now consists of collecting unemployment and playing games. Convinced that he never will be able to find a job, Sam has not even begun trying. He sees himself as the only failure in a family of high-achieving professionals. Living on unemployment, he uses credit cards to reach Level 50. He has spent more than $1,500 in three months on game time supporting several characters. One character is an evil Shaman. Another character is a powerful lord convinced that he is God's gift to women who has accumulated (or bought through gold farmers) enough virtual money, power and points to do anything he wants. The only way Sam can talk to women is through this character, or when he is drunk. His online character is a direct opposite of his real-life characteristics of low self-esteem, poor social skills and his mood problems. His virtual characters mirror his moods alternately raging or sulking depending on the status of his characters.

These extreme cases are everywhere. A gamer in his early twenties committed suicide when his *EverQuest*® romance fell apart.[13] The justice system is dealing with a teenage murderer who is blaming *Grand Theft Auto*™ for his killing spree.[14] South Korean doctors are baffled about why supposedly healthy adults play MMORPGs such as *StarCraft*® so intensely and endlessly that they do not stop to eat or drink and instead they play until they collapse and die.[15] South

[13] Winter, Joe. "Hudson Mother Seeks Answers after Son Addicted to Computer Game Shoots Himself," RiverTown.net, February 2002, <http://www.rivertowns.net/daily/hso/c020220/>.

[14] Godsey, Mark and Gabriel, Jack Chin, "Grand Theft Auto Killing Deliberately." Crimeprof [online], February 14, 2005–February 20, 2005, <http://lawprofessors.typepad.com/crimprof_blog/2005/week7/index.html>.

[15] Uncredited, "Computer Games Blamed for another South Korean Death." ABC Asia Pacific TV/Radio Australia, October 12, 2005, <http://abcasiapacific.com/news/5>.

Korea, with more than seventy percent of its population wired, is deeply concerned, yet at the same time cable programs broadcast the games twenty-four hours a day, and Internet cafés are open all night. MMORPG contests beguile players with the promise of cash prizes at marathon sessions.[16] The players ignore all signs of risk to their physical and mental health.

Extremely out-of-control gamers face multiple losses. Their behavior affects not only themselves, but as with any addictive behavior, there are negative ripple effects on the family. Mark, the adult child of an alcoholic, turned to MMORPGs and pot to escape his constant family battles. Yet, he did not escape the violence. Recently he was in the middle of a timed quest when a visiting cousin dared to interrupt him. Mark, his concentration broken, screamed at the young child, but that was not the end. He turned back to the screen to find his time had lapsed and his character was dead. Enraged, he grabbed his young cousin and threw her down the stairs, breaking her leg. Mark, completely ignoring all the commotion, immediately went back to the game in an attempt to retrieve as much equipment as possible and start the process of reviving his character. When his family returned from the hospital he only said "She interrupted me while I was doing something important. It was her fault." Mark showed no remorse, just rage. Admittedly, neither Mark nor other members of his family knew how to deal with anger except by lashing out or by drinking, yet all but Mark saw his reactions as outrageous.

Compulsive gamers continue to play despite the losses. In the previous case there was violence and substance abuse: however, not all gamers come from such dysfunctional families. In some cases the losses are small; it is only when the negative consequences accumulate that the full effect is evident.

Anthony was a straight-A student in high school and is now in college. In high school, he occupied himself with academic teams, but in his high-powered college everyone needed straight A's to be admitted. He was no longer "the brain." Every room is connected to high-speed Internet service and much class work is done online. A friend introduced him to *World of Warcraft*. Anthony, always a "good boy,"

---

[16] Kim, Victoria, "Video Game Addicts Concern South Korean Government," Associated Press Writer, October 6, 2005, <http://breitbart.com/?feed=ap&cat>.

decided to play an evil character. In the game, he became a religious leader, using power to lead others to the dark side. He chortled as his character's power grew, turning others to his bidding, hoarding his gold, seducing warriors with his words and power. His roommate, Zach, was the first to notice that Anthony was no longer following his nightly routine of dinner, class work, checking his e-mail, shower and then bed. Now it was dinner, a brief stab at class work, then the game. He still checked his e-mail regularly, but now most of his mail came from other gamers. Half the time, he never showered, and Zach noticed that many nights he was staying up all night. Soon, he was ordering meals in and skipping classes. Why go to class if the professors put the class notes online? Every time Zach asked him about it, Anthony would agree to get help, but he never did.

By the end of the semester, Anthony had accrued more gold and reached Level 53 as part of a guild, but he was totally unprepared for his exams. When he attempted to stop cold turkey in order to catch up on his schoolwork, he showed symptoms of withdrawal. He refused to talk to anyone and when someone spoke to him, he began crying and could not stop. Zach found him curled up in a fetal position in the back of the closet crying and holding his pillow over his head. Convinced that Anthony might hurt himself, Zach got some friends and they walked him to the infirmary. He was admitted and given something to help him sleep. His parents came, and Anthony went home with incompletes in all of his classes for the semester and probation for the next semester. This further complicated his life because he was home while all of his friends were either away at college or working. His parents insisted that he not sit around the house. His parents laid down the law, he had to go to counseling and get a job so that he could pay for the gas in his car.

Treatment is often effective in helping people like Anthony and Sam. The first requirement is that they are ready to change and willing to commit to therapy. It is important that there be not only a verbal commitment, but also a financial one; clients are urged to pay something even if is a minimal amount. The therapist's job is to help the individuals recognize the consequences of their decisions and to encourage helping them to look at alternative activities. Examples of these may include joining organized sports, volunteering at an animal shelter, helping children with disabilities or anything where the individual feels needed and where they meet and interact with people whose lives do not revolve around games. Truly depressed gamers with poor social skills who are anxious often find activities like these quite rewarding. Their emotional health and stability greatly improve when they feel needed by someone else in a healthy way.

There is one big question: should they abstain from the game completely? This can often be quite difficult because pop-ups appear every time they turn on the computer to do anything, including work, e-mailing a friend, searching the Web for research or paying bills. It is hard to resist the latest gaming technologies such as Xbox 360 or PlayStation 2. The latest version of their favorite games can now be accessed on their cell phones. Some people find abstinence easier than limiting their gaming time. If they wish to go back to their MMORPG, then they need to keep remembering what happened to them and contrast the feelings and thoughts that they have now with their new activities. There are programs that they can buy to block and monitor their gaming behavior. What they need to learn is how to control their behavior and be able to use their computers for appropriate reasons. They can join twelve-step groups similar to Gamblers Anonymous. There is even an online twelve-step group for MMORPG players.[17]

Sam is an example of someone who must avoid games. Faced with financial ruin, he has no money, no credit cards and no place to live. His brother, a psychiatrist, recognizing that Sam's mood swings were symptoms of a serious problem, agreed to help him. The only stipulation was that he start therapy. The therapist determined that he is acting out in the games and he must learn to change that behavior. This will involve psychological treatment and medication that will help him to stop playing.

Anthony, in contrast to Sam, recognized that his gaming behavior was problematic. Once he accepted he was a valuable person and had a lot to offer, he began to find outlets for his interests. He began tutoring students in an after-school program and decided that he wanted to teach. He has mastered several behavioral techniques that

---

[17] "Online Gamers Anonymous," December 29, 2005, <http://www.olganon.org>.

allow him to play an online game for a limited time. He uses one of many timing programs to tell him when he needs to stop. Whenever he begins to feel anxious or wants more time, he gets up, leaves the room and calls a friend. That is enough for him to take control. This shows that some compulsive players are aware that they have a problem, and actively work to correct it. Whether this recognition came because the gamer "hit rock bottom" or because a family or friend intervened and forced the issue is immaterial. The gamer is ready to change, recognizes that there is a problem and is determined to work for a solution. It is imperative that they be highly motivated to change their behavior and recognize the consequences of not doing so. If they work hard to learn behavioral techniques such as relaxation, meditation and self-stopping behaviors, they may be able to play games again, on a limited basis.

Massive Multiplayer Online Role-Playing Games, including *World of Warcraft*, are immensely attractive to people, but that attraction makes the game a problem for more than forty percent of the people who play the games. Many players enjoy the games, have fun and keep a healthy balance between their game and the rest of their life. However, in cases like those of Doug, Mark, Anthony and Sam, the game becomes their lives, negatively influencing family, friends, school and work. Once they recognize there is a problem most addicted gamers must avoid games completely while other addicted gamers can learn to manage their habit with perhaps "a game a day"; in other words, play on a limited basis. The prescription for gamers should read: Take one a day. If you are lonely, shy, bored, have low self-esteem or abuse substances there are adverse reactions that may have toxic effects on your self, family, friends, school, work and finances. If these symptoms occur, consult your therapist. Do not stop without doctor's advice. Sudden cessation may result in further damage.

DISCLAIMER: All the case histories consist of amalgamations from my private practice and from requests for help by e-mail. I do not treat patients online, but refer them to appropriate therapists. All details have been disguised to protect the individuals.

Deborah S. Orzack trained as a biologist, becoming a high-school science teacher and environmental activist. After an accident, she became a writer, editor and disability advocate as vice chair of REDD, (Rights, Equality, and Dignity of the Disabled) and is the 2006 winner of the Corey Nelson Award for grass roots disability advocacy. She has written several articles on disability issues, edited newsletters, co-authored papers on computer addiction and is working on children's books. A special friend of all animals from marine creatures to anything furry, her life is always ruled by at least one four-footed feline.

Dr. Maressa Hecht Orzack is an assistant clinical professor at Harvard Medical School. She is the author of many articles on computer/Internet addiction problems. Maressa has spoken at many organizations, including Harvard University, MIT, American Psychiatric Association, Framingham College and many middle and high schools. She has been interviewed by the NBC Nightly News, NPR: KCROW, Chronicle, Fox News, the *New York Times*, *Time Magazine*, *Boston Globe*, *Newsweek* and many local media.

ALTAHOLICS NOT SO ANONYMOUS

DORANNA DURGIN AND NANCY DURGIN

Of all the sections in this book, this one needs the least introduction. If you have read this far, you are either an altaholic or will be one soon. There are a wide range of character classes in World of Warcraft. *This means a lot more than just giving you a few choices and new spells. One thing the diversity of character classes does is to make grouping much more beneficial. Just as a military platoon will have riflemen, heavy weapons, communications, command, medics and other specialized members, a good mixed* WoW *team can accomplish the same synergy. While a party of five Paladins or Shamans can be interesting, when you penetrate the high-level dungeons, the right mix is vital. Not only can healing be a must, but crowd control is needed for any party to survive some of the nastier locales. The diversity of classes means a group can be much more powerful than just the total damage per second (DPS) of the members.*

Each class has it owns charms and shortcomings. These are discussed later, along with historical models for each of the class types. In the article below the Durgins take a light, but very accurate, look at this aspect of our addiction to WoW.

H I, MY NAME IS NANCY, and I'm an altaholic.…
I can't help myself. I want more…*more* than just my main playing character. I want diversity! I want to explore! Even though I know they're just alts. Twinks. Mules. And I know what people say about spreading yourself too thin or getting bored and boring…and you can only play one at a time unless you're two-boxing, so why bother?

> CAJE (L36 Human Rogue): What's she talking about? We don't need to be active at the same time in order to take action. We've got this nifty mail system.
> MYTE (L43 Gnome Warrior): No kidding! We're always talking to one another…trading stuff. Hey, you need this cool Silverblade I just found in the Scarlet Monastery? I can send it your way. TWINK!
> CAJE: Yeah! Hold on, I'm in the middle of sending some cash over to Drelzna. It's just a wild impulse I had. Can't really explain it.

There you go. There's one reason to bother right off the bat. Okay, so we run into a bit of game world cognitive dissonance along with it. That is, why would Caje even think to send money to a Gnome Warlock he's never met? Inside the game, the alts don't meet…don't know each other. Even characters from opposing factions get to make faces at one another, figuratively speaking…but not our alts. So to have them swapping goodies behind the scenes creates an artificial omniscient environment, and requires stepping out of the game worldview. But hey, I can live with that.

I can live with the limits on twinking, too. That is, my alts can't just grab anything my high-level character drops in their path. My Level 1 character can't wield the super-sword-of-uberness from a Level 60 dragon, even if someone feels inclined to hand him one. Doesn't bother me...in a way, it prevents things from being *too* easy—but at the same time it still allows me options to take advantage of the time I've put into the game with my main character.

> KIMA (L40 Human Mage): Check it out! I just hit Level 40! I get to buy a mount! No more walking! BO-ring! (Turns money pouch inside out.)
>
> CAJE: I'm not seeing 90 gold there.
>
> KIMA: Er...no. But I know a solution to that.
>
> NITA (L57 Night Elf Hunter): You looking at me? Fifty-seven levels deserves a little more respect.
>
> KIMA: I know a solution to that, too. Serious respect potential.
>
> CAJE: You think we ought to pool our money so you don't have to wait?
>
> KIMA: Hey, you did it for Myte.
>
> NITA: And I got my Nightsaber the old-fashioned way—I earned the money myself. I couldn't even afford to buy my Nightsaber until I was Level 50! You alts already have it easy. What took me days to accomplish only takes you hours, because you're taking advantage of my playing experience, avoiding my mistakes. And now you want my money, too?
>
> CAJE: Hey, Myte got a giant green chicken. Mechanical, at that. Is that what you want?
>
> KIMA: (horrified) No! A horse! That's what I'm supposed to get, a horse!
>
> CAJE AND NITA: (make chicken noises)
>
> KIMA: Maybe this isn't such a good idea after all....
>
> CAJE: Wait! Hold on, I have a sudden wild impulse to send you some cash. Can't really explain it....

And that's just for starters. There's plenty of lure for us altaholics, especially those of us who have been playing the game for a while. In fact, the *World of Warcraft* even *encourages* playing alts, because of its "resting" mechanic. A fully rested character gains experience at twice the rate of a "tired" character. How does your character become "rested"? By not playing! If you have alts you only play every week or so, then they will always be fully rested, which means when you do play the alts, they will gain twice as much experience for everything they do! (Well, only twice as much for killing monsters, not for quests or exploring, but that's a minor detail....)

So everybody should play alts, right?

Maybe not. If you're new to the *World of Warcraft* scene, then maybe you want to take it easy. You've got to know a lot of details to play each class of character—never mind to do a really good job of it—and if you're trying to absorb details for eight different classes at once....

Well, *ow*.

Or if you can't play quite often enough to absorb each character's skills, then it takes time to reacquaint yourself with that alt before you play it. You might never really get good with that alt. You might even never get really good at playing the next ten alts, if you pile them on too fast.

Ow.

But meanwhile, because you know the game well through your other characters, you can easily level the alt faster than otherwise would happen, especially if you take advantage of that whole "rest" thing. This could leave you with a medium-to-high-level character that you just can't play very well. You know that nightmare pickup-group you had in Scarlet Monastery? The one with the Warrior who didn't know how to hold aggro, and the Priest who was nuking instead of healing? You don't want to *be* that incompetent Priest the rest of the group is complaining about in private tells and blacklisting to their guilds, do you? Well, if you haven't put some time into leveling up that Priest alt, playing her in groups and really learning your class, then there's a good chance you will be.

Did I say ow yet?

So maybe it's best to focus first on a single class of characters, adding more as you solidify your skills. And it's easy to put an alt or two off to the side if you feel the need to catch up with yourself. Spreading yourself too thin doesn't lead to the ultimate gaming experience, but you'll never know those limits unless you hunt for them.

Hmm. Maybe "limits" isn't the term I want to use here. If there's one thing alting does, it's to expand your options to suit your gaming mood, not limit them. Feeling antisocial? Pull out a character who solos well. Feeling chatty? Grab your teamwork character. And with two opposing factions in *WoW*—Alliance and Horde—if you want to experience the full game content, you'll need to have characters on each side. Heck, you can even get tricky with it.

KIMA: Nice that we're all with the Alliance. At least she's consistent.

CAJE: I'm not so sure. There's something about that Horde Troll Shaman....

KIMA: Why would she play a Horde character? She likes us. The Alliance. *Us*.

CAJE: Don't get your robes in a twist. Maybe she's smarter than you're giving her credit for.

KIMA: (profoundly stumped silence)

CAJE: Oh, come on. *Spy!*

KIMA: You're kidding!

CAJE: You never noticed we always seem to be out of the way of Horde raids? And when that lame Undead Priest kept killing Drelzna after she accidentally triggered her PvP flag in the Crossroads, how the Troll Shaman just happened to log on and get on his case? She's using him, all right. Not that he's likely to live long...but it sure must be more satisfying to give that Undead guy grief to his face, instead of standing around making threatening gestures like we have to do. "I grimace at you!" Yeah, that's effective.

So yeah...be creative. Play your alts within their Horde or Alliance affiliations, but take the opportunity to layer their activities. Keep yourself informed of the other side's activities, and pester those who have annoyed you, unfettered by the communication restrictions between sides. You have the power! Or you *could*....

Alts can give you a handle on guilds, too. Well, sometimes you don't have the option, since guilds have different requirements for entry—some don't allow alts, or they restrict entry to high-level alts only. It pretty much depends on the guild and its purpose (raiding, social or even just people who like the idea of a big guild). There are even guilds with allied guilds for low-level alts. But having alts gives you the ability to choose your guild for the day along with the alt.

If you don't want to fool with the business of your main guild, you have a way to avoid it and keep right on playing.

Of course, with even *this* alt handling spying and *that* alt playing in a different guild, it's hard to avoid the Repetition Factor. You know, the part where you get that "haven't we been here before?" feeling. When you just start out with an alt—at least, if you've diversified nicely from previous alts—you'll have a chance at the unique quests available to the low-level characters of that race, and you'll have class-specific quests that you haven't seen before. Regardless of how many times you've been through the process of taking characters through levels, with new races you'll have new quests to explore. But then the Repetition Factor hits—for beyond the early levels, the quests become common to all. If you've done them, you've done them—you've only got the freshness of doing it with a character who has different skills and can tackle the quests in different ways.

There's still an upside to it all—if you're that experienced, then you'll also know which quests are the most fun for you, and you can skip the boring ones! Go, you!

DARLA (L6 Dwarf Paladin): I *can't* go. I can't seem to go anywhere. I'm stuck inside the Ironforge Bank. Just don't seem to want to go outside. I don't quite understand it. I used to love being outside.

CAJE: Hey, Darla, my bags are all full and I don't have time to run to the bank. I'll mail this to you, and you can just send it back to me later, okay?

DARLA: I guess as long as I'm here...(sighs) I never did get much action before this, I suppose. At least I feel useful when I can—

KIMA: Hey, Darla! Can you stash this for me? Thanks, gotta run!

DARLA: But—wait—I—! Okay, well, at least I feel useful.

Oh yeah. There's another thing. Run out of bank space? Don't want to waste playing time to run all the way to Ironforge to store those spare trade-skill components in the bank? Take one of those stalled low-level alts you maybe, kinda, shouldn't have started in the first place, and park her in the bank. She can store items from your other alts—

DARLA: (wails) I thought this would be a *temporary* gig!

—as well as buy and sell items at the Auction House.

Those alts can provide relief of another sort, too. If your main character has maxed out at Level 60, raiding could possibly be the only way to advance. You know...that multi-hour commitment to group up with forty other people to accomplish something epic, such as slaying a dragon. Except in practice, you tend to slay that same dragon every week. This is not only hard on the dragon, it also tends to diminish the epic-ness of the whole thing. And if you think it's hard to coordinate forty people in real life, you should see how fast it can get old online....

The point, of course, is that when it does get old, you can go alting for a little change of pace. Or heck, don't even wait for it to get old. Prevent raiding burnout by playing alts on a regular basis.

And that leaves me with my favorite part. Each character can have only two trade skills out of the dozen or so available in the game. If you want to try out other trade skills, or benefit from them, you either need to have a friend with that skill, or make another character with that skill. Take Alchemy...an alchemist can make potions, which can be used by any character. If you have an alt who's an alchemist, then you have someone to give any rare Alchemy components you might find, and you have someone to make potions for your other characters. Generally speaking, if you have at least one character covering each trade skill, then you've got someone to make anything you want, for free. (I really like that part. Free. Yeah.) And you have characters who can truly take advantage of rare trade skill components.

There are some limitations here, of course. The game wouldn't be any fun if it was that easy to manipulate. (No, really. It wouldn't.) The very best items can only be made by highly skilled characters, and maximum trade skill levels are limited by character level. Also, the rare components are usually only going to be found by high-level characters, and you'll need a lot of them to make something cool. So unless your trade-skill character is of a high level, gifting trade-skill components won't lead to major practical advantages. But sometimes it all works out, and meanwhile you've got all those trade skills to choose from. (Did I mention the part where you can make what you want, free?)

> DAIRINE (L12 Human Priest): Skinning and Herbalism...I'm bored. I want to make more money. Mining? Enchanting? What would be nice with Skinning and Herbalism...?
>
> KIMA: Nothing. If you're going to pick up another trade skill, you've got to lose one.
>
> DAIRINE: What? Why didn't I know about this?
>
> CAJE: (sigh) Lower-level alts. You think we're going to spoon-feed you everything? Me, I chose Herbalism right off the bat. And Alchemy. Great combination. I can collect herbs, and I can make potions with them. Did you see that killing I made—
>
> KIMA: Don't get cocky. You didn't literally kill anything over that deal.
>
> CAJE: All right, then, *I made a lot of money.* Better? When suddenly everyone wanted Swiftness and Free Action Potions to use on the new Battlegrounds? You all could have picked up the right trade skills, too, if you'd been on the ball. But I was already perfectly positioned to find the components and put them together—and set the prices really high! Ooh hoo, that was nice. I can't quite remember what happened to all that money, though. Oh, wait. I had a sudden inexplicable impulse to send some to Myte, because she needed a giant mechanical chicken.

This talk of mechanical chickens gives me the impulse to get all dry and technical for a moment—yes, it's the whole issue of having characters on different servers. Lots of reasons for that, too, starting with the simple precaution of having a different place to play if your main server goes down. Also, some servers are PvP game worlds, where characters in opposing factions can attack one another just about any time they please. On those PvP servers, you can only have characters of one faction—so if you want to play the opposite side, you'll have to use a different server.

There's also that pesky limit of ten characters per server, so if you want more alts, you have to create them on a different server. But spanning servers isn't a bad thing...not at all. It's especially useful if you have real-life friends who already play on more than one server—it gives you the chance to play with them wherever they are. And for those of us who love to take advantage of twinking, starting "fresh" on a new server gives you untwinked and untwinkable characters. It's only relevant if you have no self-control to stop yourself from twinking otherwise. Though certainly no one here would ever have that problem....

But look...don't take all this too far. The advantages of playing alts—the varied experience, the ability to cross boundaries to the other side, the twinking, the flexibility...it all takes a variety of characters, from Hunter to Mage to Warrior to Shaman to as many as suit your purpose. But if you fall into the trap of adoring a single character class and skill set....

BERT: What's she talking about?

KIMA: You. She's talking about you.

BERTIE: You mean me?

KIMA: Yes. That's the point. What does it really matter which of you is playing?

BERTWA: We think it matters.

KIMA: It's the same experience.

BERTINA: I'm a girl!

KIMA: You're still just like the others. You do the same things, have the same strengths, and you're impossible to tell apart.

BERTWO: You're just not trying. I'm going to have a defensive build, and Bert will be a dual-wielding arms build and Bertwa will use sword and shield...or was that Bertina?

KIMA: See, even *you* can't keep yourselves straight. I'm not even going to try!

There you are. None of the variety or advantages that come with playing alts, and all the boring, repetitive aspects that one tries to avoid. Plus all the boring, repetitive aspects that one tries to avoid....

True, there's something to be said for having an alt of the same class as your main, but a completely different skill build. Gives you new strengths to play around with, and if you can learn those skills you'll be better at interacting with others who have them. This only goes so far, though. And it's not as interesting or challenging as running a different class altogether.

If you've been paying attention (what, you didn't know there'd be a pop quiz?), you've seen a good solid cast of characters right here on these pages. From single-digit levels (that spying Troll Shaman) to the main, the Level 57 Night Elf Hunter. Mage, Warrior, Rogue, Warlock, Priest, Druid and Paladin…none of these are repeated. Several Humans, a couple of Night Elves, a couple of Gnomes….In other words, it's a diverse collection of levels, classes and races. Add to those characters a thoughtful collection of trade skills, and you've got the flexibility to play what you want, when you want, create your own goods, keep an eye on the opposing faction, play in groups, play on your own.…

Before I get carried away (all this talk is giving me an irresistible urge to head for the computer for some gaming), it's time to look at the big picture.

Alts No:

Repetitive. Spreading yourself too thin. Never really solidifying your skills well enough to play any given character at its best. Alts can't officially interact with each other.

Alts Yes:

Try out different skills. Relief from Raiding Syndrome. Potential faction spies. Explore additional game facets. Mules. Item and money swapping. Guild management. Playing according to your mood. Flexibility and adaptability. Multiple server options.

Hi, my name is Nancy, and I'm still an altaholic.…

Wanna come play?

Doranna was born writing (instead of kicking, she scribbled on the womb) and never quit, although it took some time for the world to understand what she was up to. She grew up attached to college-rule notebooks and resisted all attempts at separation. Eventually she got a college degree (Wildlife Illustration) and had grand adventures on horseback in the Appalachians before turning full-time writer and ending up in the Southwestern high country with her laptop, dogs, Lipizzan and uncontrollable imagination. In her copious spare time (not), she trains her dogs for and competes in canine agility trials.

Doranna writes eclectically and across genres, with a backlist in fantasy, media tie-in, anthologies, mystery and a growing collection of titles in women's action-adventure/romance. You can find a complete bibliography at www.doranna.net, along with scoops about new projects, lots of silly photos and contact info. And just for kicks, Connery Beagle has a LiveJournal (connerybeagle) presenting his unique view of life—drop by and say hello!

Nancy has been playing role-playing games for more than twenty-five years, starting with the original *Dungeons & Dragons*®. She started playing *EverQuest*® in May 1999 and has played most of the current MMORPGs, including her current favorite, *World of Warcraft*. When she's not playing games, Nancy works in computer security for a government research laboratory. She has a Ph.D. in computer science from Stanford and a master's degree in physics from Columbia.

I Play Like a Girl:
Yes, That Level 60
Night Elf Warrior Is Mine

Nancy Berman

Now, about that vive le différence. Oops, there are none. In some games there are statistical differences between male and female characters. Men are stronger or healthier, women more dexterous (anyone made them smarter too?). In a few SF RPGs there are even a few new alignments in the "none" and "other" categories of sex fit. I won't even get into androids. It has taken almost a decade, and the gradual evolution of games that interest (I've heard it stated as "are worthy of") female players, for the gaming industry to be aware of how many women are buying and playing their games. This probably should not have been as much of a revelation as it appears to have been. The reason for the revelation is that many female characters have been disguised by male avatars. Many women take male avatars just so they will not suffer from the jibes or lowered expectations of male players. Then again, there was the industry's chauvinist assumption that these are fighting games, so men must be better at playing them. Boys have "action figures" and women have dolls. (Read about Russia's WWII all-female army brigades, and be ready to shudder a lot and revise your assumptions of women as soldiers.)

Those of us from the old days of garage game companies often find little joy in the fact that our industry is now dominated by big companies and big budgets (even though we love the big games this enables them to produce). Still, one of the real benefits of this was that these new corporate types looked past our puerile-male, old-boy assumptions and realized who the audience included. They were helped along by a number of highly talented women in the field who now have the perfect right to look smug and say, "I told you that years ago." Nancy Berman is one of those women. We really should have listened....

Introduction

I
T WAS LATE and I really should have logged off, but I only had to kill a few more murlocs, run along the bridge to finish the quest, level up and then head to Stormwind to get some new spells. It shouldn't take me that long....

When I came to, I was staring at the telltale shimmering ghostly screen that told me I had died. A quick flip to the map and yep, the murlocs had savaged me and left my remains along the river. I must have clicked the mouse to start running and fallen asleep at the keyboard.

So, how cool is that? Not that I was murloc-chow but that a game could be so compelling that I'd throw common sense to the wind and play past my bedtime (we're talking waaay past my bedtime!). This probably doesn't seem strange to those of you who are male. But I'm a woman. A woman who loves playing MMORPGs. Obviously to distraction.

And what's even more amazing—I'm not alone.

What Is a "Girl Game"?

There doesn't seem to be much dispute among scholars and gamers alike that play is an integral part of human society. According to Johan Huizinga, play is a *"significant* function—that is to say, there is some sense to it....All play means something."[1] But what exactly does it mean to women? Aside from what we do as young girls and what we do with our children, that is.

Women are no strangers to role-playing. After all, it's what we do, to some degree, throughout our lives; some roles we choose and some are just part of what we do to survive. Our first experience in conscious role-playing occurs when we play make-believe. Some of us are lucky enough to be introduced to paper-and-pencil role-playing games (RPGs) by older siblings (usually as Orc fodder, but getting to roll the dice is pretty cool). From there we progress to playing these games with our own friends. Although the majority of these RPGs were developed by men, they have such flexible character design systems that it's usually no problem for a female player to develop a character she loves to play. There are disputes about the rules but rarely if ever are they based on gender bias. Even though most of the designers and players in the paper-and-pencil RPG industry are male, there has been a steady increase in female participation as writers, designers and, thankfully, as players. So why has this niche industry been more successful in integrating women while the computer game industry continues to struggle?

The mystery of male vs. female wishes, needs and playing styles seems to have baffled designers ever since software companies realized that women might actually pay money to play computer games instead of relying on the free games that come with an operating system. Over the last two decades much time and more than a little money has been spent trying to figure out how women play, what they play and why they play, in hopes of attracting this potentially significant market segment. Unfortunately, to date most companies have not enjoyed what they regard as a significant return on their investment in terms of positive reviews or cold hard cash. Fortunately, women are finally coming out of hiding and speaking up for themselves in the most effective way possible—by playing.

They are also becoming more vocal online. In June 2005, Gamasutra published a feature article titled "On Girls and Video Games,"

---

[1] Huizinga, Johan. *Homo Ludens: A Study of the Play Element in Culture.* Boston: The Beacon Press, 1950.

written by Jess Bates, who seems to believe in the stereotype that has hampered significant development in games for women, even though a fair amount of recent data seems to contradict her theories. Ms. Bates, an artist who lives in Washington, stated authoritatively that

"Most women and girls play video games infrequently at best, and usually when it involves other people—or the men in their life. Males, on the other hand, often play alone, and a large amount of males become game addicts."[2]

She went on to reference physiological differences in male vs. female eye structure, visceral reactions to stimuli and the hunter vs. nurture argument. According to her, these variances mean...

"...more than men and women just having different interests in competition. In terms of video games, it has serious implications on a player's willingness to learn manual skills in order to play, and the notion of slaying all others to win, or even the idea of playing in isolation, by oneself."[3]

Female posters on www.womengamers.com were disturbed both by the fact that Gamastura would publish that kind of article and that a woman could still believe in that stereotype. Outraged responses to Ms. Bates' editorial included a letter to Gamasutra's editor in which "Fizgig" (a poster on www.womengamers.com) wrote, "I love fragging as much as I love stealth killing someone from behind with Sam, or raiding Molten Core with my Tauren Druid, or hacking through a sea of Undead in the new *Resident Evil*®."[4]

Happily, this topic is not something that industry executives are trying to ignore or push off on an intern researcher. In his State of the Industry address at E3 2005, Douglas Lowenstein, President of the Entertainment Software Association, spoke about the need

[2] Gamastura, Soapbox: "On Girls and Video Games." Jess Bates. November 30, 2004. http://www.gamasutra.com/features/20041130/bates_01.shtml.

[3] http://www.gamasutra.com/features/20041130/bates_01.shtml.

[4] Gamasutra, Letters to the Editor, June 23, 2005. http://www.gamasutra.com/php-bin/letter_display.php?letter_id=889.

to address this problem, and in fact quoted from Fizgig's letter. He acknowledged her description of "gamer shame" (women being embarrassed to admit they play video games) and the industry's failure to combat that.

> "It's hard to argue with her complaint that our own industry, mainly through our marketing practices, reinforces the stereotype that most gamers are men. Our challenge as an industry is to break down the social conventions she described if we are to truly create, again in Fizgig's words, 'a gender neutral inclusive gaming community'... [in which my daughter] could proclaim her love of games to the world without any shame at all."[5]

There were several "women in gaming" conferences held in 2005. Ernest Adams, a speaker at a conference in Dundee, Scotland, in August, was quoted online:

> "We are soon going to be seeing massive multi-player online games that are dominated by female players," he said. "Existing online role-playing games are succeeding with women in spite of their subject matter, not because of it. When we get more games whose gameplay genuinely appeals to female players, we can expect to see huge growth there."[6]

The topics to be covered at the conference look familiar: identifying the market, how and where women buy games, the importance of art and avatars and "female entertainment criteria" (which they define as "games for girls"). Perhaps some of the mystery could be solved if designers would take a step back from what appears to be an ingrained need to make female characters sexy. Given the target market, this is probably a naïve wish, but it would appear that no real solution will be achieved until the perception at the heart of the problem has been altered. We can only hope that the conference attendees will eventually figure out what hundreds of other conferences, panels, white papers and presentations have been unable to do

---

[5] http://www.e3insider.com/newsroomArticle.aspx?articleID=N8WP7SJFMY.
[6] http://news.softpedia.com/news/Sex-change-predicted-for-computer-games-3910.shtml.

to date. In the meantime, while we wait for them to listen to us and figure out that "good game" is more important than "girl game," we want something to play now!

What Do We Play?

One need only review a game survey or two to see that a significant number of women play games like *Solitaire, Taipei* and pseudo *Mah-jong*—in essence, simple games that require no particular commitment of time or emotion. These are not social, community-building games (the kind that researchers claim women prefer) but after all, what with kids and housework and all those other things we end up doing, there is undoubtedly a perception on the part of (male) game designers that we don't have time for intense, immersive play anyhow.

As much as we would like to think that the purpose of games is to entertain us, the true purpose is like that of any other industry—to make money. There has always been a fierce battle for shelf space in the game business that has gotten worse as time passes. Games that sell are going to fill those precious slots and those are primarily going to be ones aimed at the target market (male players, eighteen to twenty-five, give or take a few years). There are usually budget games on an end cap or in a bin (you know, like 4,000 varieties of Solitaire for $9.99), and a perennial row of pink boxes involving a ubiquitous blonde in a range of activities, but when girls pass the age where Barbie™ or Hello Kitty™ is interesting, they need something else to play.

Video games seem to attract a higher percentage of female players than regular computer games, despite some writers' contention that anime or character/story-based RPGs haven't "become immensely popular among females."[7] We're not talking about *Need For Speed*™ or *Grand Theft Auto*™ or *Madden NFL*™ *2004* (although some women probably play them) but rather role-playing games with lots of gameplay and long involved storylines that stretch across several releases. In the U.S., Japanese-produced RPG video games like *Phan-*

---

[7] http://www.gamasutra.com/features/20041130/bates_01.shtml.

tasy Star and *Final Fantasy*® are popular with women, although their overall sales in this country are still barely a blip on the radar compared with, say, *Unreal Tournament*®, *Doom*™ or *Halo*®. At least they prove that there are female players out there who want to play these kinds of games and who continue to fuel the push to create games for women.

Occasionally a game pops up that has a female heroine. Does that mean women buy and play the game? Not necessarily.

Tomb Raider™, for example, has a female protagonist. A perfectly shaped, utterly gorgeous, totally kick-you-know-what female protagonist who tends to make male players go all stupid and drooly even before they had the image of Angelina Jolie in their fevered brains. But a female protagonist doth not a "girl's game" make. Very few female players (or indeed non-players) can live up to the standard set by Ms. Croft (or Ms. Jolie) and it's incredibly annoying to be wondering whether your boyfriend is thinking about you while he's playing Lara Croft or whether he's just thinking about Lara (or Angelina . . . or Lara *and* Angelina. . . .)

It would be nice to believe the statistics that "nearly half" of all video game players in America are female and represent part of the gaming industry's "new face"[8] but the fact is that the number may be closer to twenty-five percent if you discount educational software played in school and at home. An article published by the ISDN in late 2004 claimed forty-three percent, based on an indication that more women were playing video games. According to a "recent study by AOL,"[9] women forty and older spend fifty percent more time playing games than their masculine counterparts. While this statistic could also be cause for rejoicing, it most probably reflects the efforts of companies like AOL and Yahoo! to give users access to social card and board games online rather than a surge in subscriptions to an MMORPG.

Overall, this is definitely an improvement from the industry's beginnings, but when compared to the top-selling non-MMORPG computer games as of June 2005, it doesn't seem to be reflected in the

---

[8] http://www.idsa.com/releases/4-21-2000.html - survey by Peter D. Hart Research Associates for IDSA.

[9] http://wiki.media-culture.org.au/index.php/Computer_Games_-_Women_Gamers.

list (based on several retail postings)[10]: *Doom 3™*, *Age of Mythology®*, *Half-Life 2®*, *Battlefield 2™*, *The Sims 2™*, *Call of Duty®*, *Unreal Championship 2®*, *Knights of the Old Republic™*, as well as the controversial *Grand Theft Auto: San Andreas™* and the brilliant evergreen *Civilization®*.

What Do We Want?

We want the same thing any player wants: great graphics, engaging gameplay, challenges, rewards and a great story. In 2001, Meghan Fox put it very well in an article entitled "I'm Not That Hard to Write For!" when she wrote,

> *"The trick isn't to 'reevaluate what female gamers want in a virtual experience,' or to try to imperfectly delve into what Developers believe is the female psyche (Hint: not Lara Croft, even if she was good in the movie): it's to make a fun, involving game."*[11]

Obviously both the professionals and the players agree that to keep the distaff side of the subscriber base happy, a game has to offer women the chance to be more than just a pretty face or flip over a couple of cards.

It would seem that Mr. Lowenstein agrees with us too, based on his E3 address:

> *"We need games with better stories, more interesting and complex characters, games that keep you up in the middle of the night wrestling with whether you made the right ethical or moral choices, games that stay with you when you're done with them, games that make you happy when you play them, and afterwards."*[12]

Does that mean we don't enjoy first-person shooters? Some of us do but when we sit down to play an MMORPG, thanks to *EverQuest®* and *World of Warcraft*, we have come to expect a high-level package

[10] Epinions.com, Gamespot.com, Firingsquad.com.
[11] http://www.womengamers.com/articles/write4me.php.
[12] http://www.e3insider.com/newsroomArticle.aspx?articleID=N8WP7SJFMY.

that delivers on its promises. If a game company isn't going to try the "hey, it's good enough" approach with its male players, it better not try it with female players either.

There is a persistent belief that women only play MMORPGs for the "social aspects" of the game. There's no question that we appreciate the opportunity to chat amongst ourselves (read: look for non-drooly, non-kill-stealing partners), form congenial social groups (read: set up guilds) and arrange cooperative playing sessions (read: organize guild raids) but that doesn't mean we don't want phat lewtz and m4d sk1llz too!

Who Are We?

In late March 2005 Blizzard announced a 1.5 million subscriber base worldwide for *WoW,* and the boards and blogs would seem to confirm this global population. In July 2005, a thread on Allakhazam's *WoW* board addressed the issue of how many women are playing and where they are located. There were posters from Canada, Australia, Italy, Germany, Belgium, Switzerland and Sweden. One female poster noted that there seemed to be a much higher population of female players in *WoW* than in *EQ* and *EQ 2* (which I can attest to personally as well). There are a number of all-female player guilds, on both the Alliance and Horde sides. There are female guild leaders, including one who heads up a guild that definitely qualifies for uber-status with a reported fifty players past Level 60.

Some posters commented that they play *WoW* with partners and with their children, which is certainly something that appears to distinguish it from MMORPGs like *EQ.* There seems to be a "lighter" touch overall in the game that makes it less intimidating and less dark and brooding than *EQ.* Even "naked" avatars don't seem to be quite as X-rated as in other online games, which makes it more comfortable to play with children.

An even more pressing concern among players is whether there are real women behind female avatars. It was proven time and again in *EQ* that if you played a lush female (especially a Dark Elf), male players would often make extravagant displays of generosity for no apparent reason other than your physical onscreen beauty. There are also many tales, some of them fairly sorrowful, about male players who came on to female avatars only to discover that the puppet-mistress was in fact a master.

A recent post on the official *WoW* forums called for Blizzard to augment its policy to include men playing female avatars as a punishable violation. For two months, responses ranged from outraged and caustic to highly amused. Many posters tried to explain to the petitioner that *WoW* is a game, not a dating service. Other posters tried to explain that the point of an MMORPG was to role-play (the petitioner felt that cross-playing ruined the "role-playing spirit" of the game). When the petitioner revealed a belief that women should be content with being women both in and out of the game, there was a strong reaction from female posters who defended their right to play as they please, which includes being warriors and doing traditionally "unfeminine" things.

In response to a brief, very informal survey, nine of eleven female MMORPG players polled who have played or are playing MMORPGs responded:

Have You Ever Played a Male Character Online? If So, Why?

- "I've played a male character online when I used to play MUSH-ES but only as an NPC or character necessary to a story line I was running when I was a staff."
- One plays male characters because her male coworkers were playing girls.
- One plays male characters in MUD/MUSHes to broaden her RP skills.
- One did it only for role-playing purposes, while one genuinely prefers playing male characters.
- One never plays males: "I like the idea of a 'strong' female ('cause I am)."
- "Yes, only once, my friends wanted me to join 'Rainbow Pride' super group, which required a gay character. But only played him for five levels."

How Many MMORPGs Have You Played?

GAME	Publisher	Year	KB	LJ	TB	KK	ML	TM	RS	TW	NB	#
Anarchy Online	Funcom	2001				X						1
A Tale in the Desert	eGenesis	2003			X							1
City of Heroes	Cryptic Studios	2004	X	X		X	X			X	X	6
Dark Age of Camelot	VU Games	2001				X						1
Earth & Beyond	Electronic Arts	2004									X*	1
EverQuest	SOE	1999			X	X			X		X	4
EverQuest II	SOE	2004				X					X	2
Guild Wars	NC Soft	2005			X						X	2
Kingdom of Loathing	Asymmetric Publications	2005			X							1
MajorMUD	Metropolis	1995			X							1
MUSH/MUDs only								X				1
Neverwinter Nights	TSR/Quantum; Bioware	1988–1996; 2002		X		X				X		3
Puzzle Pirates	Ubisoft	2005			X						X*	2
Shadow of Yserbius	Sierra Online/ INN	1992									X	1
Star Wars Galaxies	Lucas Arts	2003			X*	X*						2
The Matrix Online	Warner Bros. IE/Sega	2005									X*	1
WoW	Blizzard	2004			X*	X				X	X	4

*Beta-tested

If You Play *WoW*, Which Race Do You Prefer and Why?

- One played as a beta tester and didn't get attached to any race.
- One prefers Gnome and Tauren females. "Gnomes are incredibly cute and can have pink hair. The Tauren storyline and characterization is the best in the game, and should be on the Alliance side."
- "Trolls, they look badass (didn't really play enough to pick up the differences between the classes)."

If You Played *EQ,* Which Race Did You Prefer and Why?

- Two preferred Dark Elves pretty much to the exclusion of any other race. One of them said she liked "the intricacies of so-called evil races. I normally play either a very chaotic Dark Elf who can't figure out what she is, or a lawful one who merely does what she can for her people." The other just liked the way they looked.
- "High Elf—she was my Barbie doll cleric. My other character was half-elf, which was basically 'Normal' in *EQ* and didn't have any distinguishing physical characteristics."
- Two preferred Dark Elves.
- "Human, I like the standard stat picks."

Have You Ever Flirted In-Game As Your Character?

All of them responded yes (and one said "always").

In Paper-and-Pencil RPGs Do You Prefer Playing a Male or Female Character?

- "I prefer playing female characters. Much the same as [another respondent], my characters all tend to be the same people. Young, clever, quick, chaotic/neutral :)"
- "I play both male and female characters. I tell myself it's because I want to explore the boundaries of my animus. No matter how diverse I try to be, though, I always end up playing (being?) the same person, whether it's male or female: strong, noisy and an emotional wreck…gosh, kind of like…me. Go figure. So, ultimately, whether or not my character has a penis isn't the issue.

What looks back at me from the bathroom mirror every morning is. :)"
- "Female but that's really because the DM prefers it that way. I wouldn't care either way."
- Two prefer playing female characters exclusively.

Give Three Reasons Why You Like MMORPGs

- "It makes me think of when I was a little kid and would run around in my Wonder Woman Underoos. I love the online community that develops because of the supergroups. And beating up on villains is always a great form of catharsis."
- "It's the best immersive escapist fantasy available. I prefer cooperative and teamwork play."
- "It's fun being someone else with other people around."
- "I love being about to 'be' in a fantasy world. I love collecting stuff and getting great armor. And I love being able to kill things, especially when I can take down a big mob all at once."
- "Social reasons (chatting, making friends). Style of gameplay I tend to like. Feeling of accomplishment."

How Did We Get Here?

In addition to women who opt to play *WoW* because they like computer games, and specifically MMORPGs, other avenues traversed to get to *WoW* include getting hooked by a boyfriend, husband, sibling, coworker, a female friend who was playing and the kids ("I just wanted to see what they were talking about....") One poster said he had gotten his girlfriend started and then had to bribe her to get his computer back.

Some players came to the game through other games like *Final Fantasy XI*®, *EverQuest*®, *City of Heroes*®, *Asheron's Call*™, *Dark Age of Camelot*®, *Neverwinter Nights*™, *Ultima Online*™, *Icewind Dale*™, *Diablo Online*® and *Lineage I/II*®. Some come through non-MMORPGs like *Lunar: Silver Star Story*, *Phantasy Star*, *Kingdom Hearts*, and *Legend of Zelda*®, while still others played *The Longest Journey*, *Wizardry, Might & Magic*™, *Bard's Tale*™, *Baldur's Gate*™, *Diablo*®, *Dungeon Siege*™, *Morrowind*®, *Prince of Persia*™, *Star Wars Galaxies*™, *Puzzle Pirates*™, and *Sims Online*™, just to name a few.

Not everyone agrees that the games listed above represent a viable option for women. Sheila Swyrtek, a member of the science & math faculty at Mott Community College in Flint, MI, wrote as recently as January 2005 (*Computer Games Magazine*) that she does not see a wide choice in available games.

Daughters of the Alliance,[13] an all-girl player *WoW* guild (and its sister guild, Daughters of the Horde[14]) has its own Livejournal™ page and they use Teamspeak. Before you think, "Awww, how cute," you should know that conversations on their Livejournal posts are every bit as technical and focused as on an all-boy guild. These ladies really know their stuff!

There are a number of girl-gamer sites out there including www.gamegirladvance, a "weblog and online journal that brings alternative perspectives to videogame culture,"[15] and www.caligirl.com, which has a section called "LadyGamers.com," an "Action and Strategy focused gaming site with a female gamer kick!"[16] Female gamers are well represented on www.livejournal.com, with at least three communities dedicated to female players and many more that have *WoW* and/or female gamers as interests.

The female gaming community takes their gaming just as seriously as men do and one example of this is www.grrlgamer.com, which claims to be "The Only Definitive Grrlgamer Since 1997." All the standard features you would find on a "regular" [male] gaming site are here: strategy guides, editorials and reviews of PC, console and handheld games—and not just of "girl" games. These ladies seem to be more or less pleased with the current fare, although they advocate increased quality and more involvement in the industry by women. The www.womengamers.com site proudly displays the tag line "Because Women DO Play," a succinct testament to the growing population of women as active players. Reading the *WoW* thread on this site is like reading any other game-related board (although men probably don't have to worry about nursing kids or driving carpool). Players complain about Priests who tank instead of heal, the difficulty

[13] http://www.daughtersofthealliance.org/.
[14] http://doth.tithin.net/.
[15] http://www.gamegirladvance.com/about.html.
[16] http://www.caligirl.net/about.htm.

in finding good pick-up groups for the high-level missions, the joy of discovering the power of ranged attacks and an appreciation for a well-balanced game that lets a player solo almost all the way to the top levels.

Who Plays Better?

This admittedly subjective assessment depends on what we mean by "better." Women seem to know how to make the best use of limited time but that may be as much from force of habit than any special skills developed from actual playing. Their secret? Quite possibly, it's an innate ability to multitask. This should not be taken to mean that men cannot multitask, but in fact women are more likely to be better at it because they have to be.

Age may be a factor in determining level of ability. According to a number of research findings, on average female MMORPG players are older than male players. (This may be because a twenty-five-year-old single male, even if he is employed, appears to have more time to spend sitting at the computer and not worrying about house-cleaning, laundry, grocery shopping, cooking, caring for the kids or cleaning.)

Objectively, the structure of a game is a major contributing factor to how quickly one can become adept, regardless of how much free time someone has to play. On *EQ*, if you wanted to get to the highest levels, you had to "play like the boys," which is to say, you needed to understand mechanics, pathing and strategy. When it came time to deal with high-end content, you had to know your role (clerics heal, fighters tank) and follow the rules (fight now, chat later.) There were certain classes that could not solo past Level 20, due to an admitted design that required players to group. Thus the behavior "traditionally" reserved for women was forced upon male players.

WoW, on the other hand, is designed to allow players to solo all the way to Level 60. Although the need for enforced socialization has been removed, there are more female players in *WoW* than in *EQ* by a significant margin. Whether this is because the game is initially more welcoming or easier to play overall (or takes itself less seriously than *EQ*) is a matter for a debate for another time.

Who Plays Nicer?

A quick scan of gaming boards and in-game chat seems to corroborate the fact that female players are less likely to give in to the sort of name-calling, mud-slinging l33t 5p34k barrages of their male counterparts. When female players do get angry, they appear to be less motivated to cast aspersions on someone's heritage, level of intelligence or sexual preferences.

Fortunately, the *WoW* designers have made it virtually impossible to steal loot from other players' kills (and bless them for that!), something that significantly reduces the motivation for angry outbursts. (Any male player who reads this paragraph and starts screaming at it has de facto proven the point that female players are nicer.)

Does being polite in a game really have any significant effect? Can male players respond to reason? Take an example in *EQ*: A small group of players (mostly women) is in Highpass Hold, trying to kill Orcs when a male player shows up, begs for admittance into the group and when he is politely denied, tries to KS (kill steal) like crazy. After trying to reason with him for about ten minutes, one of the players summons a GM. The GM shows up, the female player explains the problem in private tells, the male player says onscreen that he was just passing by and trying to help and an onscreen argument ensues about whether the place was FFA ("free for all") or available for camping. The GM gets fed up with the discussion, tells the group to leave the poor guy alone and informs the one female player that if she makes trouble again he will boot her off the server. So much for the benefits of courtesy and negotiation. (No, this is not a hypothetical story. It's the last time I ever summoned a GM I didn't know.)

Do More Women Role-Play than Men?

This is supposed to be an MMO*RPG*, after all, so who does a better job of staying "in character"? Women seem to have the edge on men here as well. Perhaps it's because they feel less self-conscious taking on a persona, perhaps it's because they seem to have a more positive response to a strong storyline that gives them opportunity for developing their own story. There seems to be in-game evidence, at least in *EQ*, that if the story is thin, women will augment it to provide a more satisfying gaming experience. Not only do women carry on conversations, and even questing business, in character, but there are ample Web sites full of female fan-fiction about *WoW*, as well as the other MMORPGs.

Another scan of boards, blogs and surveys[17] reveals comments about how much pleasure women get out of adding a role-playing element to their online gaming. Some find it to be the perfect escape from troubles in real life such as illness, depression, loneliness and bad relationships. They may admit to the addiction but feel that their personal situation warrants this avenue of escape. Nick Yee's extensive data in the Daedalus Project seems to indicate that in terms of motivation for playing, women value socializing and relationships, *as well as* role-playing and escapism. The statistic that seems most interesting, however, is that they value the opportunity to discover new places in the game and go wherever they please, which might be considered as an opportunity to act out the desire for social freedom or a wish to be freed of daily gender-based responsibilities.

Women also seem to find that their avatars offer an opportunity to try out new types of behavior that they might be too timid to test in real life or which would not be appropriate for their real-life situations. Sometimes women choose avatars and personalities based on who they wish they could be rather than who they are. (Case in point: *EQ*'s Dark Elves—who were apparently designed by a woman.) There are numerous instances of women in MMORPGs who are married in real life but "married" to a character in-game played by a person who is not their husband, and of women who are married in-game but single in real life.

The Daedalus Project notes that customization is an important feature to female players of MMORPGs. While some men may think this is because female players want to look pretty, there is equal evidence to support the notion that it's because women don't want to look like everyone else (regardless of what fashion magazines try to

---

[17] The Daedalus Project, Nick Yee.

tell them). It's amusing (and kinda sweet) that a number of male posters on the various *WoW* boards seem concerned that women won't
play Horde characters because the avatars aren't pretty enough. Or
cute enough. Or thin enough. Silly men! Anyone who thinks that all
a female player wants to do is sit around and look dainty and helpless needs to get his head out of the Middle Ages and into the modern world. We *like* hitting things and killing things and beating up
bad guys, just like the boys do!

In regard to the question about a woman's ability to deal with violent game content, in a paper entitled "Illegitimate, Monstrous and
Out There: Female Quake Players and Inappropriate Pleasure," author Helen W. Kennedy cites a quote by Aliza Sherman:

> *"I keep reading about articles and studies where experts say girls don't
> like shooting and blasting games but instead prefer quiet, contemplative
> games with well-rounded characters and storylines that stimulate their
> imagination. I'd venture to say, however, that these studies are a reflec-
> tion of how we condition girls to be passive. The image of a woman with
> a gun is too shocking, too disruptive and threatening to the male domi-
> nant order of things."* Aliza Sherman, Cybergrrrl. (Cassell & Jenkins,
> 1999: 335)[18]

Is it perhaps true that women would actually be even more violent
in games if the cultural stereotypes did not exist practically worldwide? A scary thought indeed!

One male poster on the Allakhazam *WoW* board claims that there
will always be more boys because they like blood better and get an-
grier than women. (Obviously he's young.) Another one advised
Blizzard to tout the game as being "more social" because that's what
women like. He seems to feel that *WoW's* main attraction for women
is the "virtual world type chat" but that male players aren't as interested in "flirty chatty." (Guess he never played a Dark Elf on *EQ*!)
One female poster noted that although she had never played any
games that involved killing, she was really enjoying herself!

The counterpart to this assumption in the situation mentioned
above is that a significant number of men use female avatars. Some

---

[18] http://www.lse.ac.uk/collections/newFemininities/kennedy.pdf.

don't bother to role-play but many enjoy the challenge and perhaps just a little sly satisfaction in seeing how long they can keep a fellow male player going in a flirtation. There are many stories about broken hearts and in some cases abject horror that the object of a male player's affection was actually another male player. While there are few hard statistics on this, it would appear from personal experience and anecdotal information that more men attempt this sort of in-game deception than women.

What Should I Wear?

EQ had some truly astounding avatar art, especially the famous Dark Elf women. Male players in the world of Norrath acted fairly silly around any pretty avatar but when they saw a Tier'dal woman they got positively imbecilic. Strange as it may seem, when you're fighting for your life against a deadly mob, the last thing you want is some guy standing on the sidelines sending you tells about how sexy you are—unless that gawking leads to a fit of extreme generosity!

In *WoW*, if I want to be a good guy—oops, I mean chick...uh, member of the Alliance—I can be a Human with an adequate range of expressions from startled to angry, almost all of which are beautiful (except for a distinct bias against the elderly with the unattractive "old lady" face that looks more like Sally Field playing Forrest Gump's mama with latex wrinkles than a naturally older woman). The game blithely ignores the age-old fannish question about the existence of lady Dwarves by providing a compact, well-endowed, plus-size lass who can opt for a set of braided earmuffs that would make Princess Leia weep with envy. Instead of *EQ*'s sexy Dark Elves, there are "Night Elves" who desperately need their eyebrows plucked and their ears bobbed, but move with a lithe grace (and—how cool!—can have turquoise or purple hair). Rounding out the Alliance are the totally adorable Gnomes who look like a cross between Strawberry Shortcake and Polly Pocket. There is almost no way to keep a straight face when designing a female Gnome (and maybe that's one of the secrets to *WoW*'s success with women—the game has a sense of humor!).

On the Horde (bad guy, at least to the Alliance) side, the choices require a little more tolerance about appearance. The Undead are more than stylishly slim (OK, so a few bones show, but that's what makes the cover of the tabloids, right?). The Orc and Troll maidens have a bit more flesh but they're still pretty slender. There's a lovely array of tusk choices for the Orcish ladies, besides—and everyone, Alliance and Horde alike, can choose from a variety of piercings. (Someone on the avatar design team has a real thing about piercings....) Then there are the Tauren. The Tauren are the "real women" of *WoW*. Tall, broad-shouldered, unabashedly lush, they are proud of their womanly size and flounce (OK, pound) around the plains with bovine grace as they mow down their enemies.

Conclusion

Are women playing MMORPGs? Yes. Are they playing *WoW*? Definitely yes! Are they having fun playing *WoW*? Absolutely yes. In terms of female players, *WoW* appears to have raised a bar that its successors will need to respect (and imitate) if they want to achieve the same kind of player loyalty and appreciation.

OK, it's not really THAT late. I can log on and get at least one quick mission under my belt. Wait a second! Tomorrow is Saturday! Woot! I can stay up and pound on the Horde until the sun comes up! How cool!

Nancy Berman is a freelance writer and editor with production and writing credits on forty computer and video games and more than twenty role-playing sourcebooks including *Los Angeles by Night* (*Vampire: The Masquerade*) and Alderac Entertainment's 7th *Sea/Swashbuckling Adventures* line. She has co-authored several novellas for Microsoft's *Crimson Skies*, one of which was the prequel for the Xbox game *Crimson Skies: High Road to Revenge* released in 2004. She recently completed work on a role-playing book based on the works of noted fantasy author Katherine Kurtz. Nancy is also a contributing writer for a Web site designed to help preteen and teenage girls maintain a positive attitude about themselves. She received a B.A. in English from U.C. Santa Barbara and has completed graduate coursework in English literature, costume design and folklore and mythology at UCLA. She is also a member of the Writers Guild of America-West. Nancy and her husband John are amateur chefs and avid sports fans who currently live in Reseda, California, and actively support the Horde's ongoing struggle against Alliance oppression of the Tauren people.

ADVICE TO THE WoWLORN

JODY LYNN NYE

If you have not realized it by now, I must admit to being more than just a bit addicted to WoW. I have a Level 60 Paladin, 60 Mage, 60 Hunter, 42 Priest, 35 Rogue and the odd Shaman. What that means is hundreds of pleasant, but non-productive hours, spent playing WoW. This is time I could have been writing and earning money, but wasn't. Like most self-employed writers, or in this case self-unemployed, this is a painful observation. Such a considerable amount of time spent on any activity will have some effect on those you live with.

The author of this next essay is a science fiction and fantasy author with nearly forty published books. She is also a long time gamer and back at the dawn of RPGs she typed up the original Player's Handbook *and* Dungeon Master's Guide *from Gary Gygax's handwritten notes. Keep in mind as you read below, that Jody Lynn Nye is also my wife. I am sure she is just kidding…really…I hope…right, dear?*

When you finish reading Jody's "Advice to the WoWlorn," reread the last paragraph and smile.

OES YOUR LOVED ONE spend more hours playing *World of Warcraft* online than he spends with you? Are you more familiar with his avatar than with his actual face? Can he reel off his latest statistics including Health Points, skills and gold levels more readily than he can recite your children's names and birthdates? If so, you may be dealing with a seriously addicted online gamer.

Look for the warning signs of extreme gamophilia. Your loved one may think of himself as only "interested," or "devoted," but if he has ever done any of the following, he qualifies as an addict:

- Has skipped an important family event to stay online.
- Has, if your broadband connection goes out, shot out the door looking for the nearest Internet café, no matter what time of day it was, or what state of undress he was in.
- Has made you late for an appointment, such as a dinner date, because he wouldn't walk away from the group he was with, or hadn't finished a quest/monster slaying/treasure exchange/or was just *that* close to making the next level.
- Has missed meals, milestone events (such as your child's first steps, the death of a relative, the Mars landing) and doctor's appointments.
- Becomes depressed or near-suicidal if his character gets killed during a fight.
- Has bought levels or desirable treasure items on eBay.
- Has refused to emerge from the computer room when your relatives or friends visit.
- Has refused to emerge from the computer room when *his* relatives or friends visit.
- Has skipped or been late to a business meeting because 'the group needed me. I just couldn't leave them!'

- Has stayed up all night more than one night in a row to play.
- Has quit his job or dropped out of school to stay home and build up his character's stats.

And where are you, his significant other, during all this frenzied game playing? Why, you're keeping the household running, making excuses for why he won't come to the phone or has been having increasingly disjointed conversations thereupon, raising the children, walking, feeding and cleaning up after the pets, and making sure that he eats, bathes and goes to work as close to on-time as possible (see above). Getting him home from work is no problem, believe me, unless he also has unlimited access to a high-speed Internet connection at work.

I use the masculine pronoun here, because a preponderant majority of obsessive gamers, online gamers included, are males. If your problem gamer is female, fill in the appropriate pronoun mentally. If you are the partner of an addicted female gamer, I will also suggest some strategies for you, though you are greatly in the minority.

I'm a gamer myself. I started out in the 1970s playing miniature and Role-Playing Games. Because I devoted so much time, love and imagination to those campaigns, it is hard for me to condemn any sincere player's interest in the biggest and most comprehensive RPG out there on the Internet. I can see the attractions of *World of Warcraft*. The graphics are beautiful. It's easy to maneuver around the world. The interface is relatively intuitive. It's exciting. Endless missions are available for whenever a player wants to sign on and undertake one. The monsters and assorted races are terrifically well-realized. You really have to *earn* your levels. Unlike early video games, modern ones not only never run out of quarters, but they are complex, sophisticated entertainments, suitable for occupying one's mind and hands for hours, days, months, even years. It's fun.

Still, games are played by people, and online computer gamers do not, by and large, exist in a vacuum. They were not born, fully fledged, in front of the keyboard. Before *WoW*, they had lives, in which they held down jobs, sought degrees and promotions, raised children, sold Amway products and pursued relationships with persons such as yourself. Now some have chosen to neglect those earlier responsibilities in favor of the distraction of a computer game.

But we're talking about you. *WoW* has managed to take away the person you love, and transform him into a back and a pair of furtively typing hands, and a bowed head that occasionally barks out an obscenity or chats through a headset mike with people whom you cannot see. If you are frustrated, small wonder. You are not alone. There are thousands, if not millions, like you worldwide.

One difference between computer games and other timesinks like league volleyball, softball, hunting, golf and what have you, is that one must go out to a field or a course or another off-site (meaning, not in your home) facility in order to play them. These sports can only be enjoyed at certain times of day, in certain seasons. Not so with online gaming. The field is always available, always open and, thanks to the global character of the Internet, always populated with fellow players. If none of your friends are online when you log on, it's not a problem. Almost always, there will be a questing group you can join, especially if you have a useful and desirable specialty such as healing, or you can take on a solo quest.

Here are some questions you are undoubtedly asking yourself:

What Does He See in That Game That He Doesn't See in Me?

Frankly, my dear reader, you don't offer the same challenges or the same range of visuals that a good online computer game does. How can a mere human being, however attractive or sexy or charming, compete with flying a pegasus, hopping a volcano, slaying a dragon or killing a whole bunch of trolls? Men shop with their eyes, as countless generations of women can attest. Women have had to work from this piece of knowledge for centuries, creating cosmetics and increasingly extreme modes of dress to attract that ever-roving eye, but admit it, ladies, we've been outdone.

Does He Realize How Much Time We're Spending Apart?

Actually, he does—intellectually. The game features real time, day and night. He will be aware of the movement of the sun, but these cues will not have an impact upon him, because they are on the computer screen, not shining in through the window. He will take the passage of time as another feature of the game, without observing its real-life counterpart. He'll see sunset, moonrise and, several hours later, sunrise again. However, he probably won't be aware of how many *days* he's lost.

Is There Anything I Can Do to Attract His Attention Away from the Game?

Very possibly. Your advantage is that game manufacturers have not yet inserted a tactile or olfactory component. Pheromones are your friend. His eyeballs may be glued to the screen, but most of his body is unoccupied. Using that intimate knowledge that you have amassed about him, plan your incursion. You can possibly drag your beloved away from the game, but only if you choose your moment opportunely. That moment should not be while he is engaged in combat. That interruption can and will have long-lasting repercussions. He will have suffered significant embarrassment at the hands of those other players in his party who will see his character break into meaningless, sporadic movement or, more disastrously, stand stock still as a monster wades right over his avatar, making it spew damage points into the air. The best time to intrude upon his game time is after he has cashed in the components of a successful quest, but not one that boosts his character to a new level. If he has achieved a level, he will want to take the character out again at once, as one would with a brand new sportscar or a terrific electronic gizmo, and see what fresh kinds of evil monster butt he can now kick. Any attempt you make at that stage to pull him away will almost certainly fail. He will either feel resentment, or be unable to think of anything but getting back online again. You want his attention focused upon you in a positive way. If you are determined and your timing is good, you should get it.

Here are a few suggestions for getting your gamer's attention:

Clearing the throat

This is the mildest of nudges to try and break through to your loved one. If he replies, even with a hostile bark of "What?" it proves that he is not too far gone to haul back. Be prepared to make your case at that moment, for, with the rapid-moving character of the game, his mind will snap back to the screen if you do not engage it immediately.

A touch on the shoulder

This is more serious, and may be shrugged off, or provoke a backward slap or punch.

A neck rub

Pleasurable touch can draw your loved one's attention away from gameplay in a positive manner. If you catch him at a suitable juncture, it should get good results. If you wish to engage in even more intimate contact, go for it, but realize that your gamer might be capable of multitasking on the spot.

Sarcasm

Make fun of his gameplay. Any time he makes a mistake or gets his character killed, yuk it up. The more of a spoiler you can be, the more likely he is to log out and storm out of the room. Make sure you are standing safely out of range.

Food

The smell of fresh-baked cookies or a favorite recipe, brought into the room and held just out of reach of your gamer, might do the trick. Especially good if he has run out of handy snacks.

Promise an irresistible outing

Has a movie just opened that your gamer wants to see? Is the Chili Cook-Off about to open in your town? How about the Lord of the Rings exhibition? Waving tickets under your loved one's nose ought to get him to sign off with alacrity.

Role-playing

Ask your player spouse if he wants to play "the Maiden and the Tauren" or, if he plays an alliance character, offer to play "the Night Elf and the naive Gnome princess."

Stripping off

Remove your clothing and edge into your gamer's field of view. If this does not cause his eyebrows to rise and a pleasurable grin to form on his face, it should at least evoke a promise that he will be offline within a time limit. (Warning: this method does not work on female gamers. Nor is it for the use of parents trying to get the attention of their offspring, unless they want to foot the bill for endless therapy sessions until the end of time.)

Producing catalogs or circulars from a favorite store

These should be moved temptingly into the field of view, just out of reach. (Warning: this method, while it works well with female gamers and some male gamers, will have no effect on the majority of the latter.)

A bucket of water

The fear response upon beholding such a threat is usually enough to get even hard-core gamers to start scrambling for the "Quit Game" button. There will be hardliners who will try to call your bluff. Some will employ logic, such as "it's your computer, too," or, "you were on all day yesterday, so it's my turn." These deserve it if you actually do pour it over them and their CPU.

You must be prepared for the possibility that you won't be able to haul your gamer back to real life in a way you consider meaningful. If the problem is unresolvable through any means, consider other solutions. Like widowhood in life, you as the significant other of a *WoW* player need to decide how to handle your game-induced separation. After a suitable period of contemplation, you will want to think about how you will go on to the next stage in your life.

This is not meant at all to denigrate the sorrowful experience of actual widowhood. Rather, I believe that partners deprived of their loved ones because of all-encompassing hobbies can use some of the truly bereaveds' means of coping.

Get Involved

Get your own account and learn how to play *WoW*. It's fun. It isn't that expensive of a hobby, beyond the investment in a computer with the necessary speed and graphics card and an ISP connection. Many couples have more than one computer set up at home, to permit both partners to be online at the same time or to let parents get a crack at the Internet in spite of computer-literate children at home. WoW is engaging. Hasn't it captured your loved one's attention for lo, these many months? There are many benefits. You'll meet people from all around the world. Even if you weren't a gamer to begin with, you might come to enjoy the game for its own sake. That way, when your loved one is not online, for whatever reason, you can discuss matters of interest to him from a position of knowledge. Don't laugh. Many partners have taken up their loved ones' favorite sports or hobbies for the same reason.

You can jump in and join your beloved on those quests. With simul-talk feature you can carry on a real-time conversation with him, or message one another. Talk does not have to be about the game at hand. I know many people who exchange information about their real lives while killing Dunemaul Ogres. There are even two fellows I know who talk business while their avatars are out on missions, not always in the same questing group. While you are both logged on, you do not have to be near one another to communicate, which is an advantage if you find you have completely different adventuring skills.

If you don't want to play WoW yourself, read the cheat books. Even if you are not online together, you can offer the solution to knotty problems as he encounters them. He won't resent your sitting at his elbow watching him play if you are helpful. This ploy is especially good for reminding female gamers that you exist. If you seem to share her interests, she will be more inclined to consider yours. (Warning: this technique is not always effective. To some gamers, having anyone too close to the mouse hand is comparable in distraction to having a schmoozer too close to either one of a pinball player's elbows. It throws one right off one's stroke.)

If you can evince even a mild interest in the game, you ought to find that it will provide a bond between you and your loved one.

Get Even

Perhaps you feel that you have put up with too much to be a cooperative partner to your addicted gamer. Very well, then. Take the offensive tack. Join *WoW*. Spend a lot of time building up your character. According to a recent *New York Times* article, it takes roughly twenty-five days or 600 hours of solid playing time to raise a new character from Level 1 to Level 60. Join your beloved's group on quests. Be better at slugging the monsters than he is, and be faster at grabbing artifacts. Leave him panting in the dust. He could very well lose interest in playing if all your gaming companions can talk about is how awesome his significant other is.

Pull the Plug

Online gamers are incredibly vulnerable. The servers slow down at inopportune moments. Your ISP cuts off service for maintenance. The power goes off. All of these crises can leave your gamer sitting before a blank screen, wailing to the gods that life is unfair. You've learned, by now, what moments of the game he considers most crucial (no, not *all* of them are crucial, no matter what he says). Join the pantheon of random events. When his life meter is dangerously low, "accidentally" disconnect the modem cable. By the time he resets and reboots the computer, his character will be dead. You can take some satisfaction in the amount of swearing now coming from his lair as you go about your business. After all, it was an accident. Just like any other power failure. The best thing about a 'gotcha' like that is the victim never can anticipate when the next one is coming, so you have destroyed his concentration, for good.

Provide Unavoidable Distractions

Absent yourself from the house, leaving him in sole charge of the children, the pets, elderly parents, delicate houseplants, what have you. Remember, it is not considered babysitting if they are his children, too. It's shared parenting. If he must "BRB" himself enough times on the current quest to prevent your two-year-old from tearing down the living-room curtains, the group is eventually going to go on without him, no matter how vital his skills might seem.

Make Him Fend for Himself

If you, as the significant other of an addict, choose not to maintain his household and lifestyle for him, he will eventually have to do it himself, but only enough to prevent homelessness, starvation and fatal buildup of sleep toxins.

Get a Life

If you are not interested in playing the game with him, and you're not mean-spirited enough to destroy his love of the game, accept the inevitable. He is involved with the game and wants to keep on playing indefinitely. Forgive him, and think of yourself. It would serve you best to find interests of your own. Feel free to start looking around for something that you would enjoy doing while he is playing *World of Warcraft*. Having invested so much in his own hobby, he would be selfish to deprive you of the chance to enjoy a hobby of your own. Or two. Or three. Have you ever wanted to take up a musical instrument? Join a folk-dancing group? Does travel interest you? Gourmet cooking? Have you ever wanted to start a blog? Join a chatroom? Wouldn't you like to spend more time with your relatives? Your friends? You now have blanket permission to occupy your free time in whatever way you choose. Once you have freed yourself from resentment toward your online addict, you can spread your intellectual and emotional wings, and become a more well-rounded, better-educated, happier individual.

And one day, your loved one will decide that he's had enough of *World of Warcraft* for a while. He will crawl, blinking, back out into the light of day, looking for affirmation that you are still there, and that you still love him.

With any luck, you will be on a week-long spa vacation in Hawaii.

Jody Lynn Nye lists her main career activity as "spoiling cats." She lives northwest of Chicago with two of the above and her husband, author and packager, Bill Fawcett. She has published more than thirty books, including six contemporary fantasies, four SF novels, four novels in collaboration with Anne McCaffrey, including *The Ship Who Won*; edited a humorous anthology about mothers, *Don't Forget Your Spacesuit, Dear!*; and written more than ninety short stories. Her latest books are *Strong Arm Tactics*, first in the Wolfe Pack series (Meisha Merlin Publishing), and *Class Dis-Mythed*, co-written with Robert Asprin.

Part Two

World of Warcraft
Classes

Chris McCubbin

There were Shamans before there was writing. Our first cultures are defined as Hunter/Gatherer. The concept of the Paladin dates back to Gilgamesh and has a lot of Roland in him. If you haven't read The Song of Roland, *get a good translation. It was the action novel of its day. The character classes in* World of Warcraft *are based upon traditions and heroes that often go back to before the tales were written down.*

This section takes a look at all of the different character classes that appear in WoW that were there when the game started. Two new classes, the Blood Elves and another non-human Alliance race, are planned for the first major upgrade. Along with the expected information and a few playing hints on each class, we have included an in-depth look at the background and history of each class. Each of the groups, whether as obviously of ancient lineage as a Mage or Shaman or less directly such as the Priest, has its literary and historical counterparts. In a virtual way, those of us playing WoW continue the tradition of creating heroic tales that had their beginnings in the tales of Achilles and Odysseus. Discovering these will give any player a more three-dimensional view of their character's calling and maybe even inspire a few new techniques.

PALADIN

RACES: Dwarf, Human

PREFERRED WEAPONS: One-handed and two-handed maces; later swords, axes, polearms

ARMOR ALLOWED: Cloth, leather, mail, shield, plate

POWER LINES: Combat abilities (pretty much self-explanatory), Holy Magic (heals and anti-Undead spells), Protection (buffs)

SOLO POTENTIAL: Excellent

The Paladin in WoW

Holy warrior, paragon of virtue, the Paladin's role in both *World of Warcraft*™ and the original *Warcraft* series is to be an elite commander—from the heroic generals of the original games to the perfect party leaders of *WoW*.

Undead are anathema for Paladins who can Track Undead and Exorcise Undead, a handy and powerful ranged attack.

Several class quests come up during the Paladin's career that garner various rewards. For example, at Level 20, the Paladin is given a quest to find the materials for Verigan's Fist, a very nice two-handed mace that will be useful to the Paladin for many levels.

Paladins can summon a warhorse at Level 40—no quest, no coin, no training—just, "Here's your horse!" At Level 60, Paladins can quest for their Epic Mount.

Paladins may get a free horse, but their training is expensive! The Church of Light wants to make sure that Paladins take a vow of poverty until they reach Level 45 or so. Wise Paladins make judicious use of the Auction House to supplement their income.

Ranged attacks (except some useful anti-Undead spells) and ranged weapons are *not* the way of the Paladin.

Paladins can heal and rez. If you can't find a tank or a healer for your group, a Paladin might be able to fill either or both roles. A Paladin can't tank as well as a Warrior (he comes close if he is completely specialized in Retribution talents) or heal nearly as well as a Priest (although he can do a lot if totally specialized in Holy talents), but a Paladin's abilities will do in a pinch.

Paladins are equally excellent in solo or group situations. Solo, they can take on most foes of similar level one-on-one, and then heal themselves to move on quickly with no loss of resources. This makes for fast, efficient soloing. In a group, the combination of tanking and backup healing is a basic and potent combination.

The First Paladins

The idea of the holy warrior, blessed with power by the gods themselves, is found throughout human myth. The heroic avatars of Hindu mythology are particularly vivid examples. But most of our modern concept of the Paladin can be traced directly back to medieval stories of knightly adventure. In fact, that's where we get the word itself.

The word "paladin" comes from medieval French literature. The original twelve Paladins of legend were the twelve chief champions of the Emperor Charlemagne. The word "paladin" itself comes from the Latin word "palatinus," meaning "attached to the palace," and indicating that the Paladins were under the direct authority of the emperor himself.

Charlemagne was, of course, a completely historical figure—one of the central figures of European history, in fact. And at least one or two of the twelve Paladins seem to be based on his actual historical generals. For all practical purposes, however, the Paladins of literature are fictional creations, their powers superhuman and their adventures set in a misty golden age of legend.

The traditional list of the twelve (medieval writers liked the number twelve, with its heavy associations with Biblical images, particularly Christ and his twelve apostles) makes instant sense to a fan of modern fantasy literature and fantasy games. Of course, the number is heavily weighted with noble knights, but they also included Ogier, a Danish barbarian champion, a couple of Saracens (Moslems) who converted to the Christian side and even Maugris, a powerful enchanter (!). There's also Ganelon, who in grand medieval fashion ends up betraying the emperor and his fellow Paladins. This mix of skills and backgrounds certainly foreshadows the modern role-playing guild or party.

Add into the mix a couple of other supporting characters—who, while not technically numbered among the twelve Paladins, occupied an important place in Charlemagne's legendary court—and the resemblance to modern fantasy adventurers becomes even more pronounced. These include Archbishop Turpin, a high-ranking cleric who wore armor and fought among the knights, and Bradamante (or Britomart), one of the very few female knights to appear in medieval romance.

Roland

There is definitely one star to the tales of Charlemagne's Paladins, and it's not the Emperor himself. Charlemagne's nephew, Roland, is by far the noblest and most heroic character in these tales. He has a magic horn, the Oliphant, and a holy sword, called Durandel. (Charlemagne also has a blessed sword, named Jouise, said to have been forged with a piece of the lance that pierced Christ's side at the crucifixion.)

The Song of Roland

The earliest and most important of the stories of Roland is *The Song of Roland* (*La Chanson de Roland*), the oldest surviving French poem. The poem was written about 1100 A.D. by an unknown poet, probably with the intention of drumming up support among the nobility for the first Crusade that was forming at that time.

The poem tells the story of Roland's final battle, at the Roncesvalles pass in the Pyrenees Mountains, during Charlemagne's campaign to conquer Spain.

There was a historical battle of Roncesvalles. It was a minor but embarrassing defeat for Charlemagne's forces, when a group of Basque insurgents managed to isolate and destroy the rear guard of the emperor's army (so they could loot the baggage train). It is historical fact that one Roland, Lord of the Breton Marches, was killed in the battle.

Historically, the defeat at Roncesvalles was never avenged, and Charlemagne never completely conquered Spain, instead settling for control of a strip of strategically vital cities called the Spanish March.

The battle described in *The Song of Roland* is very different. In the poem, the enemy is not a small force of ragged, greedy hillmen but rather a huge massed army of Saracen invaders, and the battle becomes a major turning point in the struggle between Christians and Moslems for Europe. In the end, the emperor gets major payback and goes on to undisputed control of all of Spain. (Charlemagne, who actually lived into his early seventies and who was about thirty-five when Roncesvalles occurred, is for some reason in the poem said to be more than 200 years old at the time of the battle.) In many ways, the campaign in the poem sounds like a series of scenarios for the original *Warcraft*™ games.

The poem describes how Roland angers his treacherous father-in-law Ganelon, who begins to plot Roland's fall. Ganelon arranges for Roland to take command of the rear echelon of Charlemagne's force as it moves through the mountains, and then tips off the Saracens where and when to hit this force.

When the Saracens attack, Roland could easily sound his Oliphant horn and call back the main body of the Emperor's force, but instead he decides it would be more chivalrous to stand with the forces he has against the vastly more numerous Saracen force. (Presumably this made some kind of sense if you were a twelfth-century nobleman.) Battle is joined, and both sides endure massive casualties, with bits of Frankish and Saracen heroes, commanders and champions raining down everywhere. Despite the odds, the battle seems to be tilting slightly in Roland's favor... until a huge force of reinforcements from Saracen Africa comes down the pass to join the battle.

Roland, in his own special way, still refuses to call Charlemagne's armies back to help. It's only when defeat to the very last man becomes completely inevitable that Bishop Turpin is able to finally convince Roland to summon the Emperor. Charlemagne arrives too late to save anyone, but in plenty of time to kill all the Saracens. God helps the Emperor out, by stopping the sun in its path until the battle is over.

When Charlemagne returns to court, Roland's wife falls over dead with grief when he tells her of her husband's death. The traitorous Ganelon is brought to trial. He almost gets off, thanks to a slick lawyer—a knight named Pinabel. However, Thierry, one of the Paladins, but known as more of a thinker than a fighter, steps up to challenge Pinabel to a duel to decide Ganelon's fate. (Pause for a moment to consider how much better the ratings for modern celebrity trials would be if they were decided by having the defense attorney and the prosecutor fight to the death.) Although Pinabel is by far the larger and stronger of the two, God is on Thierry's side and prevents him from being killed (presenting an interesting parallel to the divine healing powers of fantasy Paladins). Pinabel falls, Ganelon is convicted, drawn and quartered, and thirty of his relatives are hung.

Orlando Furioso

The other notable work about Roland and the Paladins is Ariosto's epic poem *Orlando Furioso* (loosely translated, "Roland Insane"), completed in 1516 A.D., and regarded as the greatest literary work of the Italian Renaissance. If the *Song of Roland* resembles a *Warcraft* scenario, this incredibly complex work is closer to a busy day among the upper-level *WoW* characters.

The plot is so dense and complicated that it literally defies summary, but the overall experience is very close to that found in a freewheeling, high-level fantasy role-playing game. Groups of knights join up to go on quests together, then break up and re-form to go on more quests. Evil sorcerers riding hippogriffs (an interesting parallel to *World of Warcraft's* gryphon air force) attack heroes and are repulsed. Beautiful enchantress-queens keep tabs on their favorite champions, while evil witches try to seduce them into becoming their boy-toys. Heroes and villains get burned, beaten and beheaded by the score. Orlando (Roland, in Italian) goes crazy for love of the princess Angelica (daughter of the king of India, or China, or something...even though she's described as a hot blonde) and his cousin Astolpho goes up to the moon on a flying horse to get Orlando's lost wits back. Throughout it all, a big army of pagans is laying siege to Paris. And Angelica keeps getting captured, and rescued, and captured, and rescued and captured....

While *Orlando Furioso* has all the excitement of an RPG, it also has some of the drawbacks. There's so much going on that it can get tricky just keeping track of who's doing what and why. More importantly, many of the characters are one-dimensional, and it's hard to really care what happens to them.

The most likeable character of the poem is probably the valiant female knight Bradamante, who lets nothing in this world, or the next, get between her and her marriage to her true love, Rogero (...but you've got to wonder if he's really worth the trouble). As for Orlando himself, he's the same unpredictable mess that he was in the *Song of Roland*, causing as many problems with his stubborn courage and chivalric impulses as he solves with his superhuman skills.

Galahad and the Grail

My good blade carves the casques of men,
My tough lance thrusteth sure,
My strength is as the strength of ten,
Because my heart is pure.
—ARTHUR, LORD TENNYSON, "Sir Galahad"

The tales of Roland gave us the name Paladin, and they certainly foreshadow the heroic spirit of modern fantasy literature and gaming, but the actual image of a Paladin as we know it today can be traced directly back to Sir Galahad, of King Arthur's Round Table.

There probably was a historical English overlord in the fifth century who would eventually become known to legend as King Arthur, but he is a shadowy and mysterious figure. Even more so than with Charlemagne's court, the medieval poets did whatever they wanted with the stories of Arthur's knights.

Most of the early medieval poets were French, so they invented the French knight Sir Lancelot, the embodiment of the chivalric ideal. Because Europe was engaged in the Crusades at the time, the French invented the quest for the Holy Grail (the cup Christ drank from at the last supper), a literal mission from God to motivate Arthur's knights. The Knights of the Round Table (another French invention) pursued the Grail quest with the same enthusiasm that Crusaders were supposed to feel for the conquest of the Holy Land.

The French dominated the medieval literary scene with their new genre of "romance" (which originally meant a tale of heroic adventure and dangerous love), but Arthur was a British hero, and his tales never lost their popularity in England. In the late Middle Ages it fell to an English knight named Sir Thomas Mallory to bring Arthur home by writing one of the great classics of heroic literature, *Le Morte D'Arthur* ("The Death of Arthur"), which, despite the stylish French title, broke dramatically with the fashion of the time by being written in English.

As can be seen from the stories of Roland, being a paragon of chivalry does not mean that one is perfect in every way. On the contrary, most of the great knights of romance are deeply, even fatally flawed individuals. With Roland, that flaw was a dangerously exaggerated sense of honor and capricious recklessness. For the great Knights of the Round Table (Lancelot, Tristram, even Arthur himself) their great flaw tended to be an inability to keep their hands off other people's wives. In the end, of course, it would be Lancelot's long-running affair with Queen Guinevere that would lead to the final destruction of the Round Table.

Mallory didn't take it upon himself to clean up the flaws in these classic characters, but he seems to have wanted to put at least one knight in Arthur's service who fully embodied all the positive traits of a perfect knight. He selected Sir Galahad to be the finder of the Holy Grail (the French had written Grail stories before Mallory, but they tended to star Sir Percival).

The illegitimate son of Sir Lancelot and the doomed Lady Elaine, Galahad is raised in a nunnery and trained in the knightly arts by a holy hermit. When he finally comes to Camelot, he accidentally seats himself in the Siege Perilous, the magical chair in which only the greatest knight in the world can safely sit. Omens just don't come any clearer than that, and Arthur immediately admits Galahad to the fellowship of the Round Table. Galahad soon proves himself unbeatable in combat.

With Galahad safely seated, God wastes no further time descending on Camelot and kicking off the quest for the Holy Grail. The whole Round Table scatters in search of this most holy relic, even though everybody knows that it's Galahad who's going to end up with the cup in the end.

Accompanied by his only-slightly-less-holy pals Percival and Bors, Galahad goes off on his destined quest. It's here that we get the perfect model for the modern fantasy Paladin. The saintly Galahad performs healings and miracles at every turn. Mystical portents fly fast and furious. The Archangel Gabriel gives up his sword for Galahad to use on the quest.

In the end, Galahad finds the Grail under suitably mystical circumstances and takes it to the holy city of Jerusalem, where he becomes king for a few years. Before long, however, having accomplished everything he was destined to do in his life, he asks his good friend God to please take him up to heaven, which God obligingly does.

Galahad is so very perfect—perfectly brave, perfectly skilled, perfectly beautiful and perfectly moral—that he's actually not that interesting of a character. Most of the interesting parts of his story come from the marvelous scenery in which they take place, or from the supporting characters like Lancelot and Percival. However, the concept of total heroic invincibility still lingers in fantastic literature.

Modern Fantasy Paladins

There's very little evolution in the concept of the Paladin between the sixteenth century and the late twentieth century. Many people continued to write about Galahad, Roland and their legendary like, of course (the Victorian poet Lord Tennyson was particularly interested in the idea of Galahad as the perfect champion of holiness), but nothing new happened conceptually. The fantasy heroes of the first half of the twentieth century tended to be a more rowdy, swashbuckling lot (Robert E. Howard's Conan the Barbarian, Fritz Lieber's Fafhrd and the Gray Mouser).

Some of our concepts of the Paladin can be traced to J. R. R. Tolkein's character of Aragorn, from the *Lord of the Rings* (a complex character, and one of the great heroes of modern fantasy, Aragorn also established the model for the heroic fantasy ranger, embodied in *WoW* as the Hunter character class). Descended from an ancient line of kings blessed by the gods themselves, Aragorn has mysterious reserves of spiritual power that he can call upon in conflict against evil, he carries a magic sword of great antiquity and he has the power to perform divine healing of supernatural wounds.

The final embodiment of the Paladin concept as it appears in fantasy gaming, including the *Warcraft* games, came to be in the first fantasy role-playing game, *Dungeons & Dragons*®, created by Gary Gygax and Dave Arneson. Here at last we get the full picture of the Paladin as a champion pledged to the powers of light, imbued with divine power to heal wounds and disrupt the forces of evil.

The Paladin of the dice-and-paper game *D&D* occupied the exact same tactical slot that the *Warhammer*® Paladin does today, providing an effective fusion of offensive punch, defensive strength, combat support (buffing and healing) and leadership skills.

Putting the Hammer Down

One of the most distinguishing features of *Warhammer*® Paladins— their affinity for large, blunt weapons—seems to be almost an accident. When the Paladin hero was introduced to the *Warcraft* games he was drawn with a huge mallet as his weapon—a visually impressive image that helped distinguish the character as an extraordinary figure. When the Paladin came over to *WoW*, an affinity for large hammers and maces came along with it.

From the perspective of historical tradition, a hammer is definitely an odd choice for a noble commander like the Paladin. In medieval times the mace was strictly regarded as a peasant's weapon, just one step above a club. As for hammers, they're descended from actual farm tools that threatened serfs might pick up to defend themselves against bandits or invaders. A particularly brawny medieval knight might pick up a light-horse mace or chain flail to use in battle, but only to clear away the serfs. Against other knights they'd certainly stick to lance and sword.

On the other hand, the thought of a really huge mallet impacting with your face in combat is an especially terrifying image. With sufficient power behind it, a large mace or hammer can stave in even the best armor, turning the enemy's protective edge against him. The drawback to really huge maces and hammers, of course, is that they're ridiculously slow and awkward, but what if—just imagine it—there was a warrior so huge and powerful that he could sling a giant hammer around like a sword? Somebody who could do that would be a major asset in battle, no matter what weapon he used. That's why hammers and maces tend to pop up in folklore as the weapons of the most powerful gods and heroes: Hercules carried a giant club; Thor, of course, wielded nothing but his hammer. The terror of a superhumanly powered mace attack is visually captured in the first scene of Peter Jackson's film *The Fellowship of the Ring*, when Sauron attacks the lines of the allies with his colossal spiked mace. So on the level of legendary fantasy, the big hammer makes an excellent choice for an elite champion like the Paladin.

Playing Paladins

Auras are among the Paladin's key abilities. These are group spells that add to the element or shadow resistances, decrease the chance of spell interruption, grant a very nice armor boost (very popular) and so forth. Once party members realize their armor has gone up just by staying within thirty yards of the Paladin and his Devotion Aura, they tend to stay together.

Judgment is a good thing for Paladins…and not just the mental kind. A large variety of Seals are available to the Paladin. These are spells that add Holy damage, heal the Paladin, stun your foe and so forth. There is also a Judgment spell result (the second paragraph in a Seal's description is the Judgment effect) which works against your enemies. Once a Paladin has cast a Seal upon himself, he can cast Judgment against a foe.

Proper use of Seals is the crux of successful combat. For example, Seal of Justice cast upon the Paladin increases the chance of a blow that stuns the opponent. If said opponent is known to be cowardly (runs away before the end of the battle), the Paladin can cast Judgment upon the foe, which, in the case of Seal of Justice, will prevent the foe from running away until the battle is over. Learn the Judgment result of all Seals.

Blessings are brief buffs that can be cast on the Paladin and on group members. Only one Blessing can be active at a time; some are good for Warriors, some are good for spell casters. Sometimes the

Paladin may want to change the Blessings on a fellow group member during combat.

Proper use of Blessings can spell the success or failure of your party. For example, Blessing of Might is good for tanks, while Blessing of Wisdom (increased Mana generation) or Blessing of Salvation (decreased threat) works well for spell casters. Other Blessings can help save or protect a party member. Take a moment to realize who is in your party and "bless" them accordingly. And, don't forget, they only last a short time...often only one battle.

Talents are what make each Paladin unique: Holy talents, Retribution talents and Protection talents. As a Paladin, there is the option of developing an extreme "template" or "specialization" and spending all talent points in only one area, or spreading out the points among all three areas. Holy talents may help the young Paladin stay alive, but once he/she hits the mid-teen levels, he/she needs to decide if they want to continue splitting those talent points in the future, or go all out in only one talent tree.

There are a lot of things going on during a battle. Arrange pertinent "in the heat of combat" spells on numbered hot key bars. If you have multiple characters, put similar spells (like Holy Light for a Paladin/Heal for a Priest) on the same number.

Collect equitable items that add to the Paladin's primary attributes. The Auction House is for buying as well as selling.

Talents aren't permanent. Try out a set of talents. If you don't like the way things are progressing, go to your Paladin Trainer and start over. Of course, this isn't free. It'll cost you in progressively larger amounts, but it's usually worth it in increased enjoyment and usefulness.

PRIEST

RACES: Dwarf, Human, Night Elf, Troll, Undead
PREFERRED WEAPONS: One-handed maces, wands; later daggers, staves
ARMOR ALLOWED: Cloth
POWER LINES: Discipline (defensive buffs), Holy (healing, some offense), Shadow (crowd control)
SOLO POTENTIAL: Fair

The Priest in WoW

The Priest is, hands down, the most effective healing class in the game. Their healing abilities far eclipse those of Druids, Shamans and Paladins. Humans, Dwarves, Night Elves, Undead and Trolls can be Priests. Between Priests and Shamans, the only race totally without some kind of healing class is the Gnomes.

As with all classes, much of your long-term effectiveness as a Priest will be determined by where you choose to focus your talents. Discipline talents increase the overall effectiveness of the Priest as a casting class, and are generally useful for all styles of play. Priests who choose to focus on their role as healers should concentrate on Holy talents, which increase the effectiveness and lower the Mana cost of healing spells. The Shadow talents are good for those Priests who enjoy soloing or prefer a more offensive role. Shadow talents culminate with the ability, Shadowform, which allows Priests to change their physical form and become as insubstantial as a shadow, increasing their Shadow damage and decreasing physical damage taken.

Priests can solo reasonably well. While they don't deal a lot of damage compared to other classes, they can last through the longer fights with judicious use of their array of healing spells and Power Word: Shield. Their crowd-control abilities also come in handy in solo play.

Priests are obviously a popular choice with most groups due to their ability to heal and resurrect other characters, as well as their main buff spell, Power Word: Fortitude, which increases allies' Stamina. They can also cure diseases, an extremely useful ability.

Unlike Druids and Shamans, Priests do not have a cool-down timer, nor do they use a reagent for their resurrection spell. They can continuously resurrect fallen characters as long as they have the Mana to do so.

Priests can help control a sticky combat situation through the use of Mind Control, taking one humanoid out of the fight temporarily by controlling its mind and reducing its attack speed. When controlling an NPC, you gain control of all that humanoid's abilities and spells. If you use this spell against another player character, you are only able to melee.

Priests can learn two unique spells based on their race at Level 10 and Level 20. For Dwarves, these are Desperate Prayer (10) and Fear Ward (20). For Humans, these are Desperate Prayer (10) and Feedback (20). For Night Elves, these are Starshards (10) and Elune's Grace (20). For Trolls, these are Hex of Weakness (10) and Shadowguard (20). For Undead, these are Touch of Weakness (10) and Devouring Plague (20). To learn your racial spells, speak to the Priest trainer in a major city.

Militant Priests and Fighting Monks

The gaming concept of the Priest, or "cleric," character class is a bit of an oddity. The primary character classes (Wizard, Fighter and Thief, represented in *WoW* as the Mage, Warrior and Rogue, respectively) are deeply held as ancient human-cultural archetypes. Other, more exotic classes are usually firmly rooted in either literature (e.g., Paladins) or real-world culture or history (Druids, Shamans).

Priests are a bit different. Not the idea of priesthood itself, of course—there have been priests for as long as humanity has had organized religion (longer, if you count shamanism—see **Shaman**, p. 214). But usually there's a pretty clear divide between priestly and warrior castes. In general, priests teach and exhort…they don't wear armor and bash heads. The idea of the fantasy gaming "cleric," with his healing spells and (non-edged) weapon proficiency, is basically an artificial gaming construct, based on medieval war games, and designed to fill a strategic hole in the system (the need for a mechanism to reverse damage and to control enemies).

If you dig hard enough, you can certainly find a historical tradition of warrior clerics, as well as a rich tradition of wandering healers and mystics.

Perhaps the most famous fighting priest in western literature is Friar Tuck, from the legends of Robin Hood. The portly, hard-drinking friar saw to the spiritual needs of Robin's Merry Men. He didn't wear armor or cast spells, but he could hold his own against anyone in the forest with a quarterstaff (a blunt weapon, of course), and he did tend the sick.

On the opposite end of the social spectrum from Tuck is Archbishop Turpin, from the medieval French epic the *Song of Roland*. The Archbishop was the senior cleric in Charlemagne's court, and he wore armor, wielded a sword and rode into battle with the knights. (For more on Turpin and the *Song of Roland*, see **Paladins**, p. 193.)

Below are a few more examples of holy warriors from history and legend.

Hospitallers and Templars

Although it can be argued that the Crusades of the Middle Ages were really about trade routes and political dominance (just like every other war), it can't be denied that religions—specifically European Christianity versus Islam—were the glue that held the huge and diverse coalitions on both sides of the conflict together.

On the European side, the Pope ordered the Crusades with the official goal of "defending" (actually, conquering) the Holy Land of Palestine (which, in addition to being really, really sacred to three major religions, also just happened to sit right at the hub of the trade routes connecting Europe, Asia and Africa). Under these conditions, the concept of warrior monks and priests was pretty inevitable.

During the twelfth and thirteenth centuries, the Vatican recognized more than a dozen official military orders, including the Teutonic Order, the Livonian Brothers of the Sword and the Knights of

St. Thomas. Far and away the most famous of these orders were the Knights Hospitaller and the Knights Templar.

These orders were basically armies, supported by the Vatican and directly under the command of the Pope and his representatives. Although they might be associated with a specific country or region, they did not owe any allegiance to any secular king or lord. While members of an order could be fully ordained priests, most were just lay brothers. Often, in fact, most of the order's fighters were blatant mercenaries, who gave only lip service to the religious obligations of their office. Still, many examples of true faith and devotion to the Church could be found in both the rank-and-file and the command hierarchies of many of these orders.

The Hospitallers

The histories of the Hospitallers and the Templars are intertwined, and go back to about the year 600 A.D., when the Pope ordered a hostel for Christian pilgrims to be built in the city of Jerusalem. The Hospital of St. John was enlarged in 800 by Charlemagne. About 1005 it was closed by the fanatical Moslem Caliph Al Hakim, but it was rebuilt in the 1020s.

Originally maintained by the Benedictine brothers, after the first Crusade, a new brotherhood, officially dedicated to the hospital, was founded by the Blessed Gerard in 1113 A.D. Gerard took his new order in a radical new direction, conquering territory in Palestine and levying tribute from his new subjects for the support of the hospital. The militarization of the order continued when they expanded from merely defending the hospital where pilgrims were tended, to offering armed escorts to protect pilgrims during their journey through the Holy Land.

The Knights Hospitaller wore black garments emblazoned with a white cross. At the height of their power in the Holy Land, they controlled seven major forts (the most powerful of which were Krak-des Chevaliers and Margat, both near Tripoli) and 140 estates. Their lands were divided into priories, which were subdivided into balliwicks, which in turn were divided into commanderies.

This phase of the order's history, with its dual function of defending the faithful and healing the sick, is probably as close to the concept of the fantasy gaming "cleric" or the *WoW* Priest as real-world history ever got.

The Templars

The success of the Knights Hospitaller spurred the Catholic Church to launch a new order, this one dedicated purely to military concerns. It was decided to headquarter this new unit on the Temple Mount (site of the original Jewish temple, and later—and currently—the site of the Islamic Mosque of Omar, or "Dome of the Rock"), giving it its name, "Knights Templar."

The Templars were an elite unit. There were four distinct divisions of the order. The knights were equipped as heavy cavalry and drawn from the upper classes. The sergeants were equipped as light cavalry and drawn from skilled fighters of the lesser classes. The farmers were actually managers in charge of administering lands and keeping the order supplied, and the chaplains were ordained priests in charge of traditional spiritual concerns. Each full brother of the Templars had at least ten subordinates beneath him—men at arms, laborers, clerks and so on.

The Templars were very well connected politically, and their mandate from the Pope made it easy for them to increase their wealth and political power. Their most significant holding was the entire island of Cyprus. Their concerns soon expanded beyond warfare, and led into all kinds of ventures throughout Europe and the Holy Land. In the end, it was banking that lead to their greatest power and ultimate downfall.

At the time, an increasingly urban and unified Europe was desperately in need of some sort of central banking system. The Templars filled this void. Their wealth grew exponentially—so much so that the King of France, and even the Pope himself, became alarmed.

On October 13, 1307, King Phillip the Fair of France ordered all the Templars in France arrested. Many fled to Scotland (where King Robert the Bruce was already excommunicated, and didn't care what the Pope thought about anything) or other friendly kingdoms, but many Templars were captured in France and tortured into admitting to heretical practices. There is much debate about whether the "heresies" of the Templars were complete propaganda, or somewhat distorted accounts of actual initiation rites of the order. The Pope had to take a side, and he sided with France, officially disbanding the Templars, while simultaneously issuing a secret order pardoning the surviving members from charges of heresy.

Although the Templars have been defunct since the thirteenth century, the body of myth and legend surrounding the order has only grown. There are myths that say the Templars found and hid the Holy Grail (the cup Christ drank from at the Last Supper) and the Ark of the Covenant (the golden box where the Israelites stored the Ten Commandments). Both of these myths have been celebrated in recent decades in the *Indiana Jones* movies.

A more obscure myth holds that fleeing Templars came to America a couple centuries before Columbus.

The mythology of the Templars is central to the fraternal order of the Freemasons. These mythic connections between Templars, Masons and earlier, more mystical orders has been celebrated in popular literature many times in the last few decades, most notably in Umberto Eco's novel *Foucault's Pendulum*, and in Dan Brown's massive international bestseller, *The Da Vinci Code*.

After the Templars

Even after the Templars were disbanded and the Crusaders driven from the Holy Land, the Knights Hospitaller continued to soldier on. They were given the island of Rhodes for their headquarters, but the Moslems didn't like their old enemy holding a fortress off their coast. The knights fought off two Moslem invasions in the fourteenth century, then in 1522 A.D. Suleiman the Magnificent sent 400 ships with a force of 20,000 men against the knights. Behind the walls of their city, the 7,000 knights held out against the invaders for six months, but eventually the few surviving knights surrendered and were allowed to go to the mainland.

The order was next given the island of Malta in 1530. In 1565 the Moslems tried another massive invasion to eject the knights, but this time the knights were reinforced by a large army from Spain, and it was the Moslems who were driven off with massive casualties. The Knights of Malta remained in command of the island until 1789, when Malta was captured by Napoleon. Although that marked the end of the knights as a military force, a modern Catholic fraternal organization, the Sovereign Military Order of Malta, claims direct descent from the Knights Hospitaller and remains a significant political force.

Islam: The Ribat

Islam does not have priests as such. It reveres scholars of the Qu'ran, and gives them authority to preach, teach and make legal judgments, but the Islamic *Imam* is different from a Catholic (or, for that matter, Buddhist or Hindu) priest in that he does not take any special vows setting him apart from the rest of society. Islam does, however, have a tradition of wandering monastic warriors, embodied in the medieval concept of the *Ribat*.

The original *Ribats* (from an Arabic word that can be very loosely translated as "well armed") were fortified caravansaries (way stations) established in remote wilderness areas along major trade routes, to protect Moslem pilgrims and traders. The *Ribat* was an outpost, where invaders and enemies could be spotted before they struck important cities or holy places. It was a fortress, from which forces could be sent out to engage and defeat enemies. It was a place of refuge, where travelers could seek out rest and healing. However, it was also a center of learning and spiritual discipline, where students could go to study their faith, free from the distractions of the city. The *Ribat* was also a missionary headquarters, from which wandering teachers were sent out to spread that *Ribat's* particular school of Islam.

These wandering teachers were not only well versed in religious dogma, but were also skilled warriors and healers—in short, very much like the popular concept of a wandering "cleric" in contemporary fantasy.

Far Eastern Warrior Monks and Exorcists

No examination of the tradition of warrior priests would be complete without at least a mention of the fighting Buddhist monks of the Far East, including the Sohei warrior monks of feudal Japan, and of course the legendary Shaolin Temple of China.

To American fantasy fans, there tends to be an arbitrary and somewhat odd distinction between western warrior "clerics" and eastern warrior "monks." This is understandable, particularly in the case of fantasy gaming. It's difficult to envision a game concept that could gracefully combine jovial, brawling Friar Tuck (even with some supernatural healing and protective abilities thrown in) and the building-leaping, monster-slaying martial artists of Hong Kong cinema. Still, if you take a somewhat broader view of the concept of the supernatural warrior priest—for example, defining it as "an individual who, while pursuing the spiritual disciplines of his or her faith, acquires certain supernatural abilities which he or she then uses in combat to promote the goals of that faith," then clearly the Shaolin Monk and the healer-priest of fantasy gaming have a good deal in common.

Shaolin Temple

Founded in 517 A.D. by the legendary holy man Damo (Bodhidharma), a Buddhist missionary monk from India, China's Shaolin Temple is known as the sun source of all the Eastern martial arts. Located in a strategically sensitive and well-traveled area, the monks of the temple were called upon to defend against wild beasts, robbers and foreign raiders. Over the centuries the Shaolin monks learned to turn their traditional yoga disciplines into powerful armed and unarmed combat techniques that in time evolved into the myriad disciplines of Kung Fu. Although tightly controlled by the Chinese government, the Shaolin Temple still flourishes today as a shrine to Chinese culture and tradition (and as a very profitable tourist attraction).

Sohei Warrior Monks

The Sohei were the traditional warrior monks of Japan. From the tenth through the sixteenth centuries they were one of the most potent forces in Japanese society, openly vying with the Samurai lords (and with each other) for political power. In the fifteenth century, the Sohei spawned a new popular movement, the Ikko-ikki—religious extremists who began to mobilize the common folk against the Samurai. Faced with the menace of the Ikko-ikki, the great warlord Nobunaga was forced to take decisive action against the Sohei, breaking the backs of the monasteries forever in a series of bloody engagements between 1571 and 1580.

Besides the Sohei monks, there was also a tradition of yamabushi, or "mountain warriors." These warrior hermits did not band together into large monastic communities, so they never matched the political power or notoriety of the Sohei, but they were legendary for their spiritual and martial power.

Anime Exorcists

For a fictional character that bridges the gap between Western and Eastern wandering priests, see Miroku, from the Japanese *anime* (television cartoon) and *manga* (comic book) series *Inuyasha*, by Rumiko Takahashi. Miroku is a young Buddhist monk of questionable moral fiber, but is surprisingly wise and spiritually powerful nonetheless. He also suffers under a strange family curse that makes him even more powerful, but only at constant risk to his life and soul.

In fact, the world of anime is a particularly rich source of Buddhist holy men and women who wield great mystical power without falling into the clichés of the movie martial artist. These sorts usually use *sutras* (Buddhist scripture passages, usually inscribed on strips of rice paper) to drive off and destroy demonic and Undead forces, very much like the Priests in fantasy games use their prayers to drive off evil. In American translations, they're often referred to as "exorcists," or "mediums."

Playing the Priest

Primary stats for Priests to focus on are Intellect, Spirit and Stamina, used to increase your Mana pool, regeneration rate and hit points.

Priests can wield daggers, maces, staves and wands. Wands are especially nice as a Mana-less ranged attack.

Priests are limited to wearing only cloth armor, giving them a lower armor rating than most other classes. Try to avoid aggravating the foes attacking your party!

Healing spells can draw aggro, and aggro in intense group combat is the last thing a Priest wants. Keep back from the melee when healing in combat to avoid writing an aggro check you can't cash.

Use Inner Fire when in combat to increase your attack and armor ratings. Even if you aren't in melee, the extra armor will be beneficial.

Use Power Word: Shield to quickly halt damage to yourself or your allies, or use the spell as a pre-emptive damage absorber when about to engage in a tough fight.

Learn your healing spells and learn when to use them! Renew is a heal-over-time spell that heals a small amount of Health every few seconds. Flash Heal provides a fair amount of healing in a quick burst, but it's not as Mana-efficient as using one of the longer casting heals such as Lesser Heal, Heal or Greater Heal. Balance your use of healing spells with Power Word: Shield. You won't have to heal as much if you and your allies are avoiding combat damage.

Fade is an extremely useful spell when in a group where one or more enemies single you out for aggro. Use Fade to reduce the hatred these foes have for you.

Priests can prove to be invaluable allies against casters with their Mana Burn spell, allowing the Priest to drain Mana from the foe and prevent the foe from healing itself or casting harmful spells on the party. Priests have an ace up their sleeve with the Dispel Magic spell. This spell allows them to remove two harmful spell effects from their allies or remove two beneficial spells from their enemies. Don't forget about this one!

Shaman

RACES: Orc, Tauren, Troll
PREFERRED WEAPONS: One-handed maces, staves, unarmed
ARMOR ALLOWED: Cloth, leather, shield; mail at Level 40.
POWER LINES: Elemental Combat (offensive), Enhancement (buffs),
   Restoration (healing)
SOLO POTENTIAL: Good

The Shaman in WoW

Like the Druid, the Shaman is a hybrid class, able to serve as a healer/
buffer and as a damage-dealer (either at range or close in).

Shamans are only available to the Horde races of Orcs, Taurens
and Trolls. As these are generally the larger races, especially the Tauren, they really stand out in PvP. This is also an inconvenience when
trying to navigate narrow corridors.

Primary statistics for a Shaman vary depending on your specialization.
Gear selection can be more complicated for Shamans because of this. If
you want to focus on casting and healing, then Intellect, Spirit and Stamina are your primary concerns. Shamans with a greater melee orientation
may want to focus on Strength, Agility and Stamina instead.

The Shaman's magic is cast through the power of his totems: natural objects imbued with the power of the four mystical elements—
earth (mostly defensive effects), fire (mostly offensive) and the more
nebulous air and water.

A Shaman who concentrates on developing the Elemental Combat
line has excellent solo potential. Because they have good armor and
weapon choices, and because they come from the bigger and more
powerful races in the game, Shamans have excellent combat versatility, with the ability to defend themselves physically when Mana
starts to get low.

The Enhancement line is strongly weighted toward abilities best used in groups. The Restoration line is essential to both solo and group play, but it reaches its full potential in a group setting.

The Shaman class is ideal for those who are drawn to the Horde side, but who still want a versatile class that requires thought and sophistication to play to full advantage.

Shamanism

Shamanism is the oldest known human spiritual discipline. Ten thousand years ago, Ice Age Shamans probably held beliefs and performed rituals that would be completely recognizable to a modern follower of traditional Native American or Australian Aboriginal religions.

Shamanism itself, however, is not exactly a religion. It's a spiritual path based on a certain worldview. Shamanism is based in Animism, the belief that all creation is alive in a mystical sense—that the world that we perceive is permeated and sustained by an invisible world of natural spirits, and that humans can interact with these spirits in both positive and negative ways.

An Animist believes in the spirits of nature and makes that belief a part of his everyday life (since the spirits are always there, it's wise to stay on their good side). A Shaman, however, is one who dedicates his entire life to understanding and communicating with the spirits of nature. The Shaman seeks to become a fully recognized citizen of the invisible world, able to enter it at will and to command its respect and assistance.

Shamanism focuses on the small and the immediate—the spirit of the trees that surround the town, the crops that feed it, the fire in the hearth, the water in the well. Because of this close-in focus, it's easy to reconcile Shamanistic beliefs with monotheistic and polytheistic religions that take a larger, more cosmic viewpoint. That's why the Shamanistic practices of Shinto can stay the official religion of Japan, while mixing freely with the cosmic worldview of Buddhism (originally from India) and the ethical philosophy of Confucianism (from China). It's why a *curandera* (herbal healer) in Laredo, Texas, can be both a practicing Shamanistic healer and a pillar of the local Catholic Church.

It is a big mistake to think of Shamanism as something that primitive people practiced a long time ago. Our western cultural image of the Shaman is the "witch doctor" of the cartoons, bedecked with feathers, wearing a huge grotesque mask, carrying a spear and probably boiling up a couple of hapless white explorers (still in their pith helmets) for supper. Today, those who take an interest in actual Shamanism consider such images to be not only false, but racist and offensive.

The roots of Shamanism are sunk so deep into our culture that they'll probably never vanish completely, and Shamanism remains an active practice today. Certainly it flourishes best in small, rural communities on the outskirts of our Western culture—the Native American reservation, the Australian outback, the Mexican interior. However, there's also a highly sophisticated, even urban side to modern Shamanism. In the Far East, where cultures have traditionally been very laid back about mixing and matching religions, Shamanism can become a crucial part of the dominant culture, as in the Japanese state religion, or Tibetan Buddhism, which carries a strong Shamanistic strain as part of its dogma.

Even in modern, urban America, neo-pagan and New Age spiritual movements seek to take traditional Shamanistic practices and make them applicable to everyday life. There's even a small but vocal community of "techno Shamans," who believe that the new and evolving matrix of technologically created virtual space can serve as a gateway to other and higher states of spiritual thought.

In most cultures it's probably safe to say that the path of Shamanism is associated with males, but this is far from absolute. Many Shamanistic beliefs allow both men and women to pursue the path of the Shaman (sometimes the paths for the two genders differ significantly, sometimes they're the same). The ancient Vikings considered Shamanistic practice unmanly, and only permitted women to pursue it.

The Tree

Perhaps the most fascinating aspect of Shamanistic tradition is the way it pervades all known cultures. The word "Shaman" itself derives from the Tungus people of Siberia, but if you observed a Navajo

Shaman, a Shinto priest, a Haitian *houngan* or *mambo* or a modern English witch, you'd see them all engaged in very similar beliefs and practices. The details and the names would be different, but they'd all be recognizably Shamans. Anthropologists believe that this global similarity is not a coincidence. The practice of Shamanism probably was practiced by humans before they spread all over the world, to Northern Europe, Australia, the Far East and the Americas. Everywhere that humanity settled it took Shamanistic practices with them, and these practices have stayed largely unchanged everywhere.

One central concept that can be found in almost all Shamanistic systems is the idea of the World Tree. The World Tree grows through all realities—Earth, heaven and the underworld. The World Tree is also sometimes called the *Axis Mundi* (axle of the world), because it ties all the levels of reality together. By maintaining a spiritual connection to the World Tree, the Shaman can pass from our reality into the spirit worlds to gain power and wisdom.

Traditional Shamanistic sacred places are regarded as roots of the Tree—places where the World Tree anchors itself to our reality. Traditionally, these "roots" are placed by the local people at some sort of mountain or hill, although sometimes a World Tree can be anchored to a man-made place.

Often, the myths of the World Tree will divide the universe into at least three levels—the middle world, which is the physical world we live in; the upper world, which is the home of the gods and spirits; and the underworld, which is where the ancestors live. Of course, not all Animistic traditions break down this way, and some are far, far more complicated.

The Norse called the World Tree *Yggdrasil*, while on Fiji they called it "the tree of speech." The idea of the tree even lingers in many traditions that have otherwise evolved beyond Shamanistic belief. The Hindu Bhagavad-Gita speaks of the Asvattha, or Bodhi-Tree, with its roots in the heavens and its trunk and branches reaching down to Earth. Its leaves are the Veddas (Hindu sacred scriptures). Medieval Jewish mystics who studied the Kabbala based their system around the Tree of Life, with ten *Sephirot* (levels of reality) and twenty-two connecting paths between them. In the story of the Garden of Eden, we're told that the Tree of Life and the Tree of Knowledge of Good and Evil could both be found in the garden, but the first humans were cut off from the Tree of Life when they ate the fruit of the Tree of Knowledge.

The Journey

So what makes a Shaman a Shaman? Although the way of the Shaman is a lifelong pursuit, in most traditions there is a definite point at which a Shaman is created, and that's the completion of the Shamanic journey.

The Shaman's function is to go back and forth between our world and the other worlds. The first time he does this and returns marks his full initiation into Shamanhood. This is not an easy process. While a highly experienced Shaman might be able to pass between the realities at will, the first time is always a major endeavor.

The Shamanic journey is an internal one—the physical body doesn't have to move at all. Many cultures use sweat lodges or other forms of confinement under extreme conditions to initiate the seeker. Other traditions take the "vision quest" more literally, sending the seeker out into the wilderness to wander, sometimes for days or weeks at a time. The "walkabout" of the Australian aborigine is a well-known example of such a literal journey, as are vision quest traditions among Native Americans.

Either way, the Shaman's journey is a physically daunting one. He must fast, and if possible, go without sleep. He will either engage in constant exercise, or try to remain completely motionless. Rhythmic drumming, dancing and chanting will be used to try to place himself in an altered state of existence (rhythm is a very important part of many Shamanistic rituals). He will fill his lungs with heavy, aromatic smoke and incense, and he will often ingest powerful hallucinogenic herbs and mushrooms. In some cultures the Shamanistic candidate will actually submit to beatings or other forms of torture (cutting, exposure to extremes of climate or exposure to irritating insects). All of this is designed to force the Shaman to leave his physical body behind and journey with his *astral* (spirit) body into the next world.

Just because one has a vision, that doesn't automatically make him a Shaman. In some Native American traditions, every young man is expected to go out on a vision quest. It is believed that when he completes his quest, he will be visited by his own spirit animal, which will give him his true name. At that time the spirit animal will reveal the seeker's place in life—it might be to return to the tribe as a warrior, or it might be to continue to seek the Shaman's path.

As grueling as the vision quest is on the physical body, it's nothing compared to what the spiritual body must go through to become a Shaman. Some traditions teach that when a candidate enters the other world seeking to become a Shaman, he is first ritually dismembered, then his skin is flayed off and his organs removed, until he becomes a skeleton (the ability to see oneself as a skeleton—and the symbol of the skeleton or skull in general—is very important in many Shamanistic traditions). Then the skeletonized spirit descends into the underworld where, if it can endure the abuse it receives from demons and angry spirits, it will finally be taught the secrets of the Shaman by the spirits of the ancestors. When he has learned everything he needs to know, he ascends into the overworld, where powerful spirits restore flesh and blood to the spiritual body.

Totems, Spirit Animals and the Elements

It is in the use of totems that real-world Shamans and *World of Warcraft* Shamans make their best connection. In the game, totems, powered by the four elements of nature, provide a channel which the Shaman uses to unleash and control mystical power.

In Animistic traditions, totems are physical representations of spirits, usually animals, which guard and guide the Shaman and his people. A totem can be the spirit guide of an individual, a family or an entire tribe. These images are best known to popular culture in the totem poles of the Native American tribes of Western Canada and the Northwestern United States. These ornately carved trees, sometimes twenty or thirty feet in height, were stacked with the most important totems of the tribe for maximum spiritual protection.

Totems do not, however, have to be actual images of the spirit animal. They can just as easily be a fragment of bone, fur or feather, or a piece of a nest, or a stone or other small object taken from the animal's lair or territory. The Siberian Tungus Shamans called such relics *ongons*, while some Native American tribes gathered several such items into medicine bags, which an individual would wear for protection or magical power.

Totems are one part of Animism that remains powerful far outside the realm of actual Shamanistic practice. Medieval European heraldry, for example, is extremely totemistic, as is our modern custom of naming our sports teams after animals and legendary figures.

Spirit Animals

As important as totems are, they are only a physical representation of an even more important idea, the concept of the spirit animal. The spirit animal represents one's deepest nature. A spirit totem might be an animal that the whole community relies on for sustenance (the buffalo or the salmon), or an animal that the seeker wishes to become like (a bear for strength, a horse for speed, a lion for martial power, a tortoise for patience or longevity).

Animistic cultures see no contradiction in eating an animal and making it a tribal or personal token. Native Americans believed that the animal spirits offered meat and hides to the tribe as a gift, provided that the tribe was smart enough to hunt for it, and not so greedy they took more than they actually needed. In eating the flesh of a totem animal, with love and profound gratitude, it was believed that the hunter could take in the power and strength of that spirit animal.

The actual place of cannibalism in human history is highly controversial (societies have an appalling tendency to falsely brand their defeated enemies as cannibals), but it seems certain that some ancient cultures would eat at least small, ceremonial bits of fallen enemies' (and sometimes fallen allies') hearts and flesh, as a way of honoring their strength and courage and in order to gain a portion of those virtues for themselves.

The Elements

The theory of the four elements—earth, air, fire and water (most Far Eastern cultures add a fifth, metal)—that combine to make up everything in the universe is one concept that goes back literally to the dawn of the human race. The ancient Greeks used the concept extensively in laying the foundations of modern science and philosophy. The idea of the four classical elements (as they're called) has since been echoed in pretty much every system of human magic. It's particularly important in alchemy.

It's a remarkably sophisticated way of organizing the universe. Look, for instance, at human beings. They have solid flesh—that's from earth. Inside, they're mostly liquid, that's water. They must breath to live, air. The human body radiates heat, fire. While the mixture of the elements makes up the world, the ancients also believed that certain elements exerted greater or lesser control over various objects and endeavors. By knowing which element commands a given phenomenon, the magician could take control of that phenomenon and turn it to his own ends.

An interesting ancient superstition? Perhaps. But many fantasy writers have pointed out that modern physics has proven that physical matter has four states: solid (earth), liquid (water), vapor (air) and plasma (fire). Make of this what you will.

Shamans in Literature

Until recently, Shamanism and literacy have been pretty close to mutually exclusive. Shamanistic traditions tend to flourish in rural, nomadic and unassimilated cultures where writing things down is not a priority.

Make no mistake, there are thousands of stories of heroic Shamans and their fantastic journeys between the worlds, but until very recently no one bothered to collect these stories and record them on paper. When representatives of literate cultures crossed paths with Shamanistic traditions, they tended to regard what they saw as the superstitious nonsense of primitive savages. History, as they say, is written by the winners.

Fantasy and adventure literature, which is by and large a creation of the twentieth century, picks up and amplifies these racist assumptions. The fantastic pulp writers like Robert E. Howard and Edgar Rice Burroughs tended to place Shamans in their stories primarily as villains—the mindless cannibalistic savages of the cartoons, or, at best, Machiavellian villains ruthlessly manipulating their primitive and simple followers.

Perhaps the most famous modern chronicle of Shamanism is Carlos Castaneda's books about Don Juan, a Yaqui Indian Shaman, and Castaneda's own studies and initiation into Shamanism. Castaneda wrote over a dozen books about his Shamanistic journey, but the early ones (starting with *The Teachings of Don Juan: A Yaqui Way of Knowledge*) combine a particularly clear and compelling view of Shamanistic belief, with a narrative that sometimes reads very much like a novel of fantastic adventure (whether, and exactly how much Castaneda may have embellished his experiences for dramatic effect is a long-running and significant point of contention among his admirers).

Almost equally well known (and a good deal less breathless) is *Black Elk Speaks: Being the Life Story of a Holy Man of the Oglala Sioux*, by Black Elk and John G. Neihardt. This autobiographical collaboration between an actual Native American Shaman and a respected poet offers a wealth of information about traditional Native American beliefs, the author's own journey as a Shaman and the tragic history of the Sioux people in the nineteenth and early twentieth centuries.

Voodoo is a particularly well-chronicled corner of the Shamanistic universe. Zora Neal Hurston's *Tell My Horse* is the story of the author's own initiation into voodoo practice in the 1930s. *The Serpent and the Rainbow*, by Wade Davis, is an in-depth look into the voodoo practice of zombification. Davis proves that zombies do exist in the real world, though of course they are not truly reanimated corpses. Instead, the voodoo priests use herbal preparations to put their victims in a death-like coma, from which they can be revived into a highly suggestible state that makes them easy for *houngan* or *mambo* to control. Some have complained that Davis' work shows a lack of respect for the beliefs of those he writes about, but his exploration of this legendary phenomenon is truly fascinating.

Playing the Shaman

A Shaman's most effective spell lines are instant cast, such as Purge and the Shock line. One Shock has damage over time, one has spell interruption and one has a snare effect. These are great spells to use both in PvE and PvP.

Shamans are a great class for burst damage or healing. Utilizing the Shaman class in a support role really makes them shine at later levels.

With mail armor and shields, Shamans have the third highest AC in the Horde, behind Warriors and Druids in bear-form. With weapon buffs and this additional armor bonus from mail armor and shield, a Shaman can hold his own in most melee situations.

A Shaman's talent specialization largely determines his primary role, and can surprise opponents with his strength in a specialized field. Shamans wishing to focus on their healing aspect should train in Restoration talents. Shamans wishing to focus on their damage casting aspect should focus on Elemental talents. Melee-oriented Shamans will want to put points into their Enhancement talents. The key here is that the player needs to pick out the right talents for the role they most frequently fill, and there are always trade-offs.

Shamans have the worst Mana efficiency of all the classes. The ratio of Mana to damage dealt or Health restored is poorer than that of the other pure healing or spell casting classes. Mana conservation is critical to playing a Shaman well.

Shamans have no means of crowd control or removing a foe from the fight temporarily, so choose your encounters carefully!

Shamans are at their best when using different groups of abilities rather than repeating a few abilities over and over. Play to the Shaman's strength of versatility.

Shamans have an Astral Recall ability that allows them to return to the last inn they set as their home. This works as the Hearthstone that all players receive, but doesn't take up an inventory space and can be used every fifteen minutes, although with a Mana cost attached.

Totems separate the Shamans as a unique class and are both a strength and weakness. Totems aid the Shaman and his party with their ability to benefit all nearby allies, or work as a detriment to all nearby enemies. The use of totems requires some thought and care, however, as they increase the aggro radius of the Shaman with their own aggro radius. Try not to leave unattended totems behind!

Always carry ankhs after you get the ability to reincarnate. If you're going to die and plan on using reincarnate, die out of aggro range of any mobs, so that you can safely return to life and recover from the wipeout.

A Shaman wielding a dagger and shield is generally more durable, but doesn't have the offensive output of a Shaman that uses a two-handed weapon.

Shamans gain an invaluable ability called Ghost Wolf. Research this ability as soon as it is available. This allows you to transform into a wolf and run faster! Long before the first mounts become available at Level 40, Shamans can travel quickly across the lands of Azeroth.

Shamans have many different spells and totems that have situational utility, like Water Walking (which is great in PvP to escape enemies or in PvE to bypass hostile areas). Sentry Totem is useful, to see what a named spawn is up or to watch an enemy's corpse to see whether they have released or not.

Never neglect your totems and always make sure you are fighting near your totems so that you gain the benefits. The totems become useless if you stray too far away. Also, keep track of which elements your totems use. You can have one of each element planted at the same time, but you cannot have two from the same element active. The second totem dropped will replace one from the same element already in use.

DRUID

RACES: Night Elf, Tauren

PREFERRED WEAPONS: Staves, one-handed maces, daggers, unarmed; later spears

ARMOR ALLOWED: Cloth, leather

POWER LINES: Balance (offensive spells, binds & debuffs), Feral Combat (shapeshifting and animal powers), Restoration (healing)

SOLO POTENTIAL: Very good

Druids in *WoW*

The Druids are the guardians of the natural world. Their purpose is to maintain the balance between the sentient races and the flora and fauna of Kalinda and the Eastern Kingdoms.

Strategically, the Druid is perhaps the most versatile class in *World of Warcraft*. They have a formidable array of offensive spells and excellent healing abilities. They can also change form into a bear, to act as a group tank or into a great cat, giving them a useful combination of speed, stealth and offensive punch. They have powers that allow them to control wild beasts, they command the most powerful buffing spell in the game and they have the only resurrection power that can be used during combat.

The versatility that is their strength, however, is also their weakness. Druids don't really excel in any area over more specialized classes. Their spells are no match for a true Mage, and their heals pale in the presence of a Priest. In animal form they can fight, but not with the versatility of a dedicated Warrior, and their stealth abilities are just a small taste of the skills of a real Rogue. If you're the type of player who wants to be the absolute best at some specific thing, than the Druid is not for you.

Because of the wide variety of options at his command, a Druid's choice for focusing his talents is an intensely vital part of his concept. Those who want to do most of their playing in groups will probably want to focus on the Restoration line, to make themselves viable first-tier healers, while those who prefer to solo will certainly want to dedicate their talent to Feral Combat. A Druid focused on Balance is a bit of an odd duck, but will bring useful offensive punch to both group and solo situations.

Druids can make excellent solo adventurers. It is absolutely essential, however, that a solo Druid discovers his targets' strengths and weaknesses, and tailors his attacks to the threat at hand. There's no "one size fits all" survival strategy when you're playing a Druid—you have to use your versatility to find and exploit your opponents' weaknesses.

Druids are usually not the first class sought out when forming teams. Team play tends to favor specialists, not generalists, and with a Druid you never really know what kind of asset you're getting—fighter, healer or caster. Once you're in with a regular group, however, and they know your capabilities, they're certain to come to appreciate what you bring. And don't let yourself get boxed into one role—sure, if there's a tactical hole in the group then you're the one to fill it, but never forget to use your versatility, even in group combat.

The one thing that any Druid can bring to group play is the potent one-two punch of the group buffs Thorns (damage bonus) and Mark of the Wild (armor and stat bonus). Just these two spells can make a huge difference in the long-term survival potential of a group.

Celts, Gauls and Druids

The historical Druids were a religious elite caste among the Celts and Gauls of North-Central Europe (France, some of Germany and the British Isles). Not all Celts and Gauls were Druids, but the Druids certainly dominated those cultures up until the time of the conquests of Julius Caesar (about 100 b.c.e.).

The most outstanding fact about the Druids—and perhaps the reason for the ongoing fascination with them in popular culture—is that we really know nothing about them . . . we can make any number of educated guesses, based on information from secondary sources, but we don't really *know* in the sense that we know what Rome or ancient India was like from actual members of that society, who left records of their lives. The Druids did not write their traditions down.

And this seems to be because that's the way the Druids wanted it. The Celts were not illiterate—they had their own language, written with the Greek alphabet, which was used for commercial and political purposes. The teachings and traditions of Druidism, however, were entirely oral. (The Celts also had their own sacred runic alphabet, called Ogham, but that was also never used to record the teachings of the Druids.)

Just because the teachings of the Druids were never written down, it doesn't mean they were simple. According to some sources, a Druid-in-training spent a full twenty years memorizing stories, lists and doctrine before becoming a full member of the order.

The Mystery of the Druids

Everything we know about the Druids from contemporary sources comes from Greek and Roman writers. These were not particularly friendly sources. Celts had invaded Rome in 390 b.c.e. and Greece in 279 b.c.e. At the time of Julius Caesar, he was returning the favor in a vicious war of conquest against Gaul and later, Britain. The Greeks and Romans may have reluctantly respected the Celts and Gauls, but they never liked them.

Take, for example, the question of human sacrifice. In his *History of the Gallic War*, Caesar says the Druids sacrificed humans to their gods in their sacred groves. No one else (unless they're quoting Caesar) makes any reference to this tradition. Was Caesar repeating a malicious rumor, or perhaps engaging in a bit of wartime propaganda?

In other places in his *History of the Gallic War*, Caesar also writes of the Druids with notable respect: "[The Druids] know much about the stars and celestial motions, and about the size of the earth and universe, and about the essential nature of things, and about the powers and authority of the immortal gods; and these things they teach to their pupils."

And certainly, given the time and the place in which the Druids lived, there would be nothing particularly shocking if they occasionally used ritual sacrifice as a mode of execution for a convicted criminal or inconvenient prisoner of war. But in the end, we just don't know.

Some oral traditions have survived that seem to date back to Druidic times, but these are unreliable on their face, and still more so because of the edits of meddling Christians. Most of the people who recorded popular legends in the Middle Ages were Christian monks, and they tended to put their own spin on things. There was, for example, a long-running and completely non-historical school of thought that wanted to make the Druids into enlightened proto-monotheists, in contrast to the libertine pagans of the Roman Empire. So when a medieval writer says that the Druids practiced a water ritual somewhat similar to Christian baptism, is he revealing an intriguing cultural parallel, or just engaging in some wishful creativity of his own?

Druidic Culture

There were two castes in Druid culture: The nobles, who were landowners and war leaders, and the Druids. (Well, there were also slaves, who actually outnumbered both of the other castes by a very considerable margin, but of course they didn't count.)

The Druids were divided into three distinct orders.

The **Ovates** were healers and diviners who served the people at the local level, dispensing remedies and telling fortunes. Ovates were present at birth, and again at death.

The **Bards** were historians, storytellers and entertainers. They were the memory of the tribe and their travels formed a communications web, tying the tribe together. Bards "only" had to study for twelve years to master their discipline, in contrast to the twenty years reported for Druidic training.

The **Druids** themselves were high priests, judges, astronomers and diplomats. They could be either male or female. A Druid was the social equal of a chief or war leader, and their judgments were literally the law. If the Druids disapproved of a war between two chiefs, they would physically place themselves between the two warring sides, and the lords would then be required by custom to submit to Druidic arbitration.

Celtic and Gallic society was not urbanized and centralized like Rome, but it was by no means primitive. Instead of an emperor or senate, there was a complex web of law and custom that kept every noble and Druid equal to one another. Chiefs could gain power over their peers only with the consent of all involved. Senior Druids were appointed as needed by the other archdruids. Druids were by no means muddy-legged medicine men. They were powerful leaders and learned scholars. Some sources say that no one, irregardless of rank, had the right to speak in public before the Druids present had spoken.

Like their society, Celtic religion was complex. There are several hundred Celtic deities known by name to history, but most of them are probably mere local gods. (The Gauls' religion was similar, but the Celtic beliefs are better known.) The core Celtic pantheon seems to have numbered two or three dozen gods and goddesses (thirty-three—a very sacred number to the Celts—is a likely total, but no one knows for sure). These included Arawn, god of revenge and the underworld; Bran the Blessed, god of prophecy, war and the arts; Cerrunos the Horned God, god of nature; Lir, god of the sea; Morrigan, goddess of the battlefield; Brigit, goddess of healing (later made a saint by the Catholic Church), and Rhiannon, goddess of the moon and peaceful death.

The holy days of the Celtic religion are also well known.

- *Imbolc*, the Return of Light, celebrated on February 1, marked the beginning of the growing season.
- *Beltane*, the Fires of Bel, celebrated May 1, a fertility festival marking the time when animals bore their young. The custom of the Maypole dance is a survival of this festival.
- *Lughnasad*, the Feast of Lugh, on August 1, marked the beginning of harvest.
- Most important was *Samhain*, November 1. This was the end of the harvest season, the beginning of winter, the first day of the Celtic new year and the feast of the dead. It is still observed to-

day as Halloween. (Contrary to some reports, and unlike some of the other festivals, "*Samhain*" was not the name of a Celtic god. It is strictly the name of the festival, and literally means "end of the warm season.")

Although the details of Druidic rites remain mysterious, it is reported that they worshipped in fenced groves of sacred oak trees. The name "Druid" is believed to be derived from the word for oak (which in turn is derived from an older root meaning "wisdom"). They kept "universities," where senior Druids congregated and students were trained, usually on the shores of sacred lakes.

Mistletoe was vital to Druidic practice, and it is said that priests in white robes would cut the mistletoe from sacred oaks using a golden knife or small golden sickle. Two white bulls were sacrificed at the time of the mistletoe harvest. It is believed that reincarnation was a major part of Druidic theology, and that they taught that debts incurred in this life would carry over into the next one.

Druidic Powers

According to legend, Druids could foretell the future. They were consulted before major battles and at the births of important children.

There are also stories of Druids who called down clouds of fire on hostile armies, and of Druids who caused insanity in their enemies.

The Irish hero Cuchulainn was kidnapped by the fairies and when he returned, he was obsessed with the memory of the fairy-woman Fand. The Druids brewed Cuchulainn a potion which erased all his memories of his time in the elflands, and even freed his wife, Emer, from the pain of jealousy.

When the god Midar fell in love with Etain, the wife of the High King of Ireland, he kidnapped her and took her off to a secret hiding place. The Druid Dalgm found Midar's hiding place using four wands of yew-wood inscribed with runes, though it took him a year to do so.

Beast Forms

In *WoW*, the most notable characteristic of the Druid class is their ability to take on animal forms. Somewhat ironically, this doesn't really match up with anything that we know about the real Druids.

In many Shamanistic traditions, animal spirits were of preeminent importance, and Shamans would wear the pelts of the sacred animals in order to take on the spiritual power of that creature. According to legend, some of the most powerful Shamans could actually roam the land in the form of their sacred animal (see the chapter on **Shaman**, p. 213, for more on Shamanistic practices). This seems to be the tradition the designers of *WoW* drew upon in creating the Feral Combat discipline.

It's not, however, Druidic in the least. Certainly, there was an animistic element to the Druid's practices, in their veneration of nature, but the Druidic religion seems to have been a very highly evolved polytheism, and their society was far more sophisticated and agrarian than most Shamanistic cultures. If they had any sort of tradition of skin-walking or animal totems, no record of that belief has survived to modern times.

Stonehenge

> "In ancient times, hundreds of years before the dawn of history, lived a strange race of people: the Druids. No one knows who they were, or what they were doing, but their legacy remains hewn into the living rock...of Stonehenge."
>
> —Spinal Tap

Nigel Tufnel's (lead guitar and vocalist for the legendary fake metal band Spinal Tap) famous introduction to the song "Stonehenge" was pretty much right on target with the "nobody knows who they were, or what they were doing" part, but the Druids' connection to Stonehenge is a good deal more controversial.

France, Germany and the British Isles have thousands of prehistoric stone monuments scattered around the countryside. These range from single-standing stones (menhirs, or megaliths) to the astonishing vitrified forts of England, which are literally man-made mountains. All of these have been, and often are today, pointed out to tourists as "ancient temples of the Druids." They may be ancient temples, but the European craze for stone-stacking seems to have predated the arrival of the Druids by centuries.

Stonehenge, one of the most recent and most sophisticated stone complexes, is a debatable exception. There have been many Stonehenges on the same site on Salisbury Plain, going back some 5,000 years. The first work at Stonehenge was a ditch and embankment construction, and we have no idea who created it. About 2000 B.C.E. the current residents started to bring in the smaller stones ("bluestones"). Finally, about 1500 B.C.E., the giant "sarcen" stones of the outer ring were added. This final stage of construction may have been overseen by early Druids. Some have even suggested that the final evolution of Stonehenge represents a transition point between an oppressive and obsolete culture obsessed with stoneworks, and a new, revolutionary Druidic order, with the emphasis on social order and the sacredness of natural, non-constructed holy sites, like oak groves.

Then again, maybe not. Who knows?

There is no debate that Stonehenge was designed so that on midsummer morning (the morning of the longest day of the year) the rising sun would appear directly over the oldest stone in the monument (called the "heel stone") and the first rays of dawn would strike in the center of the complex. Therefore, Stonehenge is not merely a temple, but also a precisely designed astronomical calculator. Claims that Stonehenge can also be used for more complex and esoteric astronomical calculations (for example, predicting eclipses) remain highly controversial.

Playing the Druid

Develop a rhythm for fighting. Try something like this: Starfire or Moonfire to start with. As your enemy approaches, cast Restoration or Regrowth on yourself. Knock down its armor with Faerie Fire and then shift into bear form for the bulk of combat. Heal as necessary.

Druids in cat form can prowl just like Rogues. Use this to your advantage. There are lots of quests that don't require you to fight any-thing. Sneak in, gather your quest target and sneak out.

Druids, in cat form, can also track humanoids. If you have prob-lems finding a humanoid, use this handy ability to locate your tar-get.

Druids specializing in Feral Combat with a few talent points in Restoration can move beyond the role of a simple tank while in bear form. Unlike Warriors, these Druids can soak damage, then heal and continue to soak more damage. This type of Druid is a true damage sponge.

Annoyed that you can't seem to get past all those annoying beasts that have nothing to do with your quest? Then make liberal use of the Hibernate and Soothe Animal spells to pass by them peacefully.

Feral Combat Druids really benefit from the armor patches avail-able through the Skinning and Leatherworking profession combina-tions. Restoration Druids can compensate for poorer combat abilities by using potions made from the Herbalism and Alchemist class com-binations. Balance Druids can save Mana for offensive casting by us-ing potions as well.

Never underestimate the value of a Rejuvenation or Regrowth spell cast at the beginning of combat. They can greatly extend the time needed before more healing spells.

Rogue

RACES: Orc, Troll, Undead, Dwarf, Gnome, Human, Night Elf

PREFERRED WEAPONS: Daggers, thrown weapons; later bows, crossbows, guns, one-handed swords, maces

ARMOR ALLOWED: Cloth, leather

POWER LINES: Assassination (stunning and finishing attacks used from Stealth), Combat (good old-fashioned dirty fighting), Subtlety (stealth and intrusion skills). At Level 20 you can go on a quest to get a fourth line, Poisons.

SOLO POTENTIAL: Very good

The Rogue in *WoW*

The Rogue is a dashing thief and treasure-hunter. Stealth is the first skill a Rogue learns, and it's what makes the Rogue deadly. Most of the Rogue's more effective attacks require Stealth (Ambush, Cheap Shot, Garrote, Sap). With Stealth, you can sneak past the guards and focus on the target of choice.

Rogues are excellent at working solo or in a group. A good Rogue can solo any non-elite, non-dungeon quest at orange or below—all you need is patience. You can aid your party with short-term stuns (Gouge, Cheap Shot, Kidney Shot, Blind, Sap) for crowd control, or by doing massive damage to the prime target (Ambush, Backstab, Poisons, high critical hits).

The Rogue is an expert at single-foe takedowns. If you can isolate an enemy, you can bring it down. At mid-levels, when Sap becomes truly effective, you can start to take on enemies two at a time. Sap forces one to stand there helpless while you take the other out. When "adds" come to help, you have some handy tools to help you escape.

Vanish lets you re-enter Stealth in the middle of combat. That means when things go wrong, you can Vanish and get away.

Sprint gives a significant, brief speed increase. Remember that you can run away if you have to, and you can do it faster than anyone else.

The Rogue's primary attributes are Agility (which adds to critical hit chance, armor and chance to dodge), Stamina (which adds to Health and recovery speed) and Strength (which increases your attack power and chance to hit).

Rogues begin play with knowledge of the dagger. They can throw it or use it in hand-to-hand. In time, a Rogue can train to use any one-handed weapon. At Level 10, Rogues learn to dual-wield, giving a nice boost to damage per second.

Leather armor is as good as it ever gets for a Rogue. Supplement this by keeping your Agility bonus high.

The Energy Bar is right under the Health Bar. Energy is used whenever a Rogue executes a special move. Low Energy means all you can do is normal attacks, and *that* means you're in trouble. Keep a close eye on your Energy Bar.

There is more to being a Rogue than killing. One of the first skills a Rogue can learn is Pick Pocket. You can increase your income by picking a mark's pocket before attacking it. In addition to coin, some nice items can be picked, like healing potions, special keys and lockboxes. Lockboxes are handy methods of increasing another Rogue skill, Lock Picking. Besides the nice baubles in lockboxes, there are locked treasure chests around the world, and doors in dungeons that require a special key or a talented lockpick.

At Level 20 the Rogue can gain a quest leading to knowledge of Poisons. As your level increases, your knowledge of Poisons can be trained up. Poisons can do extra damage, slow a spell caster's mind, or slow a target's movement. In the process of learning Poison, you also learn to make Thistle Tea, a concoction that will replenish your Energy like a healing potion replenishes your Health. Thistle Tea requires cooking skill.

The talent trees are where you get to make your Rogue different from every other Rogue on the planet. The three available trees are: Assassination, focused on increasing critical and poison damage; Combat, focused on increasing weapon skill and chance to hit; and Subtlety, focused on making you sneakier and increasing Stealth-related skills.

Rogues and Tricksters

People love Rogues. And for as long as there have been people, there have been stories about rogues, thieves and tricksters. These legends transcend every human culture.

Most trickster tales are humorous in nature, though some have a serious side. In some tales the trickster/rogue is trying to get something he wants; in others he's trying to help out a friend, and often he's just causing trouble for its own sake. Sometimes he gets tripped up by his own greed, but in others he gets away clean.

Often the trickster is some kind of animal. This is particularly true of more primitive societies, but civilization also has its beast fables. There's Coyote among the Native Americans, Spider (Anansi) in Africa, the Monkey King in China and Reynard the Fox in rural France. Br'er Rabbit among African American slaves was a trickster figure. Other tricksters are humanoid—in many cultures, the trickster is just "the old man." There are trickster gods in most pantheons: Loki for the Norse, Hermes and Prometheus among the Greeks.

Here are a couple of sample trickster tales, the first from Native American myth and the second from the Norse.

Coyote Steals Fire

Coyote saw that humans were naked, unlike the animals, and that they suffered in the cold of winter. Coyote decided to steal fire from the Fire Spirits, as a gift to the miserable humans. Coyote went and spied on the Fire Spirits. They saw him lurking outside his camp, but ignored him, because he was just a coyote. Coyote spied on the Fire Spirits for many days, and saw that they guarded their fire every moment of the day except one. At dawn the Fire Spirits would run into the teepees, shouting "Sister, come watch the fire!" to the other spirits inside. But Fire Spirits sleep soundly, and the replacement spirits were always slow getting out to guard the fire.

One night Coyote gathered all the animals to wait for him at the foot of the Fire Spirits' mountain. Then Coyote went up to spy on the spirits' camp until dawn. At dawn the spirits around the campfire got up and ran into their teepees shouting, "Sister, come watch the fire!"

and, as usual, the lazy spirits inside replied, "I'm awake, I'm awake. I'll be there in a moment. Stop shouting."

At that moment Coyote ran out and grabbed a branch from the fire. Holding the branch in his mouth he ran down the mountain as fast as he could. The Fire Spirits saw him running away and chased after him. One of them touched the tip of his tail, and ever after Coyote has had a smear of white ash on the tip of his tail.

Coyote shouted to the other animals and flung the branch away from him. Squirrel caught it and ran. One of the Fire Spirits grabbed Squirrel on the back, which hurt so much that Squirrel's tail curled up in pain. That's why Squirrel has a curled tail to this day.

Squirrel dropped the fire, but Chipmunk picked it up. One of the Fire Spirits raked her fingers down Chipmunk's back, leaving three black stripes that can still be seen on Chipmunk's back today.

Chipmunk threw the fire to Frog, who grabbed it and hopped off. One of the Fire Spirits grabbed Frog's tail and burned it right off, which is why frogs have no tail. But brave Frog continued on and brought the fire to Wood, who swallowed it.

The Fire Spirits gathered around Wood and begged it to return the fire. They sang to the Wood and promised it gifts, but Wood would not give up the fire. Finally the Fire Spirits gave up and went home.

Coyote went and got men and showed them how to get fire out of Wood by rubbing two sticks together. And men were very grateful to Coyote because they no longer had to suffer through the winter cold.

The Giant King's Bride

One morning Thor woke up to discover that his hammer, Mjollnir, was missing. Since this was the most powerful weapon the gods possessed, this was a major blow to the security of Asgard. Thor immediately suspected Loki, and went out to demand the return of his hammer, but under severe questioning by all the gods, Loki convinced them he wasn't guilty.

Wishing to completely remove himself from the other gods' suspicions, Loki promised to go out and find who took the hammer. He turned himself into a swan, and flew off to the land of the Giants, where he circled over the head of Thrym, the king of the Giants, and shouted, "Have you heard the news from Asgard? Thor's hammer is stolen!"

Thrym laughed and replied, "I do know that, for it was I who stole it!"

"I see," called Loki. "And what ransom will you take for the return of Mjollnir, Thrym?"

Thrym thought it over for awhile, and then replied, "I'll willingly return the hammer if Freyja, the most beautiful of the goddesses, consents to be my bride."

Loki flew back to Asgard with the news. The gods gathered and debated the problem. Asgard had to have Mjollnir back, but nobody wanted to send Freyja to such a horrible fate. Finally Heimdall, the sentry of the guards, came up with a plan. Since Heimdall had watched the Giants carefully for years, he knew how stupid they were and how little they understood the gods. He suggested that they dress up Thor in one of Freyja's dresses and send him to the Fire Giants, saying that he was the beautiful Freyja.

Thor was not greatly fond of the plan, but Heimdall and Loki convinced the other gods it was their best hope, and finally Thor agreed. They brought Freyja's finest gown, a long bridal veil, a lovely golden wig and some scented powder, and they made up Thor to pass as Freyja as best he could. Loki dressed as a handmaiden to accompany Thor. Then Thor and Loki climbed into Thor's chariot and flew off to the land of the Giants.

Giants have very peculiar ideas about beauty, and when Thrym saw "Freya" she looked just fine to him, but he was still suspicious that the gods were planning a trick.

"Why doesn't my bride speak?" Thrym asked Loki.

"Oh great king, when she was told that she was to marry you, she became so excited that she shouted for joy for a whole week. She's lost her voice."

Thrym ordered a great feast prepared for his fiancée. At the feast, Thor devoured as many cows and goats as any Giant at the table.

"Does she always eat this much?" Thrym asked Loki.

"Oh great king, with all that yelling, she hasn't been able to eat or drink for a whole week either. That's why she's so hungry."

After the feast, Thrym raised the bridal veil to give his new wife a kiss, but when he raised the veil he saw Thor's glowing red eyes glaring back at him.

"Why are her eyes like that?" he asked Loki.

"Oh great king, did I not tell you that she's been yelling for a whole week? She hasn't had any sleep in days. Her eyes will be fine once she gets some rest."

At last Thrym's suspicions were completely quelled, and he was eager to take his wife off to the marriage bed.

"Wait, oh great king," Loki interjected. "First you must deliver the gift you promised to the gods in exchange for your new wife."

In his eagerness, Thrym ordered Mjollnir brought out at once, and presented it to his bride with great formality.

Once Thor got Mjollnir in his hand, he tore off his veil and gown and killed all the Giants in short order, after which he, his hammer and Loki returned to Asgard.

Highwaymen

As I was going over the far-famed Kerry mountains,
I met with Captain Farrell, and his money he was counting.
I first produced my pistol, and then produced my rapier.
Sayin' stand and deliver, for I am a bold deceiver,

Chorus:
musha ring dumma do damma da
whack for the daddy 'ol
whack for the daddy 'ol
there's whiskey in the jar
I counted out his money, and it made a pretty penny.
I put it in my pocket and I took it home to Jenny.
She sighed and then she swore, that she never would deceive me,
But the Devil take the women, for they never can be easy.

[chorus]
I went into my chamber, all for to take a slumber,
I dreamt of gold and jewels and for sure it was no wonder.
But Jenny took my charges and she filled them up with water,
Then sent for Captain Farrell to be ready for the slaughter.

[chorus]
It was early in the morning, as I rose up for travel,
Up comes a band of footmen and likewise Captain Farrell.
I first produced my pistol, for she stole away my rapier,
But I couldn't shoot the water so a prisoner I was taken.

[chorus]
If anyone can aid me, it's my brother in the army,
If I can find his station down in Cork or in Killarney.
And if he'll come and save me, we'll go roving near Kilkenny,
And I swear he'll treat me better than me darling sportling Jenny.

[chorus]
Now some men take delight in the carriages a-rollin',
And others take delight in the hurley and the bowlin'.
But I take delight in the juice of the barley,
And courting pretty fair maids in the morning bright and early.

[chorus]

The Irish ballad above, "Whiskey In the Jar," was originally published in 1728 (and could well be a great deal older) and has remained a dependable hit ever since. The original author is unknown. In the last few decades it has been covered by numerous artists, including Thin Lizzy, The Pogues and (most recently and famously) Metallica.

This song celebrates the "gentleman highwayman" of the eighteenth century (sometimes even more euphemistically referred to as a "road agent"). These dashing, mounted figures (an unmounted thief was called a footpad) preyed on the carriages that traveled the roads of the eighteenth-century British Isles.

The outstanding feature of the highwayman was that whatever crimes he committed, he did them with undeniable style. This peculiar aesthetic is described in detail in the Alfred Noyes poem, "The Highwayman":

He'd a French cocked-hat on his forehead, a bunch of lace at his chin,
A coat of the claret velvet, and breeches of brown doe-skin;
They fitted with never a wrinkle: his boots were up to the thigh!

And he rode with a jewelled twinkle,
His pistol butts a-twinkle,
His rapier hilt a-twinkle, under the jewelled sky.

There's a wealth of adventurous fiction celebrating the Highway-man, but in this particular case the truth wasn't far behind the tales. The eighteenth-century highwayman was about as close to a fanta-sy role-playing character as any sort from recent real-world history could possibly be.

The most famous highwayman was probably Dick Turpin (1705—1739). By the standards of his highwayman brethren, Turpin was a rather rough sort—he definitely put the accent on the bandit side of gentleman bandit. His fame is largely based on his daring and suc-cessful life of crime, and his feat in avoiding capture for more than twelve years. After several years of banditry and highway robbery, Turpin retired from crime and set himself up as a horse dealer named John Palmer. He could have easily lived to a ripe old age as Palmer, if it wasn't for an unfortunate coincidence. A letter he wrote to his brother-in-law fell into the hands of a Mr. John Smith, a school mas-ter who had taught the young Turpin to read and write. The school-master recognized his notorious pupil's handwriting and Turpin was apprehended, convicted and hanged.

A much more romantic figure was Claude Duval. Born into a poor French family, he became a domestic servant at age fourteen, even-tually coming to England as a footman to an English duke. He soon started moonlighting as a highwayman, specializing in stagecoach robbery. Duval was remarkable for his stylish appearance and his im-peccable manners. He never made overt threats against his victims.

The pinnacle of Duval's career came when he relieved the Master of the King's Buckhounds of fifty guineas and left him tied to a tree, but he is most celebrated for an incident (reported to have happened at various places and to have involved various victims) where he re-turned part of a victim's loot in exchange for that personage's per-mission to dance with his wife on the roadside. Duval is certainly the model for all the romantic, chivalrous highwaymen that have popu-lated fiction ever since.

Other notable highwaymen include Jerry Abershawe, the English version of Billy the Kid, who started his own gang at seventeen and was hanged at twenty-two, and William "Swift Nick" Nevisham. Nevisham earned his nickname when he robbed a sailor in Kent in the morning, then rode to York, a distance of some 190 miles, by evening. In York, he located the lord mayor of the city and made his acquaintance, even entering into a wager on a bowls match with his lordship, thereby successfully securing an alibi. (Although he was cleared of robbing the sailor, he was soon found guilty of other crimes and hanged.)

The English highwayman tradition certainly had a lasting and profound effect on American popular culture, leading directly to the American fascination with bank robbers in the Old West (Jessie James, The Dalton Gang, the aforementioned Billy the Kid) and later during the Great Depression (Bonnie and Clyde, Pretty Boy Floyd, the Newton Boys).

Heroic Thieves & Treasure Hunters

Fictional thieves and bandits have been popular heroes for centuries. Probably the most famous in the English-speaking world is Robin Hood, who "robbed from the rich and gave to the poor." Robin Hood is probably based on an actual medieval English bandit, though much of the current myth has of course been embellished. In particular, the idea that Robin was a loyalist noble, the Earl of Locksley, fighting to defend the rightful king against his usurper brother, is a late-Victorian addition to the story.

Although not exactly a thief, the Scarlet Pimpernel, created by Baroness Orczy, is also an inspirational character to Rogue roleplayers. The Pimpernel used trickery, stealth and when necessary, his sword to rescue condemned French nobles from the guillotine during the Revolution.

Other famous fictional thieves include the French Arsene Lupin, by Maurice LeBlanc, and the English A. J. Raffles, by Ernest William Hornung (Hornung was brother-in-law to Sir Arthur Conan Doyle, the creator of Sherlock Holmes), both from the Victorian period. Simon Templar, the Saint, written by Leslie Charteris, was a reformed-but-still-wanted gentleman thief in the first half of the twentieth century. *Modesty Blaise* was a comic strip written by Peter O'Donnell and illustrated by Jim Holdaway. The title character was a sexy thief turned international super-spy, and the strip had a profound influence on the extravagant espionage thrillers of the 1960s.

Returning to the heroic fantasy genre, J. R. R. Tolkein performed a great service to roleplayers ever after with the publication of *The Hobbit*. A traditional thief would not normally be considered an appropriate hero for a children's novel in the late 1930s, but Tolkein got around this by making Bilbo Baggins a thief not by training, but by nature. It seems that due to their small size, keen eyes, quick reflexes and natural gift for stealth, perfectly respectable Hobbits just happen to be ideal thieves. Furthermore, Bilbo's mission was to recover goods that had already been stolen by a murderous dragon. Thus, in one stroke Tolkein created an enduring fantasy archetype, the halfling thief (represented in *WoW* by Gnome Rogues), and offered a viable optional motivation to those who like the idea of thief characters, but don't want to deal with the moral questions the concept raises.

Other memorable fantasy thieves are Fritz Lieber's Fafhrd and the Gray Mouser, and the *Thieves' World* stories, written by various authors, edited by Robert Lynn Asprin (later joined by Lynn Abbey) and published throughout the 1980s (additional Abbey novels were published in 2002). Stephen Brust's Vlad Taltos is a remarkably gifted assassin in a unique high-fantasy world. Brust is currently about halfway through a projected seventeen-volume series chronicling Taltos' life and adventures.

Playing the Rogue

Use your Stealth! While in Stealth, you can safely watch your enemies to find a pattern, making it easier to divide and conquer. You can find the path of least resistance to your targets. You can rob them blind without them ever knowing you were there.

Don't be suicidally hard core. If the enemies guarding your goal are too tough to safely take out, just sneak past them and forget about them—you're a thief, that's what you do.

Use your stuns. Sap doesn't work on bosses, but almost anyone else can be taken out of the fight before it starts. Once you're exposed, you can stun, which is great because stunned enemies aren't hitting you.

If it has a pocket or a lock, pick it. Mounts are expensive. Training is expensive. Healing potions are expensive. The Auction House is fun, and very expensive. Supplement your income any way you can.

Keep an eye on your Health and your Energy. Sprint and Vanish won't do you any good if you don't realize you need to use them. When you're in trouble, use your built-in escape hatches.

Inflicting big damage draws aggro. In a group, try to let your tank draw aggro before you deliver big hits. If you gain aggro and can't lose it, use the Feint skill or Vanish.

Most of your abilities have "cooldown timers," meaning you have to wait before using them again. Learn them and watch them.

MAGE

RACES: Dwarf, Gnome, Human, Troll, Undead

PREFERRED WEAPONS: Stave, wands; later daggers and one-handed swords

ARMOR ALLOWED: Cloth

POWER LINES: Arcane (defense and support), Fire (high-damage attacks), Frost (holds); later Portal (long-range movement)

SOLO POTENTIAL: Good

The Mage in WoW

Mages are a ranged-damage-dealing class that wield the forces of magic to strike down their enemies. They use either frost- or fire-based spells, as well as manipulation of raw arcane energy.

Mages are physically quite weak. They can do little damage with weapons, and can't handle many attacks before succumbing. Their strength lies in killing or incapacitating their enemies before that becomes a problem.

Mages can wear cloth armor, and only cloth armor. They are proficient with staves, and can be trained to use daggers and one-handed swords for melee. They can also use magical wands to deal ranged damage without using Mana or ammunition.

The Mage's primary stats are Intelligence, Stamina and Spirit. Intelligence raises maximum Mana, and increases the chance of spells scoring a critical hit. Stamina bolsters a Mage's weak hit points, while Spirit increases Mana and Health regeneration.

Mages reign supreme at destroying groups of monsters. There is no class with better area-of-affect abilities. For this reason alone, they are a required component of most high-level instance groups.

In a group, Mages are called upon to do more than just dish out damage. Polymorph or area-of-effect spells should be used when fac-

ing multiple enemies. Intelligence boosts, providing food and water
and teleportation home are also expected. When alone, a Mage need
only worry about keeping monsters from striking, often via Frost
spells, or simply dealing damage as quickly as possible, with Fire.

Starting at Level 30, Mages can learn to teleport to any of the three
major racial cities. At Level 40, they are able to open a portal that
their whole group can use. Both of these require the use of spell components, so be sure to always have them. Mages can also summon
food and drink from thin air, to replenish the Health and Mana of
any that need it.

Hermes Trimegistus

Hermes Trimegistus, in Western occult lore, is the first and greatest magician. Today, even among hard-core occult believers, most
don't hold that there was an actual historical person named Hermes
Trimegistus. He's more of a symbol of the universal magican. However, occult lore is nothing if not intriguingly complex, and it's quite
possible to regard the same figure as an abstract symbol, a pagan de-
ity and a historical personage, all at the same time.

The name Hermes Trimegistus (Greek meaning "Thrice-Great
Hermes") seems to have come out of an ancient Greek fad for lining
up Greek mythology with Egyptian mythology. Hermes Trimegistus
is the name for the divine entity you get when you combine Hermes
(who, in addition to his well-known gig as messenger of the gods,
was also the god of magicians) with Thoth, the Egyptian god of magic and mystical wisdom.

It must be remembered that at the time of the flourishing of Greek
literature and philosophy (the seventh and sixth centuries B.C., roughly speaking), the Egyptian civilization was already a couple of thousand years old. The Greeks, an urbane and well-traveled race, knew
the Egyptians very well, and held a high opinion of their mystical
acumen. A hint of the Greeks' regard for the Egyptians as keepers of
secret knowledge can be found in Plato's account of the sinking of
Atlantis, which he claims to have obtained from a secret archive of
Egyptian records dating back more than 9,000 years.

And it wasn't just the Greeks who regarded the Egyptians as great magicians. Even the Bible records a remarkable encounter in the Book of Exodus between Moses and the court magicians of Pharaoh. Moses is attempting to convince a dubious Pharaoh to let him lead the Israelites out of Egypt to the Promised Land. Moses goes before Pharaoh with his brother Aaron and, as a sign, Aaron throws his walking staff on the ground in front of Pharaoh where it becomes a snake. However, Pharaoh calls his magicians, and they are all able to throw their rods on the ground to produce snakes. The next day Moses turns the Nile River to blood, but the Magicians are also able to turn water into blood. Then Moses brings up a plague of frogs, but the magicians are able to produce frogs as well. It's only when Moses turns the dust into a plague of lice that the magicians are unable to match his feat and give in (nonetheless it takes several more plagues before Pharaoh actually releases the Israelites).

Hermes Trimegistus is said to have been the author of tens of thousands of ancient works. In fact, he's credited by some as being pretty much the first to write down pretty much everything. The most important hypothetical works of Hermes in occult tradition are said to be 42 scrolls which record all the training and duties of Egyptian priests. These "42 Essential Texts" were held to be the foundation of all magical thought and practice. All mystical thought and writing which claims to be descended from those 42 scrolls (which, depending on the imagination of the particular mystic doing the claiming, could be almost anything) is classified as "Hermetic" philosophy. The 42 Essential Texts were spoken of highly by the early Christian church father Clement of Alexandria, leaving open an argument ever since for those who wanted to claim to be both good Christians and Hermetic practitioners. The alchemists of the Middle Ages and Renaissance were particularly notable examples of this trend. (It should probably be emphasized, just for the record, that no ancient work currently in existence can be reliably traced to an ancient Egyptian writer named Thoth or Hermes or any variant thereof, although of course there are many ancient Egyptian mystical writings, and there are plenty of works of more or less dubious nature that claim to be the recovered wisdom of Hermes Trimegistus.)

So if Thoth, the Thrice-Great Hermes, ever did walk the earth as a mortal man, who was he? The twentieth-century psychic Edgar

Cayce claimed that his visions revealed that an architect and engineer named Thoth or Hermes escaped the destruction of Atlantis, whereupon he came to Egypt to build the pyramids. More ancient traditions say that he was Adam, the first man, or a grandson of Adam. One popular theory says that he was a contemporary and colleague of Moses, and that both men received secret mystical teachings from God, which Moses passed down to the Jewish mystics, and Hermes Trimegistus passed down to pagan magicians. Some traditions claim that the original Hermes Trimegistus had several wives and numerous descendants, all likewise named Hermes, raising the possibility of a whole dynasty of magicians named Hermes Trimegistus (which would certainly help account for his reported prolific writings).

The Magi

Our word "mage" comes from the word "Magi." The original Magi were the priestly caste of the Medes, one of the peoples who made up ancient Persia. When Cyrus established the Persian Empire in the sixth century B.C., the Magi undertook a decades-long struggle against imperial power. They were finally suppressed by the third emperor, Darius I. Although their political power was curtailed, they continued to exist as a priestly caste of the Zoroastrian religion. They were especially well known for the interpretation of dreams.

Over the following centuries, the Magi began to spread out. They were probably instrumental in bringing the influential cult of the Persian god Mithra to Greece and Rome. Because of their learning and exotic, foreign origins, many street magicians in Greece began referring to themselves as *magos*—partakers in the wisdom of the Magi. These practitioners ranged from something very like our stage magicians to out-and-out con men, and they are responsible for giving us the modern terms "mage," "magician" and "magic"—all derived from their appropriation of the name of the Magi. In the Christian New Testament, several of these false Magi are recorded as clashing with the Apostles.

By far the most famous Magi in history were the three "Wise Men" who, according to the Gospels, brought gifts of gold, frankincense and myrrh to the baby Jesus. Many of the traditions we associate with these figures are not supported by the Biblical account—for example, nowhere in the Gospels does it say there were three of them. We also don't know their names or whether they found the infant Jesus while he was still in the manger, or whether they arrived later when the Holy Family had obtained more permanent lodgings. There is absolutely no suggestion that the three were "kings" of anything.

We are told, however, that they came from "the East," and used astrology to divine the time and place of Jesus' birth ("...we have seen his star...") and that they brought gifts fitted for royalty (frankincense and myrrh are both resins used in incense, perfume, medicine and embalming preparations). These mysterious personages definitely don't seem to be pretenders, but rather Magi of the old school—mystically astute and influential in worldly matters.

Merlin

The current popular conception of a wizard—an elderly, bearded and robed man with a staff—can be traced directly back to the figure of Merlin, mentor of King Arthur and court wizard of Camelot.

Merlin appears to have been effectively the creation of Geoffrey of Monmouth, the imaginative twelfth-century historian who also gives us the definitive early account of King Arthur. Geoffrey's Merlin seems to be a conflation of two earlier legends. One is the story in the ninth-century text *Historia Britonum* about the supernatural birth of a boy named Ambrosius. The other is a series of Welsh legends about Myrddin, a hermit and prophet (referred to as a "wild man of the wood"). Myrddin may have been a real person, but possibly named Lailoken.

Geoffrey brings the two together to create a character he names Merlinus Ambrosius (it has been suggested that Geoffrey, a monk, unilaterally changed the named "Myrddin" to "Merlin," because he did not want the name to sound like the vulgar French word *merde*).

In Geoffrey's account, Merlin is the son of a nun of royal birth and a demon who impregnates her with a view toward creating an antichrist. However, the half-human infant is discovered and baptized at birth, allowing him to control his demonic nature and choose between good and evil. Nonetheless, from his father, Merlin receives an unprecedented gift for sorcery and prophecy.

Geoffrey tells how King Vortigern was being handicapped in his ongoing war against the Saxons by a fortress under construction that kept collapsing. The king's seers advise him that he should sacrifice a "boy without a father" to remove the curse. The only lad who fits this description is, of course, the young Merlin. However, when he's fetched before the king, Merlin offers a prophecy of his own, offering a contrasting interpretation of the cursed fortress (it involves two subterranean dragons engaged in a violent political allegory beneath the building). Merlin's version is convincing enough that all thought of sacrifice is abandoned.

Geoffrey also has Merlin responsible for magically transporting the stones of Stonehenge from Ireland to their present site via magic. He is said to have accomplished this feat in a single night (for more Stonehenge lore, see **Druids**, p. 231). According to Geoffrey's account, Merlin lived for at least 150 years.

Geoffrey firmly establishes the root of the connection between Merlin and Arthur—that Merlin was instrumental in Arthur's conception (by magically disguising Arthur's father, Uther, to enable him to seduce Arthur's mother away from her husband), and that the wizard later became the boy's tutor. Of course, the tale would be greatly expanded over the next 900 years, by Thomas Mallory and many others.

The traditional account of Merlin's death appears to have arisen in French tales a century or so after Geoffrey. The story goes that Merlin desired a young woman named Nimue (sometimes called Vivien, and often identified with that ubiquitous and mysterious Authurian figure, the Lady of the Lake) and took her traveling with him. Nimue made the wizard promise not to use magic to seduce her, but was still afraid of her eventual fate in his hands. She tricks Merlin into turning his powers over to her (the exact means of her trickery vary depending on the version of the story) and either kills him, imprisons him or drives him mad, again depending on the version of the story. In Thomas Mallory's definitive English work, *Le Morte D'Arthur*, Nimue imprisons Merlin forever, and then takes over his post as advisor and court wizard to Arthur.

Merlin's Children

Modern fantasy is very much in love with Mages. Of course, by far the most popular fantasy in the world right now are the *Harry Potter* stories by J. K. Rowling, which tell the story of a modern boy being schooled in magic at Hogwarts School of Witchcraft and Wizardry, with the very Merlinesque figure of Albus Dumbledore as headmaster. In fact, this seven-volume series (as of this writing, six of the books are complete) where virtually every major character is a Mage, is all by itself an excellent catalog of the various sorts of Mages found in contemporary fantasy. In addition to Dumbledore and our intrepid young hero Harry, there's the secretive Professor Snape, the fierce and brooding, but heroic Sirius Black, the compassionate and loyal Weasley family, the elegantly sinister Malfoy clan and of course the utterly decadent, immensely powerful Lord Voldemort, as well as many more.

Of course, as with everything else, Tolkien must be mentioned. His Gandalf the Gray is second only to Merlin himself as a prototype for the fantasy wizard. Although actually an immortal spiritual being of great power, Gandalf takes on the form of an old man, wandering the world with his staff and broad-brimmed hat in a constant quest to foil the plots of the Dark Lord Sauron. Wizards and their ways are a favorite target of Terry Pratchett's wit in his *Discworld* novels. The wizards of the faculty of Pratchett's Unseen University are an irresistible send-up of the stereotype of the crotchety old wizard, and the whole "magical school" genre of fantasy (many of Pratchett's tales predate Rowling's Harry Potter books, but because both authors draw on so much of the same source material, Unseen University still functions very well as a send-up of Hogwarts). Pratchett's wizards appear in most of his *Discworld* tales, but see *Sourcery*, *Lords and Ladies*, or *The Last Continent* for good introductions to these types of characters.

There are so many variations of the Mage character out there that we'll content ourselves with just one final recommendation. For an engaging nuts-and-bolts look at magic from a modern prospective, see the classic *Incomplete Enchanter* series by L. Sprague deCamp and Fletcher Pratt.

Playing the Mage

Mages should be on the lookout for gear that increases spell damage, or boosts Mana regeneration—both can be more valuable than simple stats.

Frost spells focus on skills that can slow or freeze opponents, supplemented by talents to increase this ability. The high-end talent tree provides protection against attacks via ice shields. While Frost spells may not be high in damage, they allow a Mage to stay out of striking distance and attack from afar.

Fire spells are higher in damage than their Frost counterparts, especially since several can deal additional burning damage over time. Fire talents increase the damage and critical chances of Fire spells.

Frost spells are especially effective against non-player characters, who often don't have a means to escape slow or stunning effects. On the other hand, the high damage of Fire spells is effective at quickly dispatching other players in PvP combat.

The Arcane tree provides a means to manipulate magic to defend yourself or your teammates, increase Intelligence, and cast the mighty Polymorph. Arcane talents will enhances a Mage's casting abilities, and provide bonuses that affect all types of spells.

Mana pool is your lifeblood. Be sure to have a stock of potions, water and summoned Mana gems for replenishment. If you are low on Health, Mana can be used as a shield, or to slow a monster so you can escape. But without Mana, you are helpless.

Effective talent builds usually utilize either the Fire or Frost trees, and throw in varying amounts of Arcane talents for support. While Frost and Fire combinations are possible, they are much more challenging. The Arcane tree provides powerful staples, such as improvements to Counterspell and Arcane Explosion.

When fighting in groups, start off casting slowly and let the tank attack on his own for a few seconds. Dealing a lot of damage quickly will generate too much Threat, and get yourself attacked and killed. Mages don't have any way to effectively reduce aggression once attacked, so they must avoid going overboard at all costs. If you are attacked, a quick Frost spell can be used to put some distance between you and your adversary. You should then cease casting until your tank can retake control.

Area-of-effect spells can be a very efficient means to gain experience. Learn where easier monsters congregate, so that you can wipe out whole groups at a time, earning experience much faster than one-on-one combat. Just be careful not to get yourself overwhelmed by opponents. This process becomes much easier if you have a friend to take damage or heal you.

Because instant-cast spells can be used while moving, and cannot be interrupted, they are pivotal in PvP combat. Get to know the cooldown time of your instants, so they can be cast as soon as they're ready. Since taking damage increases casting time, only use the longer spells when you are not the focus of attack.

Warrior

RACES: All
PREFERRED WEAPONS: Any
ARMOR ALLOWED: Any
POWER LINES: Battle Stance (balanced offense and defense), Berserker Stance (offensive abilities), Defensive Stance
SOLO POTENTIAL: Excellent

The Warrior in WoW

The primary attributes of the Warrior are Stamina (hit points) and Strength (attack ability), in that order. Agility (armor class) is of some use, but never more than Stamina. Any race can be a Warrior, as it is essentially a "generic" class that is defined by its talents and gear. There are three basic "flavors" of Warrior, based upon what talents are taken: Berserker, Fighter and Tank. Since WoW allows a character to re-select talent selections (for a price), Warriors can experiment a bit and evolve their "flavor" as they advance.

Warriors start out with Battle Stance, which is the generic stance. At Level 20, they can quest to pick up Defensive Stance, which reduces damage output and increases damage mitigation. At Level 30, they can quest for Berserker Stance, which increases their chance for getting criticals as well as increasing the damage taken from enemies. Some talents work in all stances, others require specific stances.

Berserkers focus on the Fury talent tree, live in Berserker Stance, typically use two-handed weapons, are all about massive damage, and are the best way to be a solo Warrior. The downsides are next-to-zero aggro management and the worst damage mitigation of the three, which make them ineffective as a group tank.

Fighters focus on the Arms talent tree, use Battle Stance, and are the utility Warriors—jacks-of-all-trades who can do a bit of everything...decent at solo, decent in a group, a balanced mix of abilities.

Tanks focus on the Protection talent tree, are almost always in Defensive Stance, and are the foundation a group is built upon. They can take the most punishment and control the most aggro of any class in the game, but their damage output is poor and it's difficult to solo...they can absorb hits forever, but they can't kill the enemy. At the highest levels, Tanks are in very high demand because no one can take the punishment delivered by the highest-end enemies like a tank.

Rage is the fuel for all Warriors. Rogues have Energy, others have Mana; Warriors channel Rage into powering their abilities. Rage is generated every time the Warrior hits an enemy, or an enemy hits him. The more Rage the Warrior has, the more he can do, so he needs to be in the mix, taunting enemies to hit him and always fighting to keep his Rage flowing. There are three talents that are Rage-related: Tactical Mastery allows you to keep some Rage as you change stances (normally Rage empties on a stance change), Anger Management slows the rate of decay on Rage (it fades over time) and Unbridled Wrath increases the Rage generated on hits.

Brawlers & Soldiers

Where to begin? Where to begin? Most of the heroic ideals that *World of Warcraft* is based on are descended from some fairly specific prototypes, but the Warrior? Warriors are everywhere. Has there ever been a human society that doesn't respect and venerate the brave and the strong? You could even say, with only a little exaggeration, that once you strip out the Rogues, Mystics and Holy Men from human legend, pretty much everything that's left is stories about warriors.

But we have to start somewhere, so why not the Bible? For the time it was written, the books that the Christians call the Old Testament are surprisingly unfriendly to heroism and derring-do. The Bible tends to be much more interested in how wise, humble and (most of all) obedient someone is, than in how well they can sling a sword.

(Not every religion has this uncomfortable relationship between physical prowess and godly wisdom. The sacred Hindu epics—Ra-

mayana, *Mahabharata* and the *Bhagavad Gita*—tend to star divinely endowed warriors who pause to reflect at length on the meaning of life and man's relationship to the divine, before hopping into their war chariots and galloping off to try their best to turn each other into hamburger.)

There are, however, a couple of definite heroic types to be found in the Good Book.

Let's start out with Samson, one of the judges who governed the Hebrew people in the centuries between the Exodus and the institution of the monarchy. Now, in general the Judges (as chronicled in the Bible book of the same name) were a pretty contemplative lot, chosen for their wisdom, piety and political acumen. Samson, however, was different. He had been given, at birth, a unique blessing from God—he would be gifted with supernatural strength, but only on the condition that he never cut his hair. Since the Israelites were, at the time, on the short end of a drawn-out war with the Philistines, it made sense to make their mightiest warrior a judge.

Samson was not, to put it mildly, of a particularly holy disposition. He definitely had a taste for partying, and he had a particular weakness for the ladies. Still, as long as his hair stayed unmolested, he remained the strongest guy there was. Every Sunday School kid learns about Samson's exploits, including killing a lion with his bare hands, escaping from an ambush in the city of Gaza by tearing the main city gates off the wall and carrying them away with him and, probably most celebrated, the time he allowed himself to be tied up and taken prisoner, only to break the ropes that tied him, pick up the jawbone of an ass and beat 1000 Philistines to death with it.

Of course, Samson came to a bad end, when he allowed the temptress Delilah to weasel the secret of his strength out of him, after which he was shorn in his sleep, allowing the Philistines to tie him up, bind him and enslave him. Having taught Samson a lesson about humility, God allows him one last burst of supernatural strength. When the Philistines bring Samson into the temple of their god Baal to mock his defeat, Samson pulls down the pillars that support the roof, killing all the important Philistines, as well as himself.

Probably the greatest warrior in the Bible is King David, he of Michelangelo's famously immodest statue. Unlike Samson, David was a thinker—a poet and musician, and a man of genuine faith. When he fought, he always fought strategically. Everybody knows the story of how, as a mere boy, he defeated the unstoppable enemy champion Goliath by refusing to play to his enemy's strengths. Instead of meeting the giant in an unwinnable hand-to-hand battle, he took him out at range, with one well-placed sling stone. In his later career, David's signature in battle was to defeat a much larger force with only a handful of men.

The early part of David's story is dominated by the murderous jealousy his predecessor, King Saul, feels toward his overly gifted protégé. David refuses to kill his rightful king (despite several chances to do so), so he has to stay on the run until Saul is slain in battle, along with his sons, clearing the way for David to take the throne. In later life David, like Samson before him, gets himself in trouble over a woman, when he betrays all his beliefs and ideals in his pursuit of Bathsheba, the wife of one of his commanders. Eventually, however, David comes to his senses and repents, and Bathsheba becomes his queen and the mother of Solomon, Israel's greatest king.

These two figures—Samson and David—exemplify a split that holds true throughout most heroic legends. Basically, there are two kinds of warrior celebrated in story. One sort is the brawler—loud, riotous and not particularly bright, he follows his appetites and his gut feelings, often to his own detriment. He's a hero simply by virtue of being stronger, tougher and meaner than anybody else. The other sort is the tactician soldier. He's disciplined, and he uses his brains as much as his brawn. Although physically formidable, he becomes a great hero by thinking his way out of problems, and never letting the situation overwhelm him. Many modern fantasy games recognize this split by making a distinction between "fighters" and "barbarians" as two different character types, but this separation is not found in *World of Warcraft*.

Greek Heroes

The popular heroes of the Greeks were all Warriors. It was a martial culture, and bravery and physical prowess were valued above all. Both brawlers and tacticians were well represented in the Greek culture.

Perhaps the ultimate example of the brawler hero is, of course, Hercules. Half-god and gifted with unmatched strength, Hercules never thinks when he can act. In many ways Hercules and Samson are the exact same character—thoughtless, arrogant and slaves to their own appetites—they are even both known for wearing lion skins as their garment of choice. It's an amazing fact of human myth and legend that the same fundamental figures keep showing up all over the world, with no obvious connections between them. Samson and Hercules are both humbled in their pride by enslavement. The goddess Hera makes Hercules go mad and kill his wife and children; to atone for that deed he must become a slave for twelve years to Eurystheus, king of Tyrens and Mycenae. It is during this time that Hercules is forced to perform his legendary twelve labors.

The other great brawler of Greek legends is Achilles. The son of a mortal father and Thetis, a water goddess, the infant Achilles was dipped by his mother in the river Styx in an effort to make him immortal. In doing so, she held the boy by the heel, so that it wasn't immersed. Although better groomed than Hercules, Achilles is also arrogant in his supernatural invulnerability, and a slave to his own passions. He is, in fact, a sulky prima donna whose self-serving pride threatens to undermine the whole Trojan War. His moodiness leads to the death of his best friend. Achilles dies when he's wounded by an arrow to the heel, his only vulnerable spot.

Among the more thoughtful soldier heroes, one of the greatest is Odysseus, the hero of the *Odyssey*. Although a brave fighter, skilled commander and legendary mariner, Odysseus is, above all, a thinker. In complete contrast to Hercules and Achilles, most of the stories of Odysseus involve him winning the day by using his head. In one of the earliest episodes of the Trojan War, Odysseus is sent to collect Achilles, who has been disguised as a girl by his mother, who does not wish him to go to war. Suspecting the truth, but unable to establish just which "maiden" is Achilles without offering deadly insult to somebody's daughter, Odysseus fills a room with all sorts of gowns, jewels and female finery, plus one fine set of full armor. By observing the maidens, Odysseus finds the one who's more interested in the armor than in the dresses, and is able to serve Achilles with his draft notice.

There are countless other examples of Odysseus' thoughtful nature in both the *Illiad* and the *Odyssey*—the famous Trojan Horse stratagem was Odysseus' idea. In addition to a quick wit, Odysseus (who, significantly, does not have any godly blood or supernatural gifts) has patience and a strong moral consistency that allows him to return to his wife and son after a ten-year siege at Troy, followed by a further ten years of cursed voyaging.

Perhaps the most perfect example of the soldier that we get from the Greeks was not a legend at all, but the remarkable Alexander the Great. By all accounts a handsome, brave and dashing warrior, Alexander was also one of the greatest military minds ever known. In a reign of just twelve years Alexander held together his father's union of the fractious Greek city states, and also conquered Persia, Egypt and most of India. He succumbed to disease (possibly malaria, typhoid or viral encephalitis) at the age of only thirty-two.

Beowulf

The very first hero of English literature is also one of the most perfect warriors known to legend. The epic poem Beowulf was composed around 700 A.D. by an unknown writer drawing on far older Scandinavian legends. Although most literary works of the time were composed in Latin, the *Beowulf* poet chose to compose in his native Old English tongue.

The Beowulf story has three parts. In the first part Beowulf, a prince of the Geat tribe, comes to the Heorot, the hall of Hrothgar, a Danish king. Hrothgar has a problem—a monster named Grendel is slaughtering his warriors. Beowulf, the top-ranked young hero of the day, has heard about the Grendel problem and comes to deal with it.

Although Grendel has been ripping through Hrothgar's big Viking warriors at a rate of up to thirty per night, Beowulf takes him on bare-handed. Beowulf ambushes the monster in the hall, and tears off his arm, fatally wounding him.

In the second part of the poem, Grendel's even more terrible mother comes looking for revenge, kidnapping one of Hrothgar's top counselors. Beowulf tracks the witch to her underwater lair and kills her there on her own turf.

In the final part of the poem, we find a much older Beowulf who has become an honored king. The aging hero forsakes his duties and comfortable existence, however, in favor of a final battle with a great dragon. In this battle both the beast and Beowulf meet their doom.

Beowulf is probably closer to the brawler archetype than the soldier. He's superhumanly tough and not much given to introspection. At the same time, he doesn't show much of the self-absorption or tragic capriciousness of Hercules, Samson or Achilles. If he comes off a bit boastful, it's just because he knows he's the baddest thing around, and is unencumbered by false modesty. Beowulf is an ideal Anglo-Saxon warrior, not a tragic hero.

Modern Literary Warriors

The swaggering, swashbuckling brawler is certainly the most popular hero in the modern-fantasy genre, so we'll only have time to look at a handful of high points.

One of the first true high-fantasy tales of the twentieth century was *The Worm Ouroboros* by E. R. Eddison, published in 1922. The protagonists of this novel are four warrior brothers of the Demon tribe (despite the name, the Demon brothers are mortal men, although men built on an epic, heroic scale). Eddison's complex, Shakespearian prose style will put off some readers, but the novel still stands as a masterpiece of fantastical imagery and the heroic spirit.

Certainly the greatest fantasy warrior to emerge from twentieth century literature is Robert E. Howard's signature character, Conan the Barbarian. Howard's many tales of Conan tell the story of his steel-thewed Cimmerian hero from his youth as a thief and pirate, through a long career as a mercenary and wanderer, until he at last finds his way to the throne of the mightiest empire of his world. Of course, a crown does not sit easy on Conan's shaggy head. Conan has been particularly lucky among popular pulp heroes in that his adaptations to other media tend to add to, rather than diminish, his mystique. These include the paintings of Conan done by master fantasy artist Frank Frazetta, the long-running Marvel comic book series originally written by Roy Thomas and illustrated by Barry Windsor-Smith and even the big-budget movies starting Arnold Schwarzenegger. While some of the creative decisions made by the filmmakers of the Conan movies can certainly be quibbled with, there can be no doubt that the young Arnold perfectly embodied Howard's hero, and made him a lasting pop culture icon.

Between 1932 and 1936, Howard published seventeen Conan stories in *Weird Tales* magazine. He finished four more that weren't published (one did appear during Howard's lifetime as a non-Conan story), and left four more unfinished at the time of his death.

Robert E. Howard was raised in Cross Plains, Texas, the son of the town doctor. A sickly child, he grew up idolizing the brawny, brawling "roughneck" oil workers that came to the town during its brief oil boom. (As an adult, Howard would take up exercise and develop an impressive physique.) Howard seldom traveled more than fifty miles from his tiny Texas home. After high school, he mostly educated himself (his only college was a few business courses that he seems to have had little enthusiasm for). He started writing for publication while still in his teens and, although pulp writers in the '30s were paid only a pittance, Howard was prolific enough that he actually became one of the more financially stable persons in town. (This was, of course, during the Great Depression, and in remote rural towns "financial stability" was a very relative commodity.)

Although one of the most promising literary talents of the pulp era, Howard's career came to a tragic end in 1936, when his mother lay dying of a long and debilitating illness. In despair, Howard killed himself with a pistol shot to the head. The story of Howard's life, and particularly his tentative and bittersweet romance with schoolteacher Novalyne Price, is told in the 1996 movie *The Whole Wide World*, starring Vincent D'Onofrio as Howard.

Of course, as with every other element of modern fantasy, J. R. R. Tolkien made a lasting contribution to our concept of the fantasy warrior. There are several notable warriors in *The Lord of the Rings*, including the tempted and conflicted noble brothers Boromir and Faramir of Gondor. Another memorable set of sibling warriors is Eomer the horse-lord, and his occasional cross-dressing sister Eowyn.

Probably the most important contribution by Tolkien to the convention of the warrior in fantasy gaming, however, is Gimli the Dwarf. Gimli in *The Lord of the Rings* (together with his kinsmen, the companions of Thorin Oakenshield in its prequel, *The Hobbit*) marks the origin of the stoical, armored and axe-wielding Dwarven warrior, which has been a staple of the genre from the early editions of *Dungeons & Dragons®*, right up to *World of Warcraft*.

Playing the Warrior

A skill that everyone has, but that is most important to the Warrior, is Defense. The Defense skill dictates how accurate an enemy will be in hitting the Warrior and, if the enemy hits, how much damage it does, and how often it gets a critical hit. Defense is in increments of 5/level, with Warriors getting a +10, so at Level 60 the max natural Warrior Defense is 310. The higher the Warrior's Defense is compared to the level of the enemy, the less likely the enemy is to hit the Warrior, much less get a critical hit (and vice versa—the lower the Warrior's Defense is, the more vulnerable he or she is). For example, at Level 60, a Warrior with a 400+ Defense skill has a very small chance of taking a critical hit from a Level 60 enemy, drastically increasing his ability to mitigate damage. Consequently, when selecting between two pieces of gear, Defense is something to be seriously considered, especially for tanks.

Warriors can wear any armor (though they should always go for the highest protection available) and use any weapon (assuming they've paid for the training). Berserkers look for high-damage two-handed weapons, fighters for a broad mix and tanks for a solid shield and good one-handed weapon. When selecting a weapon, there are a number of factors to consider, such as the stats it gives, its damage and speed and what type of Warrior you are. Tanks want stamina and speed, berserkers want massive damage and so forth.

Not all damage is melee, and the higher level the Warrior, the greater the chance of encountering non-melee damage, which means that gear decisions should eventually start including bonuses to Resists. Resists start at 0 and represent the Warrior's ability to reduce some or all of the non-melee damage aimed at him. Many Warriors carry multiple sets of gear for different types of fighting, with (for example) fire-resist gear for fire-using creatures, and melee gear for melee enemies.

WARLOCK

RACES: Gnome, Human, Orc, Undead
PREFERRED WEAPONS: Daggers, wands; later staves, one-handed swords
ARMOR ALLOWED: Cloth
POWER LINES: Affliction (debuffs, DoT, etc.), Demonology (buffs and support), Destruction (offensive damage); also pets
SOLO POTENTIAL: Very Good

The Warlock in WoW

Warlocks are crafty users of shadow magic, and are particularly keen on summoning spells. Because of this, their primary stats are Intelligence, Spirit and Stamina. They can only wear cloth armor (which is sort of like clothes, only more expensive).

Warlocks are the grown-up version of the skinny little kid in grade school who likes to spread rumors, get other people mad at each other and then watch the resultant fight from a safe distance. Since one typically doesn't get much melee practice while gleefully cackling in the corner, Warlocks tend to be pretty weak at hand-to-hand combat.

Warlocks usually use daggers or one-handed swords in the primary hand, and off-hand items in the other. Although they can use staves, off-hand items (such as those that provide Intelligence and Spirit boosts) are usually more helpful. However, the most important weapon for a Warlock is a good wand. Remember, a Warlock doesn't dirty her hands with direct combat—that's what minions are for!

The distinguishing factor between a Warlock and other magic users is the Warlock's ability to summon minions. When not washing the car or mowing the yard, minions are valuable allies that can act as co-casters, irresistible allies or disposable tanks. Minions make the Warlock a strong solo class.

Warlocks get a new minion every ten levels. While only one minion can be active at a time, minions can be dismissed and recalled at will. Summoning a minion costs one soul shard, which can easily be generated by capturing the shrieking, hopeless, eternal souls of an expiring creature. The only drawback of the shards is that they each take a slot in a bag—they do not stack.

Warlock—The Word

"Warlock" is an interesting and ancient word. Since early medieval times, its main use has been to designate a male witch (although the word "witch" is not absolutely exclusively female, it does often have that connotation in English). In this sense, popular television shows like *Bewitched* and *Buffy the Vampire Slayer* actually use the term correctly. One picaresque medieval legend says that witches ride brooms, while warlocks ride pitchforks.

The root from which the word is derived, the old English word *waerloga*, means literally, "oath breaker." (*Waerloga* is also sometimes used to refer to the devil.) Under this connotation a Warlock is seen as someone who professes pious morality in public, but secretly betrays his faith by practicing the dark arts.

Warlocks are not, then, traditionally viewed as being summoners of spirits (except in the sense that witches were believed to consort and make deals with demons at the Black Mass).

Several alternative derivations for the word Warlock have been suggested, however. One, more interesting to *WoW* players, theorizes that the word is derived from the Old Norse term *vard-lokkur*, which literally means "a summoner of spirits."

It should be noted that modern Wiccans and certain other neo-pagans, who may embrace the word "witch" (which is derived from a word meaning "wise"), regard the word "warlock" as a medieval slander, and find it offensive when applied to their practitioners.

Solomon and His Key

Although the practice in not historically associated with the word "warlock," there is a rich and ancient magical tradition involving wizards who summon spirits to do their bidding. In occult lore, the greatest of all magical summoners is held to be King Solomon.

Solomon was a real person; the third king of Israel, and the son of King David (see **Warriors**, p. 257). Under his long rule Israel expanded its borders (relying more on diplomacy and trade than violent conquest) to become a small empire. Solomon's empire was the largest realm ever ruled by the Jews, right up through the present day.

According to the Bible, Solomon was blessed with an almost superhuman degree of wisdom. He is credited as the author of the Bible books of Proverbs, Ecclesiastes and the Song of Solomon (sometimes referred to collectively as the "Wisdom Books").

Solomon is famous for his eponymous "Judgement of Solomon," where he used shrewd reverse psychology to discover which of two women, who both claimed the same infant son, was the real mother. Solomon, playing the role of the jaded despot to the hilt, decrees that the boy should be split down the middle and half given to each woman. One of the claimants agrees, on the principle that if she can't have the child at least the other woman can't either. The other is willing to give the child up to save its life. Solomon, of course, instantly changes direction and gives the child to the woman who put its welfare ahead of her own.

Also well known is the incident where Solomon entertains the Queen of Sheba, a very mysterious African potentate. His 700 wives and 300 concubines are another part of his legend.

Probably Solomon's most celebrated achievement, however, is that he built the first permanent Jewish temple in Jerusalem. And this is where his story gets all occult.

The building of the temple (early in the tenth century B.C.) is exhaustively chronicled in the Bible, and nowhere does that book suggest that it was accomplished via anything other than human labor. For centuries, however, mystics of the Jewish, Christian and Moslem faith have said that Solomon also enslaved a great host of spirits to assist with the building. Solomon is credited with summoning angels, natural spirits (djinni, see below) and even demons to work for him.

He did this, the legends say, through the power of his signet ring, the Seal of Solomon. The ring was said to be inscribed with the True

Name of God, and no spiritual being was able to resist its power. It also allowed Solomon to talk to animals.

One colorful Arab legend tells how the demon Sakhr tricked one of Solomon's wives into giving him the ring. The demon then took Solomon's form and ruled in his place for forty days (some versions of the tale say forty years) while the true king wandered the earth as a pauper. Eventually, however, Sakhr threw the ring into the sea. Imagine his surprise when the ring was swallowed by a fish, and the fish was caught and served...to Solomon. For punishment, Solomon made Sakhr build a huge mosque all by himself.

Perhaps the most important book in European occultism is the *Lesser Key of Solomon* (or *Lemegeton Clavicula Salomonis*—*Lemegeton* for short—in Latin). There was an earlier book called simply the *Key of Solomon* which concerned itself mostly with the raising of the dead and other dark arts.

The *Lesser Key* deals with summoning supernatural entities. Despite the attribution to Solomon, it was probably written in the seventeenth century (although derived from many earlier works). There are separate sections on summoning demons, natural spirits and angels, as well as guidelines for defending onself from such enemies.

The first section, dealing with the summoning of demons, is called the *Ars Goetia*. Because of this, occultists call summoning magic "goetic magic." Somewhat ironically, the Greek word "goetia" means "magician," but with a distinct connotation of fakery and humbug attached to it—more a stage magician than a real magical practitioner.

Much of the *Lesser Key* consists of lists of powerful supernatural princes, including seventy-two demons and thirty-one nature spirits, all supposedly called into service by Solomon. We'll conclude with a sample, from the popular translation by S. L. "MacGregor" Mathers, edited by the famous occultist Alastair Crowley:

> *(2.) AGARES. The Second Spirit is a Duke called Agreas, or Agares. He is under the Power of the East, and cometh up in the form of an old fair Man, riding upon a Crocodile, carrying a Goshawk upon his fist, and yet mild in appearance. He maketh them to run that stand still, and bringeth back runaways. He teaches all Languages or Tongues presently. He hath*

power also to destroy Dignities both Spiritual and Temporal, and causeth Earthquakes. He was of the Order of Virtues. He hath under his government 31 Legions of Spirits.

Djinni

Probably the most numerous and popular tales of summoning magic involve the djinni (or jinn), natural spirits from Arab legend. It is in tales of summoning and binding djinni that traditional legend most closely approaches the practices of the *WoW* Warlock. Although the Warlock's "pets" resemble Christian conceptions of demonic beings, these summoned otherworldly creatures appear to be closer in nature to the djinni.

In English, the djinni are often referred to as "genies" (as in the case in the popular Disney version of *Aladdin*, or the 1960s TV show *I Dream of Jeannie*). The word "genie" does not actually come from the Arabic at all. It's from the Latin word *genius*, which originally meant a minor spirit from whom advice or help could be obtained (which led to the English meaning of the word, connoting a powerful combination of intellect and inspiration). The Latin *genius* became *genie* in French, and when translators in the eighteenth century began translating Arab legends into European language, it was quite natural to translate the Arab word djinni into the French word with such a similar sound and definition.

Originally, the pre-Islamic Arab people believed that the djinni were the malicious spirits of the peoples of long-forgotten ancient civilizations. They were said to cause plague and some forms of insanity. They could become invisible and take the form of animals. They emerged at night and fled with the dawn. One particular type of djinni, the ghul, was said to feast on corpses. In many ways they were like European vampires.

When the Prophet Muhammad established the faith of Islam, the belief in djinni was retained. In fact, the djinni are explicitly mentioned numerous times in the Qu'ran. For example, in Surah 51:56—58:

And I have not created the jinn and the men except that they should serve Me.

*I do not desire from them any sustenance and I do not desire that they
should feed Me.
Surely Allah is the Bestower of sustenance, the Lord of Power, the
Strong.*

Under Islam, the view of djinni changed substantially. They were
no longer regarded as the malicious spirits of evil humans. Instead,
they were regarded as a distinct intelligent race, different from humans but equal to them. Although spiritually powerful, they were
not divine or infernal in nature. Rather, they were created by Allah
from divine fire and, like humanity, had the ability to choose between good and evil, salvation and damnation.

This did not necessarily mean they were friendly, or that they
weren't dangerous. Even a righteous djinni might be stern, impatient
or uncaring about the affairs of humans. And a djinni who turned
away from the path of Islam and chose evil was a fearsome thing indeed. In fact, according to Islamic teachings, Satan (Iblis) is not a
fallen angel, but a high-ranking fallen djinni. In general, the warlike
Arab Moslems regarded the djinni as rivals, more likely to behave as
enemies than friends, even if they do believe in the same religion.

djinni were regarded as beings of spirit, able to take corporeal
form, but not bound to any specific form. They could dematerialize
at will and change shape and appearance freely. Thus a djinni could
appear as monstrously hideous or supernaturally beautiful depending on its personality and inclination at the moment. They could
also easily impersonate humans or animals. They are born, they eat,
they can marry, reproduce, and eventually die. They were believed
to be able to mate with humans and produce offspring, but the exact
mechanism of such transactions is not clearly agreed upon.

Some believed that the djinni were created before Adam, and were
the first rulers of the Earth. The great ruins that dotted the Arabian
desert were believed by the locals to have been the work of the djinni, constructed before the creation of mankind. This is one reason
that even righteous djinni often hate humanity—they regard us as
thieves and usurpers.

The Moslems believe that Solomon (yes, him again) used his seal
to gather all the djinni in the world to serve him. When he was done

with them, he sealed them into a brass container and cast the container into the sea. However, at some time between the life of Solomon and the birth of Muhammad, somebody found the container and opened it, releasing the djinni into the Earth again. Needless to say, they were not too pleased with their centuries of captivity.

Solomon, or perhaps his seal wielded by another mage, also bound some djinni to other objects as well. This is the reason for stories of djinni imprisoned in lamps, rings and the like. The same power that imprisoned the djinni also compelled him to grant wishes, or simply serve the holder of the object in any way required.

Thus in Islamic stories and legends, like those collected in *The 1001 Nights*, we find wizards whose power derives from their enslavement of powerful djinni —a relationship much like that between a *WoW* Warlock and his "pets" (although referring to a djinni—even an enslaved one—as a "pet" would probably be a mistake with severe consequences).

The Summoner in Fiction

Most fictional summoners are villains. They exist as a menace for the protagonist of the story to overcome. There are, however, a few notable examples of summoning wizards who are heroes, or at least antiheroes, of their own story.

The most celebrated literary summoner is certainly Dr. Faust, who sold his soul in return for receiving a powerful devil, Mephistopheles, as a servant and companion. Of course, in the tales Faust usually finds that all he has gained from his bargain amounts to nothing, and what he has lost is everything. (Stories of pacts with the Devil go back at least to the sixth-century tale of St. Theophilus of Adana.)

Interestingly, there appears to have been a real Dr. Faust (possibly even two)—a minor German occultist who died in 1540. Although the historical Faust certainly had a sinister reputation, and once referred to the Devil as his "crony," the story of Faust's bargain can be traced back to a fantastical collection of anecdotes about him: *Historia von D. Iohan Fausten*, published in 1587. This account was a phenomenal popular success for the time, and lead to Faust becoming an enduring literary figure who stars or appears in dozens, even hundreds of stories and dramas over the next few centuries. The most popular accounts of the Faust legend are Christopher Marlowe's English play *The Tragical History of Dr. Faustus* (1600), and Johann Wolfgang von Goethe's *Faust*, published in two parts beginning in 1808. Both works combine dark humor with serious moral philosophy. The Goethe play, in particular, is a complex and provocative work that's justly regarded as a high point of nineteenth-century literature, and perhaps the all-time pinnacle of German letters.

A much more sympathetic literary summoner is found in Shakespeare's final play, *The Tempest*. Prospero is an enchanter and exiled nobleman who is shipwrecked with his daughter, Miranda, on a deserted island. On the island Prospero finds two supernatural servants—the monstrous Caliban and the powerful disembodied spirit Ariel. Both of these entities act much like enchanted "pets" from MMORPGs. The play tells how Prospero uses his servants, and his other sorcerous powers, to clear his name and engineer rescue from the island and an advantageous marriage for Miranda.

In more modern works, Michael Moorcock's tales of Elric of Melniboné feature a title character who is both a warrior and an immensely powerful sorcerer—one who does not hesitate to call up and command spiritual allies of immense power.

Terry Pratchett, the popular British author of humorous fantasy, has taken on the Faust legend in his book *Eric*, and provides a memorable variant of the wish-granting djinni in *Sourcery*. Both books are part of Pratchett's mammoth *Discworld* series.

Finally, look up Tim Powers' novel *Declare*, for a surprising view of twentieth-century history as basically a side effect of an ancient war between powerful djinni . In Powers' novel, however, the djinni are not enslaved into service by humans. If anything, the reverse is truer.

Playing the Warlock

More Warlock deaths result from Mana depletion than any other factor. Because of this, one of the more useful spells allows the Warlock to convert Life to Mana. Remember the Warlock creed, "You only need Health if you're stupid enough to take damage."

One of the primary goals of the Warlock is to be perpetually destitute. To this end, *World of Warcraft* provides a great deal of support through the following class features:

- The aforementioned soul shards—which are necessary for a number of spells—take up space, therefore reducing the potential loot room in the Warlock's bags and packs.
- Warlock spells cost about as much as other spell caster's spells, and there are a lot of them.
- While minions do not need food, water or litter, they do need spells. Minion spells are stored in grimoires (which are not free).
- Enchanting is a typical Warlock profession (especially since the Warlock can then make his own wands) but, like dwarf tossing, it is a very expensive hobby.

In spite of an impoverished early life, the Warlock will typically get a mount as soon as he reaches Level 40. This is because at Level 40, a Warlock's mount is free.

While not as powerful as Mages at direct attacks, Warlocks do get a few strong direct-attack spells, as well as some time-release spells, such as Immolate (which does what it says).

Warlocks also get a large variety of curses (debuffs), that can be cast as instants, although only one can be active per Warlock per target at a time. A typical attack strategy against an NPC (from a distance, of course) is to send a minion to attack immediately prior to casting Shadow Bolt, followed by a curse. Since the minion and the bolt get to the creature at about the same time, the enemy is likely to attack the minion rather than the Warlock. Then, the Warlock can cast Immolate, and use a wand or additional spells as needed to damage the creature from a distance.

Few things are more satisfying to a Warlock than for a creature to finally break free of a minion to try to attack the Warlock, only to drop dead in its tracks six yards away from the caster.

In situations where precise pulls are critical, curses are effective at targeting a single NPC. The Voidwalker can usually turn a monster's focus away from the Warlock while it is closing. In this strategy, Affliction spells (which cause damage over time) can be very useful, since the Warlock is not able to do as much initial damage.

The Fear spell can be a strong weapon in PvP, but it can backfire when used against NPCs. Feared creatures will wander around and potentially create a great deal of aggro before resummoning up their courage (and their friends).

Likewise, a Warlock with a minion should be careful when taking shortcuts. Minions tend to do better along clearly marked paths, but they will try their best to get back to the Warlock. If that means wandering around monster-laden halls and creating a long train of aggro, so be it. They just want to get back to their master.

HUNTER

RACES: Dwarf, Night Elf, Tauren, Orc, Troll
PREFERRED WEAPONS: Bows and guns; any hand weapon
ARMOR ALLOWED: Cloth, leather; later mail
POWER LINES: Beast Mastery (animal powers and pet control), Outdoorsmanship (traps and hand-to-hand abilities), Ranged Combat
SOLO POTENTIAL: Excellent

The Hunter in WoW

Hunters are a ranged combat/pet class that pulls pets from the wild and relies upon bows, crossbows and guns for ranged damage. There are three talent trees for the Hunter: Survival, Beast Mastery and Marksmanship.

The primary Hunter stat is Agility, with Stamina and Intelligence secondary. Stamina gives hit points (which are less important at range) and Intelligence gives Mana (even with zero Mana, the Hunter's attacks inflict effective damage). However, Agility gives attack power (which determines to-hit and damage), critical hit chance and armor class.

Hunters can use most weapons (with training), start off able to wear leather armor, and can eventually wear mail at Level 40. The transition from leather to mail is not always a clear one, as the Hunter's primary focus is his stats, so jumping into mail to get a higher armor class at the cost of fifty Agility may not be wise. When selecting gear, the primary focus should be Agility. At higher levels, increasing the chance for criticals becomes almost as important, and at the highest levels resist bonuses become a factor.

Hunters' primary role is ranged damage. This allows them to stand at maximum range to inflict damage, outside of most area-of-effect attacks (drastically reducing the healing they require), and they can sustain their damage output well after their Mana is gone (making them invaluable for long raids).

The Hunter's secondary role is that of puller. A good Hunter can separate a single mob from a pack, watch on tracking to see if a patroller is coming from around the corner and feign death if he draws too many, avoiding a wipe that other classes cannot. This requires pinpoint timing and paying close attention to how enemies behave, but a great puller is an invaluable asset for any group or raid.

The Hunter's Mystique

It somehow just comes naturally to romanticize hunters...a man on his own, taking on nature one-on-one, providing food and essential resources for family and tribe. The first heroes of early humans must certainly have been great hunters.

This mystique shows up clearly in fairy tales. Consider the woodsman who saves Little Red Riding Hood from the devouring wolf, or the stern huntsman who defies his queen to spare the life of Snow White.

Of course, in fantasy gaming nearly everything goes back to Tolkien, and the Hunter in *WoW* can be traced directly back to two key characters in *The Lord of the Rings*. The first is Aragorn, as we meet him in the guise of Strider, the stern and stalwart ranger of the north. Strider gave modern fantasy the word "ranger," and established most of the characteristics of that archetype (and the *WoW* Hunter falls firmly within the archetype of the ranger, even if the name is different).

The second paradigm of the Hunter found in Tolkein's work is Legolas, Prince of the Elves of Mirkwood, who transformed our cultural concept of "Elf" (at least within the fan community) from a tiny, winged flower-sitter to a warrior as silent and deadly as he is beautiful. The paradigm of the Elven bowman is particularly important to *WoW*, where Humans do not have access to the Hunter class.

Of the several traits that define Hunters, probably the most important is their choice of weapons. Hunters are marksmen, with a great natural affinity for bow, crossbow and gun (the inclusion of guns in *WoW* sets it apart a bit from other works of high fantasy, but as we shall see it fits in perfectly with the archetype of the Hunter). There-fore, to get a grip on the inner nature of a Hunter, we'll look at each of these weapons in turn, along with the fictional characters who best demonstrate their heroic use.

Longbows & Robin Hood

The English longbow was perhaps the most terrible weapon of the Middle Ages. Mounted knights may have ruled the medieval battle-field, but the knights feared the longbowmen, whose shafts, with only a moderate bit of luck, could take their horse out from under them, or even pierce clean through their armor. The longbow re-ally came into its own during the Hundred Years' War with France (1337–1453), when time and again a comparatively small force of massed English longbowmen decimated a much larger force of French knights and infantry before they could even close, as hap-pened in the celebrated battle of Agincourt (1415).

Up to six feet tall and usually made of yew, there is archeological evidence of longbows in use in England for as long as 6,000 years. Officially, the English longbow was accepted as part of the English military in 1280. It was actually based on a weapon that had been used against the English by the Welsh, with notable efficiency.

Because it required so much upper body strength to use effec-tively, longbowmen were highly trained specialists. Today, archeol-ogists can recognize the skeleton of a bowman by his enlarged left arm and bone spurs on his left wrist and shoulder, and right finger. A fully trained longbowman could accurately unleash twelve arrows per minute. They carried their ammunition in simple belt quivers (not back quivers) and before battle they would stick their arrows' points into the ground around them, to make it quicker to draw and fire. This practice also made it somewhat more likely that their tar-gets would suffer infected wounds. The effective range of a longbow was believed to have been somewhere between 180 to 250 yards. The best modern bows have an effective range of 200 yards.

The process of making a yew longbow, from cutting the wood to use in battle, took about four years in all, much of that time required to properly season the wood.

The longbow is a weapon of the common man. Only a very wealthy man could afford the charger, sword and armor of a knight, but any peasant could make himself a pretty passable longbow. It's a direct result of the development of the longbow that the English nobility never got to be as imperious or tyrannical as some of their counterparts on the continent. Perhaps this explains why the French never developed their own longbow units—being beaten by the English was better than succumbing to a peasant rebellion at home.

The preeminent fictional example of the swashing bowman is, of course, Robin Hood. Archer, woodsman, thief and rebel, Robin embodied all the romantic strengths and virtues of the English peasantry.

Robin Hood is first referenced in print about 1377, in a passing mention in the allegory *Piers Plowman* by William Langland. A priest boasts that he knows many tales of Robin Hood. This vividly illustrates that there was a rich and thriving oral tradition regarding Robin and his men long before any of their adventures were written down. For this reason there is no single definitive account of Robin's life and adventures, only a broad and evolving body of myth.

It seems pretty clear from the early references to Robin Hood tales that his band of cohorts—including Will Scarlet, Friar Tuck and of course Little John—were part of the legend from the very first. However, much has been added over the centuries. Robin's status as a disgraced nobleman is a later addition to the legend, for example. There's also little evidence that the early Robin Hood ever gave his spoils to the poor (though there are early tales of his helping the helpless, but not to the extent of giving away everything he stole). To the early tellers of his story, just robbing from the rich—"sticking it to the man"—was enough to make Robin a hero.

Was there ever a historical Robin Hood? In fact, there were many. There seems to have been something of a medieval fad for criminals and rebels with pretensions of style to take on the name of Robin Hood. (It's even been suggested that medieval lawmen used the name "Robin Hood" to indicate outlaws whose real name was unknown, much like the modern "John Doe.") Consequently, it probably will never be possible to determine if there was one original Robin from whom all the others, fictional and historical, ultimately stem.

Early attempts to anchor Robin in history tend to put his death between 1240 and 1280. It was later writers (beginning in the fifteenth century) who tried to push Robin back to the 1190s, the time of the First Crusade, and Prince John's tempestuous regency in the absence of his brother, Richard the Lionheart.

Crossbows & William Tell

In the hands of a fully trained expert, a longbow will always be a superior weapon to a crossbow. Not every soldier, however, is an expert archer, so the crossbow definitely has its use in combat as the ranged weapon of choice for non-specialists.

When you're defending your castle from a siege, you don't necessarily need a company of expert longbowmen (though of course that would be nice). All you really want is some means of taking out an attacking enemy before he gets to the top of the ladder. In the hands of conscripts who only have brief training, or infantrymen who only occasionally need ranged combat capability for defensive purposes, a crossbow has many advantages over a longbow.

First of all, a longbow is a delicate precision instrument, while a crossbow is a sturdy machine. A crossbow is easier for ordinary troops to maintain in good condition, and can be more efficiently mass produced. Also, by nature of its construction, a crossbow provides a stable platform for aiming, making it more accurate for non-specialists.

Bows are not easy to load and fire. While a proficient archer can fire faster than a single-shot crossbow ever could, non-specialists find it easier to load and fire a crossbow at a constant rate. Furthermore, a crossbow can be pre-cocked and put aside until needed, ready to fire at a moment's notice.

Perhaps most importantly, a bow's power is limited by the archer's upper body strength, but a crossbow's power can be augmented with a variety of mechanical aids. A simple lever can do wonders. Larger crossbows use foot straps, allowing the user to put his whole body's strength into cocking the weapon. A longbowman can penetrate plate armor, but a really big crossbow can rip through a shield wall or siege tower.

But even though crossbows are easier to use than longbows, that doesn't mean skill doesn't count. By far the most celebrated cross-bowman in song and story is the legendary Swiss revolutionary William Tell, he of the celebrated overture that was hijacked by an American masked gunman.

In the fourteenth century, the Austrian emperor was asserting control over parts of Switzerland. In the town of Altdorf the newly appointed Austrian bailiff put his hat on a pole and ordered that every local who passed the pole bow to it. When Tell was spotted walking past the pole, he was arrested. The bailiff, named Gessler, gave Tell a choice for his sentence: either be put to death, or shoot an apple off his son's head with his crossbow. If Tell succeeded in shooting the apple he could go free.

On November 18, 1307, Tell shot the apple off the boy's head with a single shot. But when the bailiff asked Tell why he had two bolts in his quiver, Tell replied that if he had missed and killed his son, he would have used the second bolt to kill Gessler. The bailiff was so enraged by this impertinence that he ordered Tell re-arrested. Tell was bound and brought on a ship across Lake Lucerne to Gessler's castle. During a storm on the lake, however, Tell managed to escape, whereupon he went on to the castle. When Gessler arrived, Tell shot him. Tell's deeds inspired the people to rise up in rebellion against the Emperor's occupation.

As far as can be told from history, William Tell never existed. There are actually a number of Germanic tales and legends about heroes forced to shoot objects off their sons' heads, and Tell's story appears to fall into this tradition. There are no independent records of the existence of Tell, Gessler or even the rebellion Tell supposedly sparked. To many Swiss, however, Tell remains a very real figure, and stands as a symbol of their country's pride and independence.

Rifles & Natty Bumppo

Including guns as a weapon choice in *World of Warcraft* was a rather audacious decision. For whatever reason, our concept of "high fantasy" stops somewhere after the invention of full plate armor, but short of the development of gunpowder as an effective combat measure.

Still, in a world where Mages can blast fireballs at each other at the drop of a wand, a single-shot musket is hardly going to upset the balance of power, and guns fit in well with the Dwarf race, especially their character as craftsmen and gadgeteers.

Historically, it took several centuries before gunpowder weapons surpassed the longbow and crossbow as the battlefield soldier's personal weapons of choice. Consider for a moment the Three Musketeers, from the Alexandre Dumas novel and its countless adaptations and spin-offs. A musketeer is a specialized combat rifleman—that function is right there in the name, a soldier with a musket. But how often do we picture the musketeers using firearms? Instead, we think of them as swashbuckling swordsmen.

The function of early firearms on the battlefield was not so much to wreak destruction on the enemy—bows were still more accurate and efficient killing machines. Rather, the noise and smoke from the firearms created an effective psychological weapon, frightening the enemy and creating chaos in his ranks.

The perfect exemplar of the gun-toting WoW Hunter in fiction is probably Natty Bumppo, the Deerslayer, from James Fenimore Cooper's *Leatherstocking* novels. Of course, the correspondence is not precise. For starters, Bumppo is human (there is a sad shortage of classic adventure fiction featuring dwarves with blunderbusses). Also his weapon of choice is the Kentucky long rifle, which is a much more advanced example of single-shot rifle technology than the WoW guns seem to be. Nonetheless, Bumppo almost perfectly captures the mixture of woodlore and marksmanship that mark the Hunter.

Bumppo's adventures are chronicled in five novels, collectively referred to as the *Leatherstocking Tales—The Deerslayer, Last of the Mohicans, The Pathfinder, The Pioneers* and *The Prairie*. These books tell the story of Bumppo's life on the American frontier of the eighteenth century, from his twenties to his eighties. Cooper seems to have loved coming up with picaresque nicknames for his most famous hero— thoughout the novels Bumppo is referred to as Deerslayer, Pathfinder, the Trapper, Killdeer, la Longue Carabine and Leatherstocking, among others. The justification for this is, as a wanderer all his life, Bumppo travels among many tribes and nationalities, each of which bestows their own nickname on him.

Although he lives in a time of revolution, Bumppo is not a revolutionary, unlike Robin Hood and William Tell. Though not a soldier himself, he works for them as a scout and hunter, doing his duty without too much thought to the politics of his employer. Bumppo is the equal of any Indian in woodcraft, and surpassed by no man alive as a marksman. The Kentucky long rifle is a weapon of legendary accuracy and stopping power, and Bumppo is its absolute master. What he aims at, he hits, and what he hits is dead.

If there's one element of the *Leatherstocking* tales calculated to make modern readers uncomfortable, it's their view on race. Cooper wrote the books between 1823 and 1841, at a time when racism was an inescapable part of the American character. In many ways Cooper's views were ahead of their time—he firmly believed that a man's worth was based on the content of his character, and that no man was better than another simply because of the color of his skin. In the books, this principle is embodied in the Indian Chingachgook, the title character of *The Last of the Mohicans*, and Bumppo's best friend and longtime companion. At the same time, Cooper had some views on class and race mixing that will probably make most modern readers squirm. By the fourth or fifth time that Bumppo proudly declares himself "a man without a cross" (meaning that, despite his living among the Indians and mastering their ways, he himself is of pure European stock with no Indian blood), the modern reader starts to wish he'd just shut up about it already.

Nonetheless, the *Leatherstocking Tales* remain wonderfully vivid adventure stories, and perfect evocations of the spirit of the American frontier.

Bumppo hardly stands alone in the annals of adventure fiction as a heroic, rifle-wielding hunter and explorer. If you prefer tales with a stronger fantasy element than Cooper's firmly historical novels, you should definitely check out the tales of Solomon Kane by Robert E. Howard (best known as the creator of Conan the Barbarian). Kane is a Puritan mercenary of the sixteenth century—a solitary, moody and haunted man who stars in more than a dozen short stories, most of which were originally published in the legendary pulp magazine *Weird Tales*. (The Kane stories are currently most conveniently collected in the Del Rey paperback *The Savage Tales of Solomon Kane*.)

In the stories, Kane fights dark and ancient magic across several continents, armed with his rapier, flintlock pistols and musket.

In the nineteenth century, the European big-game hunter and explorer—often referred to by the racist sobriquet "Great White Hunter"—became a fixture of popular fiction. Probably the greatest literary big-game hunter was Allan Quatermain, created by H. Rider Haggard. Quatermain has a habit of finding lost cities and races, and all his stories have a definite mystical flavor to them. The most famous of the many Quatermain books Haggard penned is *King Solomon's Mines*. Recently, interest in Allan Quatermain has surged thanks to his inclusion as one of the main characters in Alan Moore's popular *League of Extraordinary Gentlemen* comics.

Playing the Hunter

Survival is the utility tree that upgrades the Hunter's traps, self-buffs and melee. Few Hunters invest in this tree because Hunters are not an optimal melee class, and traps are primarily used while soloing, but there is still value in this tree.

The Beast Mastery tree upgrades the Hunter's pet to be more effective. This is also primarily a solo-Hunter tree, as pets become less effective at higher levels and, in many instanced areas, are a detriment, so investing in this tree means the Hunter will eventually need to pay to respend his talents.

Marksmanship talents increase the Hunter's ability with ranged weapons. This is the tree for Hunters who either work often in groups or see their pet as something to hold an enemy off long enough for them to destroy it. This tree significantly increases the damage per second the Hunter is capable of generating at range.

It is imperative that Hunters keep their pets' skills up to date. Most pet skills are trained by the Hunter, who learns them from other animals, so Hunters need to regularly (every five to eight levels) stable their current pet and go tame pets with the desired skills, then train them to their current pet. The pet skills are Bite (small DPS, low Mana), Claw (high DPS, high Mana), Growl (taunt aggro), Cower (lower aggro), Dash (sprint) and Dive (sprint for flying creatures). The higher level the pet, the higher level the abilities it can learn, and the more effective it is.

While most classes do not have "optimal" crafting professions, the Hunter does have one...Engineering. A Hunter Engineer can make his own guns, bullets and—most importantly—carry Goblin Jumper Cables, which allow a Hunter to Feign Death when a party is overwhelmed, get up, and have a decent chance of resurrecting the Priest, who in turn can resurrect the party and get things going again.

Key Points for Hunters

Always have plenty of ammunition and food for your pet.

Always control your pet. Many areas have odd pathing or have the party jumping off ledges. A pet that makes its own way down to the party, trailing a dozen enemies behind it to overwhelm the party, does not endear the Hunter to the group.

Keep the pet in the right mode (usually Passive in a group) and dismiss it if you are unsure how it will behave in a given situation.

Always control your aggro. The high DPS of a Hunter can also be a downside against a single target, causing the enemy to charge across the party to the Hunter. Even with a successful Feign Death, the party has to chase after it, risk having it area-of-effect the cloth-wearing party members, and so forth. Use special attacks sparingly, pace your damage over time, and Feign Death often to shake off any aggro you may have picked up. The desired effect is to do the most damage possible without ever capturing the enemies' attention.

Acknowledgements

Thanks to

Jody "Gallatin" Cochran, Whisperwind Realm, for her advice on playing a Druid

Christopher "MacAllen" Pinkard, for his advice on playing a Hunter

Chris "Lord Pixie" Karel, for his advice on playing a Mage

Raini "Arlaine" Madden, Whisperwind Realm, for her advice on playing a Paladin

Andrea "Cryth" Silva, for her advice on playing a Priest

Max "Shragul" De La Garza, Feathermoon Realm, for his advice on playing a Rogue

Stephen "Tarhorn" Reinsborough, for his advice on playing a Shaman

Ken "Sidnin" White, for his advice on playing a Warlock

Christopher "MacAllen" Pinkard, for his advice on playing a Warrior

Printed in the United States
by Baker & Taylor Publisher Services